# Public Funding of Higher Education

# Public Funding of Higher Education

## Changing Contexts and New Rationales

Edited by
## Edward P. St. John
and
## Michael D. Parsons

The Johns Hopkins University Press
*Baltimore and London*

© 2004 The Johns Hopkins University Press
All rights reserved. Published 2004
Printed in the United States of America on acid-free paper

Johns Hopkins Paperbacks edition, 2005
9 8 7 6 5 4 3 2 1

The Johns Hopkins University Press
2715 North Charles Street
Baltimore, Maryland 21218-4363
www.press.jhu.edu

*The Library of Congress has cataloged the hardcover edition of this
book as follows:*

Public funding of higher education : changing contexts
and new rationales / edited by Edward P. St. John and
Michael D. Parsons.
      p.      cm.
Includes bibliographical references and index.
ISBN 0-8018-7973-6 (hardcover : alk. paper)
1. Education, Higher—United States—Finance.   2. Public
universities and colleges—United States—Finance.   3. Federal
aid to higher education—United States.   4. Government aid
to higher education—United States.   I. St. John, Edward P.
II. Parsons, Michael D. (Michael David)
   LB2342.P795 2004
   379.1'18'0973—dc22                    2004000140

ISBN 0-8018-8259-1 (pbk : alk. paper)

A catalog record for this book is available from the British
Library.

# Contents

# Public Funding of Higher Education

# CHAPTER ONE

# Introduction

## Edward P. St. John and Michael D. Parsons

In the late twentieth century the underlying rationale for the public funding of higher education in the United States broke down. Policymakers routinely questioned college officials' claims that allocating tax dollars for higher education, either in the form of direct subsidies for instruction or of funding for university-based research and development, promotes economic development and social equity. Such rationales are no longer accepted without question. Furthermore, the argument that federal and state funding of need-based grant programs were necessary to maintain equal opportunity has also been routinely discounted in the policy process as lobbyists argue for their piece of a declining education budget. Instead, these older rationales are undermined by criticisms from new conservatives who assert that colleges are wasteful and therefore overpriced, as well as from new liberals who argue for school reform as an access strategy. As a consequence, there was relatively rapid movement toward privatization of public colleges and a transformation in emphasis in federal student aid from equal access to middle-class affordability through loans and tax credits.

Thus, the politics of higher education are more contested now than was true for most of the twentieth century. In the early twenty-first century, the old rationales for public funding are subject to challenge, creating a complex situation for administrators who argue for increases in public funding as well as for researchers attempting to understand the new policy context. In this book, scholars and practitioners address the complexities of the new policy context with the goal of informing policymakers, professors, and students about the changing nature of the politics of higher education. As an introduction, we review some of the reasons that the old political consensus broke down and then focus on the ways that a reconstructed understanding of the policy context can inform advocacy for institutions, research funding, and student aid. We conclude by suggesting a framework for examining the new policy context and the new rationales for public funding.

## Breakdown of the Old Consensus

For most of the past century there was a political consensus both about the rationales for public financing of higher education in the United States and about the structure of the relationship between government and institutions. By the end of the 1800s, the states' role of funding public colleges and universities had been firmly established, partially as a result of state responses to the land grant acts (Johnson 1989). During the 1900s, state support of higher education expanded with the growth of state university systems and the addition of teachers' colleges and, later, other comprehensive colleges, community colleges, and other publicly subsidized colleges and universities. In the 1960s and '70s, the federal government acquired a major role in funding need-based student aid as a means of equalizing educational opportunity.

Underlying these developments was a broad consensus about the social and economic valuation of the public's investment in higher education. Liberals supported these developments because they valued the expansion of educational opportunity; conservatives supported the expansion because it promoted economic development. The two positions were not inconsistent, and they actually reinforced one another even when there were disagreements about which funding strategies were desirable. However, in the past two decades these common-ground assumptions have given way to a new form of conflict about higher education finance and accountability. To illustrate the breakdown in the old consensus, we need only ponder the arguments of the new conservatives and new liberals who are critics of public policy in higher education.

In the 1980s, the new conservatives began to argue that higher education was unproductive (Finn 1988; Finn and Manno 1996) and that student aid was ineffectual (Bennett 1987). These criticisms alienated the higher education community, which began to seek alternative explanations for rising prices. However, that there were few credible counterarguments to these criticisms made it easier for the new conservatives to gain majority support for the reduction in federal need-based grants and the increase in loans (St. John 1994). This new critical attitude caught the higher education community ill-prepared, and it was ineffectual in its efforts to lobby for higher education programs (Parsons 1997). Essentially, this new conservative position valued economic development over social development. This position dominated federal higher education policy throughout the early 1990s and had a substantial influence in many states as higher education was increasingly defined as a private, rather than a public, good.

By the middle 1990s, a new liberal position emerged, a development that began to bring a new, possibly temporary, balance to the higher education discourse. This position argued that there were losses in access attributable to the new federal student aid policy (McPherson and Schapiro 1997) and that the majority of voters supported maintaining the public investment in student aid (Cook 1998). It essentially valued the social development aspect of higher education spending along with the new economic goal, which enabled new liberals to hold ground in the policy debates about student aid, avoiding further reductions in grants in spite of the election of a Republican majority in Congress (Cook 1998).

However, the new liberal position lacked a rationale for increasing government funding for students and institutions. Given the assault on need-based grants, analysts shifted their argument to academic preparation. New liberal advocates argued for the funding of programs that encouraged students to enroll (e.g., Gladieux and Swail 1999), leading to funding of a new federal program, Gaining Early Awareness and Readiness for Undergraduate Programs (GEAR UP). They also argued that student financial aid was not enough (Gladieux and Swail 1999; King 1999) as equity-based student aid programs lost their support and new inequalities emerged, including a diverging of educational opportunity between high-income and low-income students (Advisory Committee on Student Financial Assistance 2002; St. John 2002). And institutions began to develop incentive-based budgeting systems that encouraged faculty to seek external funding (Priest et al. 2002).

This new context differs from the old progressive consensus in several ways. Prior to the 1980s, the logic used to advocate for higher education investment bundled together the social and economic development goals, justifying public expenditures on higher education because it was both a public and a private good (e.g., Honeyman, Wattenbarger, and Westbrook 1996). The major point of disagreement was about the extent and type of new investment necessary to expand opportunity (a social goal) and stimulate economic development (an economic goal). The new conservative position of the 1980s undermined the liberal progressive consensus, arguing that the public investment had gone too far, that increases in investment resulted in income transfer and contributed to the economic slowdown (Hansen 1983). This conservative position of valuing economic goals, rather than merely arguing against new investment, fueled an argument for decreasing the public funding of higher education.

In contrast, the new liberal position reconstructed the value of the social development goal of higher education policy. Arguments for new programs that provided encouragement to students (Gladieux and Swail 1999; King 1999) were reasonably effective. However, research that documented that the cuts to need-based aid had been too deep (McPherson and Schapiro 1991, 1997) went largely unheeded.

A new policy puzzle has been created by this newer debate. There is substantially less common ground than there had been from the late nineteenth century through the 1970s. Rather than viewing higher education as promoting both social and economic development, the economic development goal now dominates federal policy, while the new liberal position essentially claims victory if it holds ground against further cuts (Cook 1998). Privatization of public institutions and loans for undergraduates, both part of the globalization process (Henry et al. 2001; Slaughter and Leslie 1997), offer few alternatives for advocates of public funding.

## Rethinking Theory and Practice

Unfortunately, higher education advocates and policy researchers have rarely pondered the theory problems associated with the new political context in higher education. Historically, the role of rationalization and advocacy went without critical examination largely because of the old consensus. However, in the new context both the advocates—those who argue for funding of higher education programs and institutions or those who argue for reductions in such funding—and the researchers who analyze the effects of these policies need to think more critically about how they use theory to rationalize policy choices. If such reflections are communicated, they might help build a sounder base for policy discussions, creating a shared understanding among proponents of different ideological positions. In the new context it is important to think about the uses of rationales and evidence. Reflection on theories that explain or underlie the policy discourse can help inform this type of critical thinking and analysis.

## *The Underlying Theory Problem*

The politics of higher education policy analysis have been under-theorized, especially when compared to other disciplines and fields. The lack of theory to explain policy process and policy choices in higher education has been attributed to several factors, but two stand out. One is the evolution of educational policy studies as a field separate from its parent discipline, political science. As educational policy developed, scholars implicitly adopted pluralism as their guiding theory, but their rationales for funding were adapted from economics. Coupled with rationalism in organizational theory and empiricism in inquiry, the pluralistic assumptions made in educational policy analysis and research became so strong that scholars seldom acknowledged theories. Theory had become embedded in the codes and models; thus, scholars tacitly used these frameworks to analyze policy.

If higher education policy scholars had critically examined their approaches to policy analysis, they would have discovered the ideology embedded in those codes and models of analysis. Laurence H. Tribe did just that in his seminal essay, *Policy Science: Analysis or Ideology* (1972). Tribe argues that the guiding ideology of policy analysis was the belief that policy choices were "essentially technical in character" and that policymaking was a matter of rational choice (p. 66). In making choices, researchers used value-neutral methods to insure objectivity. Social questions about gender, power, privilege, and values were excluded as policy analysts focused on techniques. Douglas J. Amy (1987) took Tribe's criticism a step further, suggesting that policymaking is not only a function of methods and methodology but of the education of policy analysts. Policy analysts are trained to leave moral and ethical questions to the domain of policymakers. While many of the positivist principles that guide policy analysis have been questioned and discredited, those principles remain embedded in higher education policy analysis today and contribute to its under-theorization.

The second factor explaining the stunted development of theory in higher education policy analysis was the growth of the political consensus that came to dominate the federal higher education policy arena. With the passage of the Higher Education Act (HEA) of 1965, everyone seemed to become a Deweyan. With appropriate federal support, education could end racism, promote social justice, end unemployment, win the space race, and bring about other untold social and economic good as America built the Great Society. Republicans expressed doubts at first, but in a few short years the primary difference between

Republicans and Democrats was one of means rather than ends. Richard M. Nixon would become the first president to make a nationally televised address on education. A common language and shared values helped provide coherence, unity, and logic to the policy arena. Since almost no one questioned the basic philosophical underpinning of problems and issues, conflicts tended to arise over specific solutions. For example, whether loans should be given via direct lending was not an issue of loans, but of how to deliver loans. The same was true of the loan-grant imbalance. The issue was not student loans, but the proper balance between loans and forms of grant aid. The guiding assumptions and beliefs remained unchallenged, with only the solutions open to question and conflict.

The consensus that had guided the policy arena since the 1960s began to erode in the 1980s and broke down in the 1990s (Parsons 2000). Loan defaults, pressure for tax credits, a renewed emphasis on merit aid, a shift from educational opportunity to middle-income support, a decline in public support for social justice, the rising costs of higher education, and other trends forced policymakers to question the old consensus. Surprisingly, the erosion of consensus did not produce the explosion of competing theoretical and methodological approaches associated with similar shifts in other disciplines (e.g., history or philosophy). One change increased attention to federal science policy in the 1990s, but access and equity still ordered much of the research agenda for higher education policy. Policy advocates continued using old rationales, while policy scholars made only incremental moves away from traditional models of policy analysis.

In this context, some researchers and advocates began to rethink liberal and conservative arguments about public funding. Michael Mumper's *Removing College Price Barriers* (1996) and Constance E. Cook's *Lobbying for Higher Education* (1998) are excellent examples of the new liberal arguments. Recent analyses (Callan and Finney 1997; St. John 1994) have presented ideas that emphasize responding to new market conditions, if not privatizing public universities (Kidwell and Massy 1996; Priest et al. 2002). These arguments carry forward new conservative assumptions about reducing taxpayer support.

Mumper's work, framed by access and equity, looks at what government has done and why the efforts have not reduced price barriers. While no theoretical framework is acknowledged, Mumper is explicitly analyzing the impact of institutional arrangements and interactions on public policy. The recommendations for reform focus on improving public funding. Cook (1998) uses interest-group theory as a framework for analysis but also focuses on institutional performance and how it might be improved. Specifically, she is interested in how effectively the Washington-based higher education associations represent the interests of their members. She found that, from the perspective of campus presidents, the associations were somewhat out of touch with the campuses. Like Mumper, she focuses on improving institutional arguments about funding higher education. Neither work attempts to break away from earlier frameworks to arrive at new understandings of higher education policy.

The new conservative rationales are more critical of the status quo than are the new liberal rationales. Conservatives offer the market as a neutral arbiter. William Massy and colleagues (e.g., Kidwell and Massy 1996) have added to the arguments of others who have advocated for budget and administrative strategies that introduce market forces into universities. This takes a step further than do prior authors who have suggested that institutions view their assets in the way that a private corporation would view asset strategies (e.g., Simsek and Heydinger 1992). Among other things, this means selling some assets and contracting for services, from food service to administration of student services. While such recommendations are controversial, the new conservative vision is gaining support. It calls for reengineering administrative services, including downsizing and outsourcing, and restructuring academic processes to meet the challenges of the changing higher education market (e.g., Johnson and Kidwell 1996).

In *Public and Private Financing of Higher Education* (1997), Patrick M. Callan and Joni Finney offer another view, one that balances aspects of the new conservative and new liberal rationales. From their perspective, reduced public funding is driving the move toward privatization. Institutions can respond either by downsizing or by privatizing. They recommend privatization as a way to avoid, or at least limit, the influence of ill-designed public policy. Privatization will allow institutions to respond to the market and position themselves to achieve their academic goals and aspirations. Callan and co-authors argue that higher education policies should focus on the "balance between institutional interests and market forces" (Bracco et al. 1999, p. 42).

Both arguments are open to the charges that Tribe made against policy analysis more than a quarter of a century ago. Neither can capture or explain the dynamic changes in the higher education policy arena; both approaches are "essentially technical in character" and view policymaking as a matter of "rational choice" (Tribe 1972, p. 66). Unfortunately, theory is often dismissed as lacking application or relevance outside the halls of academe. However, the construction and application of theory is important for three very practical reasons.

One reason is that today's university leaders operate in a "political university" (Rosenzweig 1998). The myth of the university as a reflective institution removed from the external world of politics and policy is just that, a myth. Higher education is enmeshed in policy. University leaders in the second half of the twentieth century spent much of their time thinking about policy, responding to policy directives, and attempting to influence government policymakers. Without theory to explain and predict the policy process, university leadership becomes a series of disconnected, reactive events mired in a swamp of interacting, overlapping, and at times conflicting federal and state policies. Theory offers an opportunity to influence policy proactively.

Another reason for the importance of theory is that with the erosion of common ground in the policy arena, the already limited use of theory has been displaced by ideology presented as policy analysis and serving as a rationalization for policy positions. Absent theory, policy analysis seems to be moving into noncommunicative camps reminiscent of the culture wars in literature. Ideological rationalizations can become self-serving tautological arguments. In this intellectual climate, analysis from rival camps is dismissed as ideological. Theory will not bring competing approaches to a common framework of beliefs; however, it can lead to common frames of analysis with ample room for robust and rigorous disagreement.

Finally, theory creates a space to gain distance and perspective. Without theoretical distance and space, policy analysis can become, as suggested above, nothing more than a rationalization for a policy paradigm intent on selling ideas and positions. Theory cannot promise truth and objectivity, but it can allow the space and distance needed for critical analysis. In this sense, theory can at least offer policy analysts and researchers a critical stance for testing claims about truth and objectivity. Therefore, one goal of this volume is to build a better understanding of the theory of policy development and the practice of lobbying for higher education.

## *Rationalization in Advocacy and Policy Research*

While we think that openness, truth, and objectivity are desirable in the public discourse, we also realize that these are difficult in practice, given the pervasive role of political ideologies and institutional interests. However, the old shared beliefs about liberal progressivism have been sufficiently shattered that we do not expect a new consensus to emerge in the short term. Therefore, it is important to build an understanding of the role of advocacy in policy development along with the roles of rational arguments for funding and of confirmatory policy research in this process. We consider the process of *reframing*, that is, rethinking the use of rationales and research evidence to inform policy development, as integral to constructing more workable policies in higher education.

With the breakdown in the consensus in higher education, it is important for the policy analysts to think through how research is used to inform the policy discourse. By examining the rationales used to argue for public funding in relation to empirical evidence about the truth of the implied claims, it may be possible to develop better-informed rationales to illuminate the political nature of policy decisions. In this way we can move from an abstract use of theory to explain the policy process to a pragmatic use of theory to advocate for better-informed policy choices.

The federal student aid programs for higher education were developed to pursue the goals of expanding equal educational opportunity and promoting economic development. In her study of institutional lobbying for the *Higher Education Act,* Sheila Slaughter (1991) found that most institutional lobbyists appealed to human capital arguments in their appeals for new programs and public funds. Within states, most of the planning for higher education was handled within a broad consensus that included master planning, coordination among diverse constituents through coordinating boards, and rationalized funding formulae. The costs and benefits of higher education were commonly understood in most states. The major concerns were how to fund institutions adequately in periods of tax revenue shortfalls and how best to optimize the use of state dollars to promote the common goals (Berg and Hoenack 1987; St. John 1991). However, with the breakdown of the old consensus, there is no longer a common set of assumptions among policymakers and institutional advocates.

In the early 1980s, colleges and universities began an era of strategic planning. Institutional leaders and board members began to rethink their missions in relation to the expected downturn in enrollment. Many private colleges and some public universities began to emphasize quality improvement and marketing. The underlying assumption was that with fewer students, campuses would need to become more attractive to traditional students, develop new programs that appealed to nontraditional students, or both (Keller 1983; Norris and Poulton 1987). Institutions also adapted their financial strategies to these new strategic aims. Indeed, colleges and universities began a sustained period of raising tuition to reinvest in educational activities and student aid (St. John 1992, 1994). These practices had a new embedded rationale, one that placed institutional interests ahead of the older assumptions about the common good. These new strategies may have been hastened by the decline in federal funding of need-based grant programs and a failure of states to keep pace with the rate of subsidies to public colleges and universities, but they also marked a new dimension of institutional advocacy.

When the new conservative criticisms advanced by the Reagan administration are examined in relation to the emergence of these new institutional strategic initiatives, the underlying reasons for the new divisions in beliefs become more visible. In the middle 1980s, at the same time the strategic planning era was taking shape, the federal government began to reconstruct its commitment to higher education. As the federal government was formalizing its use of loans as a strategy for funding college students, the level of student debt climbed (Fossey and Bateman 1998). During this period, a substantial portion of the burden of paying for college shifted from taxpayers to students and their families (Kramer 1993) as the states continued to decrease their support per student in public colleges. In spite of the restructuring of college costs, however, enrollment continued at levels that were substantially higher than most national projections.

In retrospect, these developments further illustrate the breakdown in the old consensus. A new strategic environment had emerged by 1990, with colleges taking more market-oriented approaches that reflected the changed role of government and the need to compete for students. A new set of government financing strategies had also emerged. For example, the western states that were facing enrollment expansion began to explore alternative paths, such as funding electronic university programs, increasing public funding for students in private colleges, and other approaches that would reduce taxpayer costs of meeting anticipated demand.

These developments also raise questions about the future of the policy discourse, including questions about the role of rationalizations for public funding, how they will change, and whether new forms of policy research will evolve. It is highly probable that the contested terrain will continue into the early twenty-first century as colleges pursue their strategic, adaptive behavior in the midst of contradictory and clashing state and federal policies on higher education. Indeed, in this new context higher education lobbyists and government agencies often independently pursue separate agendas, seeking new coalitions on each project that requires cooperation. This would involve a continuation of the current strategic environment, with college and university leaders advocating for their own institutions in the face of legislative concern about the costs of higher education.

It is also possible that taxpayers, government policymakers, and college administrators will evolve a new consensus that reflects the new challenges and opportunities they face. This would involve creating a more open discourse, one that breaks the bonds of current rationales and addresses the strategic aims of institutions as well as the interrelationships between interests in existing systems and the new interests of states in expanding postsecondary education options at a lower cost. This would also involve building new understandings of the consequences of various approaches to the development and expansion of new systems of higher education. It would require a rethinking of the ways information and analyses are used in support of strategic planning within university systems and state agencies.

Regardless of which path evolves, however, we need to begin exploring new rationales for public funding of higher education. The breakdown of the old consensus illuminates the need to develop new, theoretically grounded perspectives on policy development in, and public funding of, higher education. It also illustrates that there are times when institutional interests may come into conflict with new state initiatives aimed at building lower-cost systems. In this context there will be conflict between traditional values and the newer values of activist public officials. Therefore, our second goal in this book is to build a better understanding of the ways policy research can inform political decisions about higher education policy.

This collection of essays explores the applicability of an alternative theoretical lens to the study of policy research in higher education and examines alternative rationales for funding. Habermas (1985, 1987) argues that most action is strategic, aimed at achieving goals. Consequently, most advocates construct rationales to support their own positions, their own goals. Many policy analysts have documented the global decline in social welfare and education funding along with increased emphasis on the privatization of these services (Henry et al. 2001; Teaford 2002). In *Development and Crisis of the Welfare State,* Evelyne Huber and John D. Stephens note: "Our claim that class (gender) interests are socially constructed and that changes in class (gender) power rela-

tions operate in part through changes in consciousness—the changing preferences—of the population provides us with the key link in our argument that
it is the long-term pattern of partisan government that is critical for welfare
state development" (2001, p. 28). They examine the influence of change in political majorities of elected officials on funding for social welfare programs in
developed democracies globally, using regression analyses, and they examine
case histories of the changing rationales for public funding. The dominant ideologies held by the new political majorities in national elected bodies (Huber
and Stephens 2001)—and by state governments in the U.S. (Teaford 2002)—
have de-emphasized equity in favor of privatization, a value reflected in both
social and educational policies.

Habermas (1985, 1987) also argues for and demonstrates a communicative
approach that involves discerning the claims made using different rationales,
examining evidence related to those claims, and reconstructing understandings that might inform new patterns of action based on those new understandings. In the policy arena, the application of this method has been described as a "critical-empirical approach" (Miron and St. John 2003; St. John
and Hossler 1998; St. John and Paulsen 2001). It has potential for bringing evaluative evidence that is not bound into any single rationale into policy discussions (Teddlie 1998), but it is seldom used in policy analysis. The standard approach used to frame policy problems limits the wide use of a critical-empirical
approach. Researchers tend to frame problems within a single theoretical perspective, which means that they typically construct studies to test a single rationale, rather than to test multiple and competing claims (Miron and St. John
2003). Moreover, most practitioners' construct new rationales in support of
their evolving positions based on a review of evidence, but they tend not to
have an open mind about competing rationales.

Our position is that if policy researchers recognize the politics and strategic nature of policy research, they can construct studies that inform policymakers who hold different points of view. Providing empirical evidence related
to conflicting claims can create new understandings. Researchers who take this
approach can address new challenges that emerge from policies implemented
based on ideological or political decisions. Such research can inform further
adaptations in policy.

As editors, we took a first step toward a critical-empirical approach by ask-
ing expert scholars and informed practitioners to critically examine political rationales that are widely used in state and federal policy along with the argu-

ments that are now being used by university lobbyists. We asked the contributors to begin the process of rethinking the rationales that institutional advocates use to lobby for higher education and researchers use to study the politics of higher education. Three overarching questions guided us and the contributors:

*How do theories of the policy process inform research on higher education policy and political advocacy for higher education?*

Specifically, we were interested in contributing to an understanding of the politics of higher education that incorporates an understanding of the distinct roles of lobbying and research. Therefore, we asked scholars whose research can inform an understanding of policy to address specific topics related to the politics of higher education.

*How have shifts in political ideologies over the past two decades, along with the incremental privatization of public higher education, influenced the rationales higher education advocates use to lobby for public support?*

The high tuition creates a different environment for advocates of public and private higher education. For most of the twentieth century, states were primarily concerned about public universities. However, with the increasing privatization of public colleges, states and the federal government need new ways to think about the future of the state systems that include both public and private universities. Thus, it is important to consider how the new context informs and transforms the rationales used to advocate for new policies in specific issue areas related to the new common goals, such as student aid or desegregation.

*How can researchers interested in higher education policy engage in research that can better inform policy development?*

While this preliminary definition of the new policy context and statement of possible common goals inform this initial study, how might they inform researchers who are concerned about the policy implications of their research? In this sense, we are interested in the ways this preliminary statement of goals might inform new directions in policy research.

The chapters in this volume provide a basis for suggesting a new common ground for education public policy, one that recognizes the new preferences of the public at the same time that alternative rationales are articulated and examined. The analyses herein can inform readers about these questions. The authors address specific topics related to federal policy (Part I), policy in the states (Part II), and the rationales institutions use to argue for public funding (Part

III). In the introductions to each part, we consider how the chapters can inform readers about the role of theory in research on political advocacy, how political ideologies influence the rationales that are used to argue for funding, and how policy research can inform policy development in the policy context. In the final section (Part IV), we consider the theory and practice of lobbying in this new context and suggest strategies for conducting applied policy research that can inform policy development.

REFERENCES

Advisory Committee on Student Financial Assistance. 2002. *Empty promises: The myth of college access in America.* Washington, DC: Author.
Amy, D. J. 1987. Can policy analysis be ethical? In *Confronting values in policy analysis: The politics of criteria,* ed. F. Fischer and J. Forester, 45–67. Newberry Park, CA: Sage.
Bennett, W. J. 1987. "Our greedy colleges," *New York Times,* 18 February.
Berg, D. J., and S. A. Hoenack. 1987. The concept of cost-related tuition and its implementation at the University of Minnesota. *Journal of Higher Education* 58 (3): 276–305.
Bracco, K. R., R. C. Richardson Jr., P. M. Callan, and J. E. Finney. 1999. Policy environments and system design: Understanding state governance structures. *Review of Higher Education* 23 (1): 23–44.
Callan, P. M., and J. E. Finney, eds. 1997. *Public and private financing of higher education: Shaping public policy for the future.* Phoenix, AZ: American Council on Education and Oryx Press.
Cook, C. E. 1998. *Lobbying for higher education: How colleges and universities influence federal policy.* Nashville, TN: Vanderbilt University Press.
Finn, C. E., Jr. 1988. Judgment time for higher education in the court of public opinion. *Change* 20 (4) (July/August): 35–38.
Finn, C. E., Jr., and B. V. Manno. 1996. Behind the curtain: Higher education in the U.S. *Wilson Quarterly* (Winter): 44–53.
Fossey, R., and M. Bateman, eds. 1998. *Condemning students to debt: College loans and public policy.* New York: Teachers College Press.
Gladieux, L. E., and W. S. Swail. 1999. Financial aid is not enough: Improving the odds for minority and low-income students. In *Financing a college education: How it works, how it's changing,* ed. J. E. King, 177–97. Westport, CT: Oryx Press.
Habermas, J. 1985. *The theory of communicative action,* vol. 1, *Reason and the rationalization of society.* Translated by T. McCarthy. Boston: Beacon Press.
Habermas, J. 1987. *The theory of communicative action,* vol. 2, *Lifeworld and system: A critique of functionalist reasoning.* Translated by T. McCarthy. Boston: Beacon Press.
Hansen, W. L. 1983. The impact of student financial aid on access. In *The crisis in higher education,* ed. J. Froomkin. New York: Academy of Political Science.
Hearn, J. C. 1993. The paradox of growth in federal aid for college students: 1965–1990.

In *Higher education: Handbook of theory and research,* vol. 9, ed. J. C. Smart, 94–153. New York: Agathon Press.

Henry, M., B. Lingard, F. Rizvi, and S. Taylor. 2001. *The OECD, globalisation and education policy.* Amsterdam: Pergamon.

Honeyman, D. S., J. L. Wattenbarger, and K. C. Westbrook, eds. 1996. *Struggle to survive: Funding higher education in the next century.* Thousand Oaks, CA: Corwin Press.

Huber, E., and J. D. Stephens. 2001. *Development and crisis of the welfare state: Parties and policies in global markets.* Chicago: University of Chicago Press.

Johnson, E. L. 1989. Misconceptions about early land-grant colleges. In *ASHE reader on the history of higher education,* ed. L. F. Goodchild and H. S. Wechsler. Needham Heights, MA: Ginn Press.

Johnson, S. L., and J. J. Kidwell, eds. 1996. *Reinventing the university: Managing and financing institutions of higher education 1996.* New York: Wiley.

Keller, G. 1983. *Academic strategy: The management revolution in American higher education.* Baltimore: Johns Hopkins University Press.

Kidwell, J. J., and W. Massy. 1996. Transformation in higher education: Beyond administrative reengineering. In *Reinventing the university: Managing and financing institutions of higher education 1996,* ed. S. L. Johnson and J. J. Kidwell, 3–32. New York: Wiley.

King, J. E. 1999. Crisis or convenience: Why are students borrowing more? In *Financing a college education: How it works, how it's changing,* ed. J. E. King, 165–76. Westport, CT: Oryx Press.

Kramer, M. 1993. Changing roles in higher education finance. In *Background papers and reports,* ed. J. P. Merisotis. Washington, DC: National Commission Responsibility for Financing Postsecondary Education.

McPherson, M. S., and M. O. Schapiro. 1991. *Keeping college affordable: Government and educational opportunity.* Washington, DC: Brookings Institution.

McPherson, M. S., and M. O. Schapiro. 1997. *The student aid game: Meeting need and rewarding talent in American higher education.* Princeton, NJ: Princeton University Press.

Miron, L. F., and E. P. St. John., eds. 2003. *Reinterpreting urban school reform: Have urban schools failed, or has the reform movement failed urban schools?* Albany: State University of New York Press.

Mumper, M. 1996. *Removing college price barriers: What government has done and why it hasn't worked.* Albany: State University of New York Press.

Norris, D. M., and N. L. Poulton. 1987. *A guide for new planners.* Ann Arbor, MI: Society for College and University Planning.

Parsons, M. D. 1997. *Power and politics: Federal higher education policymaking in the 1990s.* Albany: State University of New York Press.

Parsons, M. D. 2000. The higher education policy arena: The rise and fall of a community. In *Higher education in transition: The challenges of the new millennium,* ed. B. Fife and J. Losco, 83–107. Westport, CT: Greenwood Publications.

Priest, D. M., W. E. Becker, D. Hossler, and E. P. St. John, eds. 2002. *Incentive-based budgeting systems in public universities.* Northampton, MA: Edward Elgar.

Rosenzweig, R. M. 1998. *The political university: Policy, politics, and presidential leadership in the American research university.* Baltimore: Johns Hopkins University Press.

St. John, E. P. 1991. A framework for reexamining state resource management strategies in higher education. *Journal of Higher Education* 62 (3): 263–87.

St. John, E. P. 1992. The transformation of private liberal arts colleges. *Review of Higher Education* 15 (1): 83–106.

St. John, E. P. 1994. *Prices, productivity and investment: Assessing financial strategies in higher education. ASHE-ERIC Higher Education Report No. 3.* Washington, DC: George Washington University, School of Education and Human Development.

St. John, E. P. 2002. *The access challenge: Rethinking the causes of the new inequality.* Policy Issue Report #2002-1. Bloomington, IN: Indiana Education Policy Center.

St. John, E. P. 2003. *Refinancing the college dream: Access, equal opportunity, and justice for taxpayers.* Baltimore: Johns Hopkins University Press.

St. John, E. P., and D. Hossler. 1998. Higher education desegregation in the post-*Fordice* legal environment: A critical-empirical perspective. In *Race, the courts, and equal education: The limits of the law,* vol. 15, *Readings on equal education,* ed. R. Fossey. New York: AMS Press.

St. John, E. P., and M. B. Paulsen. 2001. The finance of higher education: Implications for theory, research, policy and practice. In *The finance of higher education: Theory, research, policy, and practice,* ed. M. B. Paulsen and J. C. Smart. New York: Agathon Press.

Simsek, H., and R. B. Heydinger. 1992. An analysis of the paradigmatic shift in the evolution of U.S. higher education and its implications for the year 2000. Presented at the Association for the Study of Higher Education, ED352923. 72pp. MF-01; PC-03.

Slaughter, S. E.. 1991. The "official" ideology of higher education: Ironies and inconsistencies. In *Culture and ideology in higher education: Advancing a critical agenda,* ed. W. G. Tierney, 59–86. New York: Praeger.

Slaughter, S. E., and L. L. Leslie. 1997. *Academic capitalism: Politics, policies, and the entrepreneurial university.* Baltimore: Johns Hopkins University Press.

Teaford, J. C. 2002. *The rise of the states: Evolution of American state government.* Baltimore: Johns Hopkins University Press.

Teddlie, C. 1998. Four literatures associated with the study of equal education and desegregation in the United States. In *Race, the courts, and equal education: The limits of the law,* vol. 15, *Readings on Equal Education,* ed. R. Fossey, 237–58. New York: AMS Press.

Tribe, L. H. 1972. Policy science: Analysis or ideology. *Philosophy and Public Affairs* 2 (1) (fall): 66–110.

# Part I / The Changing Federal Context

The chapters in Part I provide a perspective on the changing nature of the federal policy context. First, John R. Thelin provides a historical view of the evolution of the federal role in educational policy. Institutional lobbying generally focuses on funding for institutions. Historically, as Thelin argues, the federal government provided funding for some programs thought to be in the federal interest (e.g., agricultural research), and over time, federal investment in research has expanded substantially. Direct funding for institutions is limited to a relatively small number of institutions; therefore, most institutional lobbying is for specific research programs.

Thelin uses a historical perspective to examine the evolution of institutional lobbying. From this perspective, the underlying pattern of going to the public for money remains largely unchanged even if the arguments of advocates have changed over time. This idea—that college advocates seek public support—remains a dominant theme in research on public policy in higher education. The authors in this book explicitly recognize this theme.

Second, James C. Hearn and Janet M. Holdsworth examine the transformation in federal student aid policy in the late twentieth century using a critical view of the policy process. They situate their analysis in an understanding of the political nature of this process. Student financial aid was the primary federal role in higher education in the 1960s and 1970s. However, for the past two decades, federal policy has been adrift, as Hearn and Holdsworth aptly describe. While the early student aid programs were rationalized using economic theories, the newer policies have evolved without a compelling rationale and without a substantial research base. Hearn and Holdsworth illustrate some of the ways that political beliefs dominate in the policy process. Indeed, they illustrate how ideology, rather than research, now drives major policy changes.

Finally, Clifton F. Conrad and David J. Weerts and examine the evolution of the federal agenda in college desegregation and consider aspects of the agenda that remain unfinished. The federal courts continue to play a role in enforcing constitutional principles in higher education. Conrad and Weerts focus on the shift in the rationales on which the federal courts have based their decisions about desegregation of public systems of higher education. Their analysis considers the role of the federal courts in shaping both state and federal policy, and considers how Supreme Court decisions influence litigation. They also point to social justice issues that were not adequately addressed in litigation over desegregation.

Conrad and Weerts walk a difficult line as they attempt to sum up the status of litigation on desegregation. Clifton Conrad was an expert witness in many of the cases they review. With David Weerts, one of his former graduate students, he grapples with the status of this litigation. They conclude that part of the agenda has been reached, but part remains unfinished.

In combination, these essays not only illustrate the complexity of federal policy but also show that a unified theory may not be possible. Political theories may inform the general understanding of the policy process, but economic theory and educational research also inform federal policy. If the courts are responsible for protecting the rights of citizens, this means theories of social justice must also be a central component of policy development.

These essays illuminate the pervasive role of institutional self-interest and political ideology in policy development and research. This is a challenge that faces all policy researchers: to convey an awareness of the political and ideological complexities of policy research. What is compelling about these chapters is that all of these authors are aware of the political nature of federal policy and attempt, in their own ways, to deal with this complexity in their essays. How policy researchers contend with this challenge influences whether and how policymakers will use their research.

# CHAPTER TWO

# Higher Education and the Public Trough

A Historical Perspective

## John R. Thelin

On July 20, 2001, virtually every major daily newspaper ran front-page headlines announcing, "U.S. Cuts off Johns Hopkins' Funding." Each national network's evening newscast also devoted prime time coverage to this story in which "Johns Hopkins University of Baltimore, the nation's largest recipient of U.S. government medical research money, was ordered to cease all federally funded research on humans yesterday after the June 2 death of a volunteer in an asthma experiment" (Zitner 2001).

The stakes were high. At the Johns Hopkins University, for example, about 2,400 federally funded research experiments were underway. The university had federal research and development expenditures of $770,580,000 for the 1999 fiscal year—roughly half of that university's annual operating budget (NSF 2001). For all of American higher education, the total federal grants and contract expenditures were over $18 billion. The controversy underscored the dramatic success story of federal research funding in universities. The current stature and scope of the federal research presence is illustrated by the recollection that immediately after World War II the entire National Institutes of Health budget was about $250,000 and was focused on maintaining venereal disease research studies that relied on U.S. sailors in port cities as their source of subjects and data.

While the presence of federal research grant dollars—and related concerns about regulations—certainly was the most dramatic development concerning federal support for higher education, it was not the whole story. At about the same time that the Johns Hopkins University story made headlines, the higher education "trade" paper *The Chronicle of Higher Education* published less spectacular but important annual progress reports on government funding issues. Several state governments announced plans for reduced rates of support for their public colleges and universities (Hebel 2001). At the federal level, student financial aid plans were embroiled in negotiations (Mulhauser 2001). Meanwhile, parents, university presidents, and federal agency directors annually debated and probed the rising costs and prices of going to college as both tuition charges and available student financial aid increased each year (Thelin 1985).

Within this gallery of articles about government support for higher education, one conspicuous piece dealt with federal legislation and its campus beneficiaries. According to this article, numerous colleges and universities were "Feasting at the Pork Barrel" as Congress gave colleges nearly $1.7 billion in earmarks in 2000–2001 (Brainard and Southwick 2001; Brainard 2002). Taken in isolation, these recent articles about higher education suggest public outrage or crisis, but that impression can be deceptive. A historical perspective on such matters as federal research grants or student financial aid programs suggests a slightly different interpretation.

Relying on historical analysis adds an irony to the topic, namely, the insight that the exposés tend to affirm rather than reform such federal appropriations for higher education. Over time, the recurrent headline stories simply become part of the long-term predictable annual ritual. For example, the previously cited August 2001 article about the higher education federal research largesse is almost an exact replica of an article that appeared a year earlier. In July 2000 the headlines read, "A Billion-Dollar Pork Barrel"—with the added commentary, "A swelling surplus in the federal budget leads Congress to earmark a record amount for buildings, research and other academic projects in the 2000 fiscal year" (Brainard and Southwick 2000).

Monitored across several years, these articles provide off-handed testimony to a significant historical development: the public acceptance of massive state and federal support for higher education. While critics may object to the practice of a U.S. senator slipping a "rider" into a huge highway construction bill that quietly allows for his or her state university to receive two million dollars for an asphalt research institute, the same individuals hardly expect the practice to stop. Nearly all groups on the political spectrum expect government support for higher education now and in the future. The arguments tend to be about the fine-tuning of who, how, and where. Just as each spring brings newspaper reports about the swallows returning to San Juan Capistrano, so it is that in summer they write about the migratory patterns of the nation's capitol. The Republican elephants and Democratic donkeys are joined by the metaphorical campus pigs returning to the federal trough in Washington, D.C.

This rhythm of politics and higher education is comparable to the life cycle of federal entitlement programs initiated during President Franklin D. Roosevelt's New Deal administration. In the late 1930s, proposals for social security were denounced by Republicans and championed by Democrats. In 2001, both parties and virtually all citizens presume that social security is part of our national fabric. Indeed, one concern is not that any political group will push to eliminate the program—but rather, the worry is that at some point the success of the program will exhaust it. Government support for higher education in the twenty-first century faces a comparable paradox of success and popularity, punctuated by the familiar annual stories dealing with funding cuts or excesses.

Taken together, these articles about current and recurrent themes illustrate the major contours of government support for American higher education. From this core sample one can glean the following key points: government support for higher education in the United States is substantial; it is also expected—with predictable requests for more funding or complaints about reduced increases in funding. These articles also provide good clues to the two divergent government areas supporting higher education: sponsored research and development grants and contracts; and undergraduate student financial aid programs, including scholarships and loans. State governments, in contrast, have come to provide annual appropriations for operating budgets usually tied to student enrollments and capital construction costs. Both federal and state financial investments are large. However, postsecondary education spending as a percentage of a state government's budget is substantial—one of the highest priorities in most states. In contrast, federal higher-education-related expenditures, although large in dollars, remain a miniscule part of the congressional budget.

These different categorical responsibilities provide a snapshot of contemporary policies and practices. The historical question is, How did we reach this interesting hybrid American arrangement? Merely chronicling a success story is bad historical writing. Instead, these developments must be reconstructed to suggest the distinctive and significant nature of public funding for higher education—one that includes institutional reliance and regulation. This type of historical inquiry also helps us reconsider our most obvious beliefs and policies. For example, about twenty-five years ago Chester E. Finn Jr. raised a fundamental point in his book *Scholars, Dollars, and Bureaucrats:* While fiscal 1977 federal expenditures for higher education amounted to nearly $14 billion, the federal government did not have a comprehensive and unified policy toward higher education (Finn 1978). To compound this enigma, the Tenth Amendment of the U.S. Constitution states that powers not expressly delegated to the federal government are reserved to the states or the people. Wouldn't this pertain to higher education? When connecting past and present policies, the primary requirement is to steer away from the fallacy of inevitability—that is, we ought not presume that the current pattern of public funding for higher education was destined to turn out the way it did. So, briefly, it is useful to go back to the start of American higher education.

## Back to Basics

The most amazing fact about government support for American higher education is that it occurred at all. Going back to the colonial era, it is important to recall that the mercantile purpose of a colony—sending raw materials or profits back to the mother country—made building colleges in a colonial outpost an unusual investment for the British crown, where performance tended to be monitored by import-export data. The raw materials of sugar cane, spices, cotton, indigo, and tobacco as well as the finished products of rum and molasses—not bachelor's degrees conferred—literally were the coin of the realm. Prisoners, conscript laborers, and slaves—not students and faculty— were the human capital that most dominated policy discussions about Great Britain's imperial economy of the seventeenth and eighteenth centuries. For example, one supplicant for royal monies petitioned the court of King William and Queen Mary, pleading that the monarchy's support for a college in the New World might help to save souls of infidels as well as colonists. The king's attorney general, whose job was to act as a filter and buffer for numerous requests, responded curtly, "Souls! Damn your souls! Raise tobacco!" (Rudolph 1962).

Fortunately for the history of government-supported higher education in America (and later, the United States), a few exceptions to the rule of imperial economics and policies existed. The Crown did find some interest in supporting colonial colleges that purported both to save souls and to instill clear thinking. In an unusual reversal of standard practice, the Crown and colonial governors earmarked taxes on tobacco to support building a new college rather than to fill the coffers of the Crown! Similarly, building lucrative roadways and canals was the linchpin of colonial productivity, but the Crown and every one of the New World colonial governments dedicated transportation taxes, tolls, bridge fees, and surveying licenses—as well as sales taxes—to help found and maintain a college in each colony.

Imperial policies made a college charter in the British Empire, whether at home or abroad, an extremely difficult document to obtain. However, a royal charter was not merely a license to operate; it was comparable to a marriage in that both parties had serious, perpetual commitments to one another. It meant that the royal and colonial governments had an obligation both to oversee and to fund a college. Consequently, colleges in the American colonies were relatively well supported. One is hard-pressed to find another public works project or institution that received as generous support as the colleges. Surviving academic buildings on the historic campuses provide a good example. Usually the "college building" was the largest public building in a colony. Colleges certainly received far more funding than did elementary schools, public health, or employee benefits of that era.

Another legacy from England's institutional regulations and laws had evolved by the eighteenth century: government allowances for perpetual endowments. Colleges, as one of the major recipients of endowment gifts from alumni and supporters, gained considerable financial leverage and stability from this policy. In contrast, the French government distrusted the accumulation of capital in private institutions and required endowments to be dispersed and spent in a relatively short time, such as five years (Sears 1922).

## New Ground Rules for a New Nation

The colonial precedent for strong government support of higher education was modified—and almost lost—with the formation of the United States. Most Americans feared a centralized national government with the power to tax for special projects. Congress did, however, initiate the practice of awarding each new state a substantial land grant for establishing academies or colleges. In contrast, between 1790 and 1820 numerous proposals, endorsed by prominent leaders, floated the idea of creating and funding a "national university." But this never materialized. With the important exception of the federal role in establishing and supporting the U.S. Naval Academy at Annapolis and the U.S.

Military Academy at West Point, college building and funding fell exclusively under the states' domain.

This new nationalism hardly meant lack of interest in higher education by the states. To the contrary, many governors and legislatures granted charters to petitioning groups, especially in the younger states of what was then called the West and the South—Michigan, Ohio, Indiana, Kentucky, Tennessee, Georgia, and North Carolina. In contrast to the British approach, however, the new state governments seldom tied substantial or regular funding to their conferral of a college charter. One finds an erratic, uneven record of state support—ranging from occasional lottery proceeds to deeding of cheap land to colleges. State governments often played favorites, rewarding one college with a lottery award while another college got the consolation prize of desolate swampland. Such short-run favoritism often had the opposite effect for colleges years later when poorly funded institutions owned real estate that later escalated in value.

If a source of relatively stable government support for higher education in the early nineteenth century existed, it was probably at the local government level. Mayors and city founders along with real estate developers offered inducements of land, buildings, and money to persuade a college to locate in their township. Higher education perhaps set a precedent for the late-twentieth-century practice of American cities' relying on public subsidies and tax breaks to court professional sports teams to their metropolitan area.

## The Private-Public Conundrum

One consequence of the peculiar state approach to chartering but not actually funding colleges was confusion between the present-day notions of "private" and "public" institutions. In retrospect, it raises an interesting and perennial question: Does being a state institution necessarily mean that the institution receives state funding? Another question involving a subtle but important distinction must also be asked: Does a state's failure to provide funding to a "public" college result in the forfeiture of state control?

One finds in both past and present a great variation from state to state in the treatment of higher education. The scope of support ranges from enjoying status as an entitlement in one state to an individual investment choice in another. California, for example, took great pride for over a century in its tradition of charging no tuition at its state colleges and universities. On the opposite side of the continent, New Hampshire's tradition kept taxes low and charged full tuition at its state university. Most states now provide a subsidy of sorts when a student who is a resident of the state enrolls in a state institution, but even this general tendency is interpreted with a range of policies across the fifty states.

An interesting variation on the state subsidy theme is the development of institutional incentives. Many state governments provide tuition grants to students that are portable to an array of institutions within the state. For example, the California Scholarship Commission started a program in the 1950s whose scholarships became known as "Cal Grants." The honor of being a California State Scholar included the financial tool of choice. In some states—for example, Massachusetts and New Jersey—state governments even allowed their state scholars to carry their tuition grants to institutions in other states, public or private!

## Land Grants and the 1862 Morrill Act Legacy

Any comprehensive history of American higher education must pay homage to the 1862 Morrill Act for having fostered the land grant colleges. This seminal legislation has come to be associated with inclusion of the "useful" studies and with widespread access into higher learning—agriculture, engineering, mechanics, and mining—compressed into the familiar "A&M" acronym. The funding formula was intriguing: each state was apportioned land grants based on its number of congressional seats. The proceeds of the land sales were to be used within five years to support and maintain "at least one college where the leading object shall be, without excluding other scientific and classical studies, and including military tactics, to teach such branches of learning as are related to agriculture and the mechanic arts, in such manner as the legislatures of the States may respectively prescribe, in order to promote the liberal and practical education of the industrial classes in the several pursuits and profession in life. . . ." Shortly thereafter, thirty-seven institutions were designated as "land grant" colleges. In some cases, a state legislature opted to graft the new programs onto a historic college. Elsewhere, states created wholly new state land grant colleges. Either way, most of these institutions remained relatively small in enrollment, modest in funding, and limited in scope as of 1890.

The relative silence of state and federal governments on matters of campus enhancement in the 1880s did not necessarily mean lack of government interest in technology, applied science, or research. There was no presumption or imperative that colleges or universities would be the institutional sites for large-scale government projects. The federal government created its own scientific infrastructure, with such components as the U.S. Coast and Geodetic Survey and the U.S. Geological Survey, along with the Department of Agriculture's Weather Bureau. Historian Daniel J. Kevles concluded that the Geological Survey enjoyed international praise for the quality of its scientific work. Its annual budget of $500,000 between 1881 and 1884 was substantial. Federal scientists faced continual review and criticism from impatient members of Congress who favored research that had practical, predictive value (Kevles 1998). Despite such repeated scrutiny and complaints, the federal government's investments in ongoing scientific surveys and research remained strong.

The groundwork for funding federally sponsored projects at colleges and universities may have been put into place by the Morrill Act of 1862, but a serious, enduring national policy for funding university research remained a nascent endeavor until about 1890. Eventually, a wave of related federal legislation expanded on the advances made by the 1862 law. Thanks to the effective lobbying and organizational acumen of George W. Atherton, president of Pennsylvania State College from 1882 to 1906, the designated land grant colleges were effective in consolidating and enhancing the original Morrill Act (Williams 1991). Hence, one must look at Atherton's leadership role in the formation of the Association of State Universities and Land-Grant Colleges as a lobbying endeavor that led to passage of the Hatch Act in 1887, the second Morrill Act of 1890, and even later legislation to track the flow of federal funds to such activities as experimental research sites, agricultural and home economics extension services, and large-scale sponsored research. It was the second Morrill Act of 1890, for example, that explicitly authorized the funding for historically Black land grant colleges (Wright 1988). This trend of collective action and federal support for agriculture as a part of higher education continued well into the twentieth century. As one noted economist concluded, "Political lobbying brought legislative results" (Cheit 1975).

## Characterizing the Federal Presence

The succession of major federal legislation between 1887 and 1920 that benefited the state land grant colleges both established and illustrated some important features. First, this "horizontal funding" cut across several institutions by emphasizing particular fields. Second, such appropriations were thematic—focusing on addressing some issue or topic, such as agricultural productivity or finding a way to prevent wheat rust, deemed worthy of prolonged national attention. Later, in World War I, American campuses used such funding to bring together military officers for intense training. And in World War II, the federal government tried a new approach: relying on the expertise of faculty at multiple campuses to join forces with military, business, and other academics on high-priority projects. The Manhattan Project and the development of the hydrogen bomb provides an example of such collaboration. It included numerous other projects as well, ranging from weapons development to nutrition research, cryptology, cartography, and foreign language instruction and cultural analysis.

## State Governments and Enrollment-Driven Funding

An overlooked but important approach to higher education public policy took place at the University of Illinois in the early 1900s. Compared to adjacent Midwestern states such as Ohio, Michigan, and Wisconsin, Illinois had not provided robust funding for its flagship university. The University of Illinois's president, however, lobbied persistently for regular, reliable state funding. Keeping the Illinois legislature informed of proposed projects while providing accurate estimates of anticipated costs became a central part of his strategy. Counter to the conventional presidential practice of understating costs to the state, Illinois's President James took time to explain why proposed new units would be expensive but worthwhile (Slosson 1910). This approach generated long-term benefits far beyond the specific appropriations the University of Illinois received that particular year.

Indeed, after 1910 the fundamental achievement of state governments and higher education was the practice of annual appropriations, increasingly defined by standards and formulae. In general, state governments provided basic funding for their state colleges and universities—encouraging undergraduate education and professional courses for entry-level positions in business, engineering, teaching, and public health. Few state legislatures provided extensive research time for faculty. Advanced studies and doctoral degree programs remained on the margin of state priorities.

Coincidentally, changes in demographics and educational policies in the post–World War II era provided fertile ground for state university finance stability. Thanks to such policies as the GI Bill and the 1947 Truman Commission Report, Americans received both a taste and a tease of expanded educational opportunity. Furthermore, the increased birth rate of the late 1930s and the 1940s meant that after World War II, states could anticipate a rapidly expanding cohort of students to proceed through their respective state K–12 educational systems. In some cases, the large number of WWII veterans who migrated to different states intensified the already existing population pressure. The result was that in California and New York, two highly populated and education-minded states, governments faced an immediate and long-term crisis: how to best accommodate the forthcoming wave of annually increasing college applicants.

In California, the state government embraced a policy of reliance on property taxes for higher education and reaffirmed a commitment to "no tuition" charge at the state's public colleges, universities, and community colleges. Ironically, making good on this promise was, for California's General Assembly and governors, less a problem of money than it was of the logistics of time. How could a responsible and responsive state government build and accommodate fast enough? The mutually beneficial solution was to place increasing reliance on per capita student-enrollment-driven funding. For university presidents and trustees of the 1950s and 1960s, this was attractive. Demographic projections indicated that the size of the student cohort would continue to increase for several years. Meanwhile, each added student cost the campus less to educate, since there was what economists called an "increasing returns to scale." State legislators, meanwhile, could reassure voters in their home districts that, indeed, the state college and university system would have seats in the lecture halls and laboratories for their sons and daughters who wanted to go to college. Enrollment-driven funding was well matched to a period of economic and demographic growth.

The acceptance of enrollment-driven funding by state legislatures and state institutions alike was no small accomplishment. Such an achievement did, however, run the risk of imposing a misleading sense of standardization and security on higher education in the second half of the twentieth century. On closer inspection, however, reliance on enrollment-driven funding proved to be risky. No state university was completely protected from the perils of a changing state economy or the vacillations in public and legislative opinion regarding state institutions. As an analysis by Mary McKeown and Daniel Layzell has shown, the state-by-state variations in what was meant by enrollment-driven funding suggest a concept that was sometimes shaky in practice (Layzell and McKeown 1992).

## The GI Bill of 1944

American colleges and universities received an unexpected and not wholly welcomed windfall in 1944 when Congress passed Public Law 36, the Servicemen's Readjustment Act—popularly known as the GI Bill (Kiester 1994). The novel features of this legislation were as follows: first, it was entitlement—the government guaranteed financial aid to any veteran who had served after 1940 and met other conditions. Second, the scholarship monies were portable, carried by the eligible student to the institution of his or her choice. An important corollary was that an institution had to be documented as eligible—a regulation that gave a boost to regional accreditation since it was a proxy for federal government approval.

The GI Bill laid the groundwork for the proposition of increasing access and affordability through portable student aid grants. It resulted in $5.5 billion in funds going toward higher education expenses. Out of 14 million eligible veterans, 2.2 million opted to use their GI Bill benefits. The fact that interest in the program by eligible students far exceeded predictions had lasting implications for government support of higher education. Amidst the post hoc celebration, however, it is easy to forget how uncertain passage of the act was— and how unknown would be its consequences. Many college and university officials had reservations, even opposition, to the act. What they really wanted was a resumption of "business as usual"— "real" college life of the late 1930s. The implication was that the immediate measure of providing a financial aid system for returning veterans to a wide range of institutional choices was not necessarily intended to represent a permanent change in higher education or in programs sponsored by the federal government. That it did signal a permanent, significant change in public policies was in large part due to the influence of two books published immediately after World War II.

## Policies Following World War II

The most important works about higher education published in the late 1940s addressed the issues of government relations and public policies for funding colleges. Vannevar Bush's report, *Science: The Endless Frontier* (1945), and the Report of the President's Commission on Higher Education, *Higher Education for American Democracy* (1947), chaired by George Zook both provided a rationale for the major federal initiatives toward higher education for several decades. This apparent cohesion, however, is a bit misleading because at the time of publication, their respective arguments were disconnected and perhaps even antagonistic. In sum, they represented "federal policies" toward higher education as distinguished from a unified, integrated "public policy" for higher education. The value of these works, however, rests in the fact that prior to their publication a concerted and enduring federal presence in American higher education really did not exist.

Vannevar Bush's *Science: The Endless Frontier* made a case for continuing federal support of large-scale science research into peacetime and for a domestic economy. Bush, a president of the Carnegie Institution and a physicist with strong ties to MIT, had headed up the wartime Office of Scientific Research and Development. His report indicated the appeal of a new model of federal involvement in "Big Science"—namely, reliance on competitive, peer-reviewed grants submitted by scientists at universities to carry out government projects. This contrasted with proposals that the federal government build its own laboratories and research agencies and infrastructure. Over time, the federal government would do both, but the innovation of competitive research and development grants advocated by Bush would be the genesis of the "federal grant university." Bush's argument also helped create policy structures that would characterize serious large-scale scientific research for decades to come.

If Bush's report symbolized the manifesto of "big science as the best science," matching individual talents with government priorities, then the 1947 Report of the so-called Truman Commission represented the federal government's increasing interest in educational equity and access. Just as *Science: The Endless Frontier* encouraged the extension of federal research support into peacetime, so did the Truman Commission Report suggest ways in which the federal government could—and should—extend the principles of the GI Bill beyond an intense, short-term program. Sound policy for the future called for an array of programs that would increase college choices and affordability to an entire generation of American citizens coming through the primary- and secondary-school pipeline.

While all commission reports succumb in part to the blandness of compromise and generic discussion, the Truman Commission Report managed to forcefully assert the analyses and recommendations that became the blueprint for subsequent federal policies involving student financial aid and the general expansion of postsecondary educational opportunity. When viewed from the perspective of 2000 and beyond, it reads like a script for a succession of now familiar and famous programs. It presaged, for example, the *Brown v. The Board of Education of Topeka, Kansas* case and included discussion of the inequities and injustices of discrimination in education on the basis of race and income. Its chapters provide an early commentary on the imperative for legislation and programs ranging from the New Frontier through the Great Society and into the era of Pell Grants and guaranteed student loans that today we coagulate as "social justice." Furthermore, the report contained a lengthy discussion of community colleges. As with all commission reports, there was no imperative that its recommendations be linked to legislation and implemented. One explanation for this was that for President Harry Truman, commitment to expanding educational opportunity lost out in priority when faced with a hostile Congress, an unsupportive press, and urgent matters of national defense. Ironically, state governments—not the federal government—would take the initiative in carrying out many of the recommended measures. By the 1960s, however, many of the ideas and agencies first envisioned in the Truman Commission Report reached fruition as federally mandated and federally funded programs.

## Sponsored Research and the "Federal Grant" University

The primary legacy of the immediate post–World War II discussions and legislation was the acceptance of permanent, ongoing support of advanced research and development by a variety of federal agencies. The consequence for higher education was the creation and nurturing of what Clark Kerr in 1963 called the "Federal Grant University"—about fifty major institutions that received the bulk of federal research funding (Kerr 1963). For relative newcomers to large-scale research, the federal government funded such programs as EpScore to provide seed money for under-represented regions and institutional categories. In the main, however, competitive peer review of research grant proposals by established scientists and scholars characterized most federal agency sponsored research. The arrangement was sufficiently productive to classify the period from 1945 to 1970 as "Higher Education's Golden Age."

Signs of tarnish in the "golden age" appeared by the mid-1970s. From the point of view of the established large research universities, the federal government offered signs of retreat from its patronage. Even though annual research and development appropriations may have increased in actual dollars, the research community argued that years of double-digit inflation and a decrease in the *rate* of funding increases had effectively stifled an invaluable "big science" research effort. Illustrative of this line of argument was Robert M. Rosenzweig, whose 1982 book *The Research Universities and Their Patrons* reflected his experience as Stanford University's vice president for government relations and, later, as president of the Association of American Universities (Rosenzweig and Turlington 1982).

## Federal Student Financial Aid, 1972 to 2002

The federal government's role as a relative latecomer in student financial aid provides a curious fact in the history of American governmental support for higher education. With the important exception of special, intensive programs targeted to select populations—military veterans, the children of veterans, and disabled students—prior to the 1970s federal student aid programs were relatively small, limited, and specific. Even the famous Higher Education Act of 1965 dealt primarily with extraordinary appropriations for facilities construction and campus libraries. After 1972, however, one finds a proliferation of well-funded entitlements—an alphabet soup of the BEOG, SEOG, and SSIG. Decoding the acronyms, these included the Basic Educational Opportunity Grant (soon renamed the Pell Grant in honor of Senator Claiborne Pell of Rhode Island), the Supplementary Educational Opportunity Grant, and the State Student Incentive Grant. Some would argue that such legislation was an outgrowth of other civil rights laws in that these programs expanded affordable access to higher education. Less known is that the massive federal student aid programs created in 1972 were the product of compromise and unexpected opportunity.

As suggested by earlier discussion of the "Federal Grant" universities of the 1960s, America's established colleges and universities—both public and private—had for years enjoyed prestige and popularity among citizens and elected officials. University presidents and leaders of higher education lobbying groups in Washington, D.C., were confident that eventually they would be successful in obtaining direct institutional funding from federal agencies. This optimistic mood of the mid-1960s, however, started to erode in large measure due to the student unrest and campus demonstrations. Another problem with direct federal aid to institutions was that politicians were left in the unenviable position of having to say "no" to some institutional applicants. No member of the legislature relished the prospect. Furthermore, if prestige and merit were the criteria, institutional grants would most likely have been geographically maldistributed. This would be another source of political tension among the "have" and "have not" congressional districts.

Resolution came from an unlikely source. A new, relatively small cadre of student activist groups had discovered working within the system. Lobbying, rather than rebelling or disrupting, provided an effective vehicle for change that helped shift institutional appropriations to student financial aid programs. Why was this attractive? First, a student grant would be an entitlement: if a college student qualified according to published, known criteria, he or she would be guaranteed to receive the award. Second, federal student aid would be "portable"—the student as recipient became a consumer, carrying with him or her federal grant funding redeemable at numerous state institutions. The student (probably the son or daughter of a happy voter and taxpayer), not the federal government, made the choice. This forced colleges to compete for student aid recipients—and institutions could blame only themselves, not a congressional subcommittee, if large numbers of students did not bring their federal grants to "Alma Mater." Significantly, this genuine landmark in public policy and higher education support emphasized direct grants—not loans.

The federal student aid programs worked reasonably well for about six or seven years. By 1980, however, some new situations amended both the programs and their image. Politicians during a reelection year scurried to respond to complaints that federal student aid programs tended to favor lower-income groups and neglected the "Missing Middle Class." To correct that allegation, members of Congress favored guaranteed student loans, thus bringing commercial banks into the partnership. The loans, virtually an entitlement, were a predictable success. Banks liked them, as did students and their families. Why wouldn't a family take advantage of low-interest guaranteed loans that had few restrictions? The public relations problem occurred when stories surfaced about individuals using the loans to finance noneducational endeavors. The real long-term problem, however, was that federal loans increasingly supplanted federal grants as the hallmark of undergraduate student aid programs.

## The Wear and Tear on Traditional Policies since 1980

By 1990 a customary lament of state university presidents was, "Once we were state supported. Then we were state assisted. Now we are state located." Administrators argued that state governments had persistently reduced their customary share of state appropriations. State colleges and universities had to make up the difference of costs by raising the price of tuition, or state legislatures could cap tuition charges as a way of reassuring parents and voters that state colleges were "affordable." Unfortunately, the latter strategy ignored the rising costs of educating a student and required the state college or university to continually absorb the difference. This was the plight described by Thomas Wallace, president of Illinois State University, in his papers for the American Council on Education and in his article for *Change* magazine (Wallace 1993).

The funding formula of state appropriations plus institutional tuition charges could work well only if both sides operated in good faith. In an interesting shift from conventional practice and wisdom, Wallace went so far as to argue that a tradition of low tuition charges at public institutions was dysfunctional both to institutions and to students if the state government chronically underfunded its share of the appropriation. This practice left institutions severely strapped for the resources necessary to meet the cost of educating a student. The student, in turn, was short-changed by a false sense of economy: large classes, fewer course offerings, reduction of fields of study, and so on.

## Indirect Support through Tax Policies

Most of the historical discussion has emphasized direct funding from government to higher education constituencies. Often overlooked are the enormous benefits colleges and universities have enjoyed through indirect sources—namely, tax exemption. One reason this warrants consideration is that it is not an inalienable or unchanging benefit. Many large universities offer their host communities money for public services as both a goodwill offering and a political move to ensure that local public services are not denied to the institution. The current legal tax exemption for most universities allows them leverage in determining how much money to contribute to the local government (Kay, Brown, and Allee 1988). However, this situation is subject to reinterpretation. A good example is a recent court decision in Vermont invoking a precedent from over a century ago. The State Supreme Court ruled that land owned by an educational institution did not automatically qualify for a tax exemption. Rather, universities and other schools needed to use the property for educational purposes to receive the tax break (Blumenstyk 1988; Therrien 1990; Van Der Werf 2001).

## Conclusion

Whether one examines the 1862 Morrill Act or the 1944 Servicemen's Readjustment Act, federal government support for higher education displays a distinctive characteristic: it often is a convenient means for the U.S. government to attain larger national goals. The 1862 Morrill Act promoted western land development of a distinctive style. The GI Bill defused problems of the postwar labor market. Research funding during the Cold War era and beyond provided pieces of a broadly defined national defense apparatus.

In recent decades, however, this perspective showed signs of change. Thanks in large part to the extended writings of economist and university president Howard Bowen, Americans—including governors, state legislators, and U.S. representatives and senators—increasingly viewed funding for higher education as a social investment for the public good (Bowen 1978). For example, by the mid-1980s virtually every gubernatorial candidate across the country vowed to be an "Education Governor." An important and persistent corollary emphasized by university presidents and the national higher education associations housed in Washington, D.C.'s One DuPont Circle was that the costs of compliance with federal and state regulations had been unreasonable (Fields 1979). According to the higher education establishment, they were needlessly rigid and tended to underestimate voluntary compliance. On balance, the regulations hampered the ability of colleges and universities to deliver the services and expertise associated with its stature as a national asset and social service (Bok 1980). Above all, academic leaders argued that higher education had been reasonably effective and efficient in both educating students and carrying out research projects. When assessed in comparison with other federal and state initiatives—ranging from aerospace contracts to highway construction— American higher education was a government bargain, a national treasure, and a source of international admiration.

This mixed tone between capitol and campus has continued into the twenty-first century. One must remember the net gains in the threshold of government funding for higher education in all its varieties. In 1950 even the president of Harvard University seriously discussed with senior professors the proposition that Harvard might not apply for or accept federal research grants. Such a suggestion in the new millennium would seem laughable, an indication of the integral role government funding plays at virtually all American higher education institutions.

ACKNOWLEDGMENT

The author wishes to thank Eric Moyen, a Ph.D. candidate in educational policy studies at the University of Kentucky, for his research and editorial assistance.

REFERENCES

Blumenstyk, G. 1988. Town-gown battles escalate as beleaguered cities assail college tax exemptions. *Chronicle of Higher Education* 34 (41): n.p.

Bok, D. 1980. The federal government and the university. *Public Interest* 58 (Winter): 80–101.

Bowen, H. R. 1978. *Investment in learning: The individual and social value of American higher education.* San Francisco: Jossey-Bass.

Brainard, J. 2002. Another record year for academic pork. *Chronicle of Higher Education* 49 (5) (September 27): A20–A21 and A24.

Brainard, J., and R. Southwick. 2000. Congress gives colleges a billion-dollar bonanza. *Chronicle of Higher Education* 46 (47) (July 28): A29–A44.

Brainard, J., and R. Southwick. 2001. A record year at the federal trough: Colleges feast on $1.67 billion in earmarks. *Chronicle of Higher Education* 47 (48) (August 10): A20–A38.

Bush, V. 1945. *Science: The Endless Frontier.* Arlington, VA: National Science Foundation.

Cheit, E. F. 1975. *The useful arts and the liberal tradition.* New York: McGraw-Hill.

Fields, C. 1976. Higher education's Washington lobbyists. *Chronicle of Higher Education* 28 (4) (March 19): A1 and A11–A13.

Finn, C. E. 1978. *Scholars, dollars, and bureaucrats: Federal policy toward higher education.* Washington, DC: Brookings Institution.

Hebel, S. 2001. Public colleges feel impact of the economic downturn: Many are being forced to enact large tuition increases; others face budget uncertainty. *Chronicle of Higher Education* 47 (45) (July 20): A21–A22.

Kay, D., W. A. Brown, and D. J. Allee. 1988. *University and local government fiscal relations.* A study conducted by Cornell University.

Kerr, C. 1963. *The uses of the university.* Cambridge, MA: Harvard University Press.

Kevles, D. J. 1998. A time for audacity: What the past has to teach the present about science and the federal government. In *Universities and their leadership,* ed. W. G. Bowen and H. T. Shapiro, 199–240. Princeton, NJ: Princeton University Press.

Kiester, E., Jr. 1994. The GI Bill may be the best deal ever made by Uncle Sam. *Smithsonian Magazine* 25 (8) (November): 129–39.

Layzell, D. T., and Mary P. McKeown. 1992. *State funding formulas for higher education: Trends and issues.* Paper presented at the Annual ASHE Conference, Minneapolis.

Mulhauser, D. 2001. Financial assistance for students rose sharply over the past four years. *Chronicle of Higher Education* 47 (48) (August 10): A51.

National Science Foundation (NSF). 2001. Top institutions in federal research-and-development expenditures, fiscal 1999. *Chronicle of Higher Education Almanac Issue, 2001–2* 48 (1) (August 31): 30.

Rudolph, F. 1962. *The American college and university: A history.* New York: Knopf.

Rosenzweig, R. M., and B. Turlington. 1982. *The research universities and their patrons.* Berkeley: University of California Press in conjunction with the Association of American Universities.

Sears, J. B. 1922. *Philanthropy in the history of American higher education.* Washington, DC: U.S. Government Printing Office.

Slosson, E. E. 1910. *Great American universities.* New York: Macmillan.

Thelin, J. R. 1985. Why does college cost so much? *Wall Street Journal,* 11 December, 32.

Therrien, L. 1990. Getting Joe College to pay for city services. *Business Week* (July 16): 37.

Van Der Werf, M. 2001. Vermont court says educational use is test for property tax exemption. *Chronicle of Higher Education* 46 (46): A35.

Wallace, T. P. 1993. Public higher education finance: The dinosaur age persists. *Change* 25 (4) (July/August): 56–63.

Williams, R. L. 1991. *The origins of federal support for higher education: George W. Atherton and the land-grant college movement.* University Park, PA: Pennsylvania State University Press.

Wright, S. J. 1988. The Black colleges and universities: Historical background and future prospects. *Virginia Humanities Newsletter* 14 (spring): 1–4.

Zitner, A. 2001. U.S. cuts off Johns Hopkins' funding. *Lexington* (Kentucky) *Herald-Leader,* 20 July, A12.

Zook, G. F., ed. 1947. *Higher Education in a Democracy: A Report of the President's Commission on Higher Education.* New York: Harper & Bros.

# CHAPTER THREE

# Federal Student Aid

The Shift from Grants to Loans

## James C. Hearn and Janet M. Holdsworth

Federal student financial aid programs for postsecondary education attendance have expanded remarkably in scope and volume in the past fifty years. In the early 1950s, there was virtually no federal student aid available for the masses of Americans who had not served in the armed forces. Now, generally available federally supported aid totals nearly 50 billion dollars, and the federal aid programs serve increasingly diverse purposes, institutions, and students.[1]

Over the remarkable half-century of growth, the national aid programs have passed through several phases with varying patterns of philosophical and fiscal emphasis. Many observers of this evolving history look to the mid-1970s as something of a "golden era" in federal student aid policy, notable both for an emphasis on need-based grants rather than loans and for relatively high levels of consensus among policymakers, leaders in different postsecondary sectors, and student aid officials. There can be little question that since the mid-1970s the grant emphasis in federal policy has evaporated (see Hearn 1993, 2001a, 2001b). As the College Board (2000b, p. 4) has noted, "Over the past quarter century, federal student aid has drifted from a grant-based to a loan-based system, producing a sea change in the way many students and families finance postsecondary education." Similarly, there can be little question that since the mid-1970s the level of consensus surrounding federal aid policy has declined significantly. In the face of dissension around aid policy goals in recent years, former SUNY chancellor and financial aid authority Bruce Johnstone (1999, p. 3) has argued that "the fabric of the American 'system' of financial assistance and tuition policy seems to be unraveling." Of course, it is easy to oversimplify and romanticize the aid programs' past glories, but aid experts agree that the current context is quite distinct from that of the mid-1970s.

Interestingly, however, it may be most accurate to view the grant emphasis and relative harmony of aid policy in the mid-1970s as more an aberration than an early state of grace from which policymaking has fallen. The first major investments in generally available federal student aid came in the form, not of grants, but of student loans under the National Defense Education Act, enacted in Eisenhower's second term.[2] Student loans, including those under the new Guaranteed Student Loan (GSL) program, were also major elements in the federal Higher Education Act of 1965. That act was passed only after heated negotiation among parties holding widely different views of the proper federal role in education. The reauthorization of the Higher Education Act in 1972 was by any definition a divisive battle among starkly contrasting views and interests (Gladieux and Wolanin 1976), with those favoring institutional control via campus-based delivery of expanded aid programs challenged by those favoring student choice via the initiation of "portable," nationally standardized calculations of aid eligibility. Although the latter side arguably won in these debates, the case was not closed: even during the putatively halcyon 1970s, there were alternative delivery approaches in place for student loans. Over the years since the 1970s, we have witnessed declines in federal attention to broader concerns like the effectiveness of overall aid policy (see Advisory Committee on Student Financial Assistance 2001) and increasing willingness to experiment on a variety of new fronts (e.g., tax credits, merit-related aid) without abandoning older programs.

Thus, when we look past the 1970s into the 1980s and beyond, we see a *return* to dissensus and to a lesser prominence for grants. The current dominance, volume, and fiscal magnitude of loans in federal policy is certainly unprecedented, as is the level of concern over the implications of students' loan burdens, but some important foundations of this context were in place well before the 1970s.[3]

Putting this history in the context of this volume, one would be hard-pressed to argue that there has ever been common policy ground regarding federal student aid, or federal student loans in particular. Absent a coherent, persuasive, and enduring defense for the more expensive choice of emphasizing grants, federal policymakers have allowed loans to become the dominant vehicle of national student-aid policy. The shift to loans can be captured in five major themes. First, growth has been ongoing in the student-loan programs for decades, but especially since the mid-1970s. Second, a wide variety of policy rationales has been used to initiate and defend the loan programs. Third, the programs have suffered from an ongoing absence of tight oversight and evaluation. Fourth, the programs have been consistently subject to policy disputes concerning goals, participants, and delivery systems. Fifth, policy has been developed incrementally, year by year, rather than on the basis of longer-term strategic and philosophical considerations. These themes in the growing federal involvement in student loans are explored in this chapter.

## Growth

As noted above, *growth in the student loan programs has been dramatic since the 1950s, and especially since the mid-1970s.* Since the mid-1970s, loan aid has risen spectacularly as a proportion of all federally supported aid and as a proportion of all aid (College Board 1993, 1995, 2000b). In constant-dollar terms, loan aid increased 125 percent over the 1990s, while total grant aid increased only 55 percent (College Board 2000b). The rapid expansion of the loan programs has affected not only the efficiency and effectiveness of the programs themselves but every other aspect of federal student-aid policy. The growth in dollar volume and number of loans may be attributed to an interrelated complex of factors.

Colleges and universities have been facing rising costs as well as pressures on several sources of institutional revenue (e.g., state funding, medical operations). This squeeze has stimulated increases in tuition charges in both public and private institutions (College Board 2000a; U.S. Department of Education 2001). Despite these tuition rises, undergraduate enrollment rates have been extraordinarily strong (Hearn 2001a). Clearly, the public increasingly recognizes the importance of obtaining postsecondary education (Harvey and Immerwahr 1995). In turn, the rising prices and strong enrollments have prompted greater demand for student aid. Because Congress has resisted raising taxes or reallocating other funds to expand grant or work-study programs, the growing demand for student aid has been translated into a growing demand for student loans (Gillespie and Carlson 1983; Kramer and Van Dusen 1986; College Board 1993, 1995). Although attenders naturally tend to prefer grant aid over loans, the public has long accepted loans as an alternative for facilitating college enrollment.[4] Thus, in the context of limited supplies of grant and work-study funds, the simultaneous rises in enrollment and tuition have stimulated loan demand and growth.

Growth in loan volume has also been encouraged by federal legislation promoting college affordability. Policymakers created the unsubsidized Stafford loan program under the 1992 reauthorization of the Higher Education Act (HEA) and increased the maximum loan limits under the 1998 HEA Amendments with affordability in mind. Those reforms have clearly served to fuel the growth in loan volume in recent years (Fossey 1998; Cunningham and Parker 1999; College Board 2000b; Redd, 2001).

Although reforms have occasionally chilled an otherwise welcoming regulatory climate, the government has rarely done anything to discourage significantly the participation (and profiting) of financial institutions. Kramer and Van Dusen note a particular irony here: "The great concern in the early years of the [GSL] program was how to fix the accelerator, not the brake—how to increase access to the program and overcome barriers to its growth," but attention since the late 1970s has been paid, in contrast, to selective slowing of program growth (1986, p. 14). Of course, little slowing has occurred. Until terms for outside lenders are made notably less inviting, or until the original indirect GSL program is abandoned fully in favor of direct lending (an increasingly unlikely event), the prospects for greatly lessened involvement of the private financing sector may be minimal. The continuing involvement of private providers has unquestionably increased available loan funding.

At the same time, borrowing has become easier. Recent mergers and acquisitions within the loan industry itself are often defended on the basis of ease of borrowing: students benefit from a "seamless" borrowing system in which one organization makes, guarantees, and collects on their loans (Burd 2000). Such a system may diminish competition within the loan industry and could result in rising costs to student borrowers, but it arguably provides an easier, more inviting, and more "customer friendly" borrowing process for individuals (Burd 2000). In fact, a number of analysts (King 1999; Redd 1999, 2001) suggest that the growing ease of borrowing has led many middle- and upper-income students to borrow more in the unsubsidized loan program than they actually need to meet their educational costs.

Dramatic changes in legislation, in regulatory or fiscal conditions for private lenders, or in other aspects of the student-loan environment may at some point greatly slow the decades of growth in the loan programs. Absent such developments, however, the prospects for continued program growth remain strong.

## Varied Rationales

*The federal student loan programs have been initiated and defended on disparate and sometimes conflicting grounds.* Among the many observers noting this second theme in loan program history are Friedman (1962), Hartman (1971), Dresch (1982), Woodhall (1988), Breneman (1991), McPherson and Schapiro (1991), and Cunningham and Parker (1999). Policymakers and policy analysts have viewed loans as an element in social policy, supplementing other forms of aid for the disadvantaged. They have also seen loans as an element in economic policy in that they may aid the workings of credit markets, promote a skilled and flexible workforce, and help in the recruiting of students into significant jobs with arguably insufficient labor supply.[5]

These social and economic rationales are interlinked. For example, loan programs can use credit markets to improve the efficiency of governmental student aid directed to those with financial need. Government stimulation of private credit markets through loan guarantees, cost allowances, and interest subsidies can increase the overall supply of funds for higher education attendance and thus increase enrollment rates at little substantial, long-term expense to governments. Work since the early 1980s (e.g., see Tierney 1980) has suggested that loans do promote attendance. They do so less powerfully than outright grants, but also at appreciably less expense. One can argue that, as a government investment, loans have an overall cost/effectiveness profile superior to that of grants despite their weaker enrollment effects. That argument grows in strength when one remembers that, even among students whose attendance the government wishes to aid for some societally justified reason (e.g., economic development), the individual returns from postsecondary attendance may be significant enough to warrant all aided attendees having to repay some portion of their government assistance. In sum, because loans do work in promoting attendance, and because individuals, regardless of background, receive substantial returns from attendance, fully subsidizing the attendance of some (via grants) at the expense of foregoing partial subsidization of the attendance of many more may not always be a prudent policy choice. It is one thing to compare loans and grants purely on grounds of the power of their equity effects, but it is something else to compare them in terms of public costs versus public and individual benefits.

Thus, the social and economic rationales for loans as a policy instrument may be plausibly connected. Other less tightly linked rationales also abound, however. Some policymakers and analysts have argued that loans are superior to other forms of aid because they may encourage productive labor and a sense of social obligation after graduation. That is, one can view loans as an element in educational policy promoting the development of good economic citizenship.

Finally, loans have been defended on political grounds as a form of aid more politically feasible than grants. At potentially low cost, they can address the priorities of several constituencies, including both the needs of the disadvantaged for access to higher education and the liquidity needs typical among middle- and upper-income families with college-aspiring members.

Thus, the list of rationales for federally supported student loans is varied. Together, the rationales are not fully consistent with each other or with the development of one kind of student loan program. For example, the optimal structure of loan programs addressing middle-income families' liquidity concerns may differ substantially from the optimal structure of programs aimed at promoting educational opportunity for the disadvantaged. Any program seeking to fulfill both goals at once is likely to perform less than ideally at both. That, precisely, was the criticism frequently raised against the Guaranteed Student Loan program in the 1980s and early 1990s (Gladieux 1983; Hansen 1987; McPherson and Schapiro 1991). As new federal loan programs have been initiated in more recent years, specialization has been improved, but some overlaps remain: each program has been asked to meet purposes somewhat in synchrony and somewhat in conflict with those of other programs.[6] Thus, familiar problems have persisted.

Of course, it is important to note also that the various rationales for federal loans have occasionally been combined productively. One prominent example has been the use of several of the rationales in support of significant guaranteed student loan availability for students in private colleges and universities (Gladieux 1989). Still, the imprecise philosophical underpinnings of the programs have consistently proved a source of unease. Loans have been defended on a number of grounds, and those grounds can both complement and conflict with each other.

## Limited Oversight and Evaluation

*The federal student loan programs have suffered from an ongoing absence of aggressive managerial oversight and evaluation.* This third theme in the history of the loan programs is most often raised by those who call for hard evidence on programmatic effectiveness and efficiency (e.g., Hansen 1987; Hartle 1991). Providing such evidence has proven quite difficult, and the federal government's scrutiny has too frequently been inadequate. The high costs of providing such scrutiny are central to this theme. As the loan programs have expanded, the federal government has faced increasing fiscal pressure. Since its inception in the late 1970s, the U.S. Department of Education has consistently been constrained by small budgets and often threatened with extinction. Under those conditions, it has been unable to devote sufficient resources to oversight and evaluation.[7]

One aspect of this historical theme is perhaps almost archetypal of the current dilemmas of government programs with heavy private-sector participation. If you wish to institute and maintain a federal program dispensing federal funds but relying critically on private-sector actors, tight monitoring for waste and abuse is imperative. Clearly, the need for such monitoring is paramount in the traditional guaranteed student loan programs in particular. Yet the federal climate has not been conducive to funding in-depth data gathering, evaluation, or quality control in those programs. Those programs have provided loan money essential to college attendance to millions of people, but they have done so without steady, comprehensive management attention and analysis.[8]

When problems in loan programs have grown to the point of public and political visibility, audits, additional rules, and other forms of oversight have been instituted, but these have often been late and inadequate to solving the issues at hand (see DeLoughry 1990; Flint 1991). Recently, some postsecondary institutions have expressed concern over the Department of Education's expanded power and authority to oversee or regulate complex and costly loan programs that already create major administrative burdens on campuses (Merisotis 1998). This bridling by institutions no doubt stems from a history of disappointments on some campuses with the department's capability to oversee aid programs fairly and effectively. Interestingly, however, while the federal government has aggressively specified the rules of the game, it has most often tended to leave the day-to-day action on the field mainly to the players (schools, banks, guaranty agencies, students, families, etc.), allowing them to play the game largely unrefereed. That is, much of the federal oversight takes the form of summative, punitive action after the fact rather than ongoing monitoring of transactions occurring under the loan programs' aegis.

Of course, problems of oversight and evaluation are characteristic of the entire federal effort in student aid. In this arena, program evaluation studies have frequently been abandoned or underfunded, to the disappointment of analysts (McPherson 1988; Hearn 1993). Financial management problems, inadequate financial information, and unreliable student-level and aggregate data continue to challenge the Department of Education despite recent efforts to improve management information systems (Zook 1995; GAO 1995; GAO 1997; Fossey 1998; Hearn 2001b). What is more, while there has been some improvement in the management information systems and research base supporting the student aid programs, many policymakers are willing to invest in these programs without sufficiently *using* extant evidence on how they might best fashion that investment. This problem, one of some policymakers' attitudes toward using available data and research, parallels a reluctance to seek out new data and research. Work by Wildavsky (1979) and others provocatively addresses this ongoing and very fundamental question in government policy-making.

The information-base and information-use problems challenge all of student aid policy. The problems are especially troubling in the student loan arena, however, because the dollars involved are so large, because program profusion and complexity are so great, because the effects of these problems endure well beyond students' departure from school, and because so much of the sphere of loans is invisible to federal eyes.[9] Recently, Congress provided the Department of Education with the power to bar institutions from loan programs and created expanded incentives for institutions to lower default rates (Burd 2001; Babyak and Glickman 2001). Since 1991, over one thousand institutions (mostly proprietary institutions) have lost the privilege of participating in the loan program (Burd 2001). Borrower default rates have declined in the past decade because lenders and guarantee agencies have provided more debt-management and fiscal counseling to borrowers and offered them more flexible repayment options (Burd 2001). On the other hand, as Merisotis (1998) notes, the optimal nature of the federal presence in this arena is a delicate issue. While oversight and evaluation of federal loan policies and programs are improving, much remains to be done.

## Continuing Policy Disputes

*The federal loan programs have been subject to continuing policy disputes concerning appropriate goals, participants, and delivery systems.* In many respects, this fourth historical theme flows directly from those preceding it. Although the loan programs' overarching purposes may be described with disarming simplicity (e.g., facilitating college attendance by allowing deferred payments for attendance), the devil is in the details, as the saying goes. Policy arguments concerning critical operational matters have been a constant feature of the loan programs.

One example of the unresolved disputes continuing to trouble this field comes from the for-profit institutions. The growth in participation in the proprietary sector since the early 1970s and the growing attention to defaults and fraud in that sector have led some to call for either the retargeting of the federal aid programs on "higher education" in its traditional sense or the development of separate financial aid policies that address the distinct needs of fundamentally different types of postsecondary institutions and the students they serve (Wood 1997). The proprietary sector has fiercely resisted such proposals. A second ongoing tension continues between the public and private sectors of traditional two and four-year higher education. Because loan program specifications can have widely varying impacts on the two sectors, owing to their different pricing structures and somewhat different clientele, public/private conflict tends to arise whenever new loan programs or regulatory changes are proposed. A third longstanding dispute involves the debate between those who favor a controlled volume of loans limited to a low- or middle-income clientele with clearly unmet financial need and those who favor expanding volume, a largely unlimited clientele, and little attention to whether a loan was actually used for liquidity purposes or outright need (see Hansen 1987). A final dispute concerns the role of private profit-seeking banks and lending agencies in the system. The emergence of direct lending has brought to the fore a host of issues concerning the place of markets and profit motivation, as opposed to governmental direction and control, in the expansion of financial aid availability (Dean 1994; Burd 2001).

Although it would be naive to argue that there was unanimity around the loan programs at *any* point in their history since the 1950s, it seems fair to observe that the divisions since the mid-1970s have been especially stark. As noted earlier, those who described an aid "community" or "coalition" largely agreeing on student aid issues in earlier years have taken to lamenting the breakdown of consensus in more recent times.[10] The most fundamental description of the erosion of consensus in federal loan policy has been that of Kramer and Van Dusen (1986). In the early years of the federal student aid programs, they argue, the packaging of student aid was based on several generally accepted principles: the expectation of a level parental contributions for student attendance equal to the parents' ability to pay as determined by agreed-upon need-analysis methodologies, the expectation that students would contribute "self-help" funds drawn from their own savings and earnings, and the tenet that total aid would not exceed the difference in costs and parental/student contributions. Kramer and Van Dusen argue that the guaranteed student loan program from virtually its inception interfered with and blurred each aspect of this longstanding consensus among aid administrators, the government, and students and their families. In a more recent revisiting of the same issue, Kramer noted that the growing reliance on student loans is undermining the longstanding assumption of the aid community that grants are the proper way to equalize educational opportunity: "Grant programs reduce inequality of resources, but loan programs perpetuate it when low-income graduates owe more than their affluent contemporaries" (1991a, p. 25). Kramer goes on to argue that this undermines the rationale of leveling-up that was central to the consensus of earlier years.

## Incremental Policy Development

*Federal loan policymaking has consistently been incrementalist in nature.* Some might challenge this fifth and final theme in loan program history. Notably, there are instances of federal loan policy changes based in debated, informed, and planned long-term policy decisions. In the past decade alone we have seen such innovative developments as the emergence of the federal direct-lending programs and the commitment to unsubsidized loans as a policy approach. Nevertheless, integrated policy development has been as hard to achieve as ever. In most respects, loan policy changes have been the product of incremental, often reactive policy deliberations driven by immediate fiscal and political pressures. In the 1980s, for example, Congress repeatedly acted simply to preserve existing loan programs in the face of a hostile administration rather than to re-examine any of the core tenets or operational characteristics of those programs. In the 1990s, Congress and the administration agreed to begin a direct-lending initiative, but it did so only in the context of maintaining preexisting, privately supported delivery options for guaranteed loans. Thus, even seemingly critical changes may be more likely to emerge as an accretion of marginal decisions than as fundamental reconsiderations.

In this light, it seems reasonable to question whether there really has been a seismic philosophical shift toward loans in the federal programs (as some of the recent literature implies) or simply a largely unconsidered but steadily increasing tilt toward loans by a Congress with limited money and limited tolerance for philosophical debate. Consistently politicized incremental policymaking, not deliberations focused on strategic goals for the longer term, has resulted in the current loan explosion.[11]

Many analysts have noted the historical tendency toward incrementalism in federal financial aid policy (e.g., see McPherson and Schapiro 1991; Hearn 1993). Notably, Mumper (1996, pp. 73–74) has argued that

> in their efforts to remove college price barriers, policy makers did not act as a unitary force carefully implementing a comprehensive plan. Rather, the growth in the student aid programs emerged from more or less constant negotiations among an ever-changing cast of characters making small, periodic, incremental revisions. As new problems or circumstances emerged, adjustments were made in each of the programs and in the relationships among them. As these events unfolded over three decades, no one individual or viewpoint was able to dominate the process. Hence, today, no side can claim credit for the programs' successes and none must accept blame for their failures.

This general point holds especially true for the burgeoning loan programs. In an environment in which student aid is not very high on the attention list of federal policymakers, and an environment in which the resources and energy for fundamental retooling in education may simply not be available, the loan programs have lived from year to year in a strange purgatory: regularly "exposed" as flawed by the popular press, Congress, and analysts, yet rarely significantly changed.[12]

## Conclusion: The Rising Centrality of Loans in Federal Policy

The current tone of reluctance and regret in discussions surrounding federal student aid is historically striking. Analyses of federal student aid written in the mid-1970s tended to portray the history and performance of the aid programs positively, emphasizing upbeat themes of progress, growth, and control (e.g., Fife 1975; Leslie 1977). Analyses written since that time tend to focus on disorder, inequities, complexity, inefficiency, misdirected regulations, stalemate among key constituencies, political strife, and the need for major reform.[13] Certainly, the continuing debates over grants versus loans as vehicles of educational opportunity, direct versus traditional forms of loan provision, the use of tax breaks as aid mechanisms, the place of merit in aid efforts, and other philosophical issues indicate that very little can be assumed to be constant. Indeed, as Spencer has perceptively argued, we in higher education may be in a new era in which even "the federal commitment to 'access' for low-income students can no longer be taken for granted" (1999, p. 116).

This rise in disillusionment with federal student aid policy has directly paralleled the rise of the loan programs as elements in that policy. Contemporary criticisms of federal student aid seem most frequently to focus on problems in the loan programs. Of course, this parallel timing may be a coincidence,[14] and even if there is some substance to the connection, the discovery of a parallel begs the question of causation. Is the increasing use of loans a response to disappointment over the effectiveness and cost of other forms of student aid? Is the disillusionment with the federal aid programs partly a response to their declining grants focus? Are the perceived problems with the loan programs mainly problems of inefficiency in delivery, or are they more fundamentally problems stemming from a loan emphasis itself? What other factors (e.g., rising societal questioning of direct government assistance programs across health and welfare domains as well as education) might be feeding both the disillusionment with federal student aid and the growth of federal loans? Any conclusions regarding the parallel must remain rather "soft." Many observers suggest, nonetheless, that the parallel has some substantive basis (e.g., see St. John 1994b).

Unquestionably, the growing loan emphasis and the parallel growing emphases on meeting the needs of the middle class and on shifting responsibility from parents to students represent the most fundamental changes in the federal programs since the mid-1970s. Otherwise, the federal aid programs themselves have not changed so greatly (Keppel 1987; Mumper 1996). The demographics of postsecondary students have certainly changed since that earlier period, with more students older than 22 (and in parallel, more financially independent students), more students with dependents, and more part-time students (U.S. Department of Education 2001). These changes have been dramatic and have perhaps fueled a sense among policymakers that college attenders are no longer such an identifiably youthful and needy population. But it is important to remember that student loans are provided in great number to the masses of students of traditional age and not simply to the "new student" population. The transformation of aid policies is not simply a demographically based phenomenon.

Insofar as our concern is with the student aged 18 to 24, the shift to loans may be viewed conceptually as a shift in generational responsibility for paying for college. As noted earlier, one of the core tenets of the aid programs before the late 1970s was the notion that parents had a responsibility for a major portion of the costs of their children's postsecondary education. Need and eligibility calculations for the grant and work-study programs assumed substantial parental contributions and left little room for the substitution of federal aid for those expected contributions. In the early years of the guaranteed student loan programs, many parents even took responsibility for paying off their children's loans (Kramer 1991b). Now, however, students are clearly paying for more of their college education. Because they, rather than their parents, are paying so much and accumulating debt levels so great, it is unlikely that their own children will have the same prospects of receiving aid from their parents that the student generations of the 1960s and 1970s did.[15]

McPherson and Schapiro see the burden of paying for college across generations as an "intergenerational compact" and worry over the consequences of breaking that compact: "The symmetry between own-generation and next-generation payment holds so long as each generation agrees to perpetuate the chain. Any one generation can get off scot-free by accepting its parents' largesse and refusing to help its own children" (1991, pp. 174–75). Hartle characterizes the changes of the past two decades similarly: "The United States, in effect, has decided to shift the burden of financing higher education to students themselves. The social compact that assumed that the adult generation would pay for the college education of the next generation has been shattered" (1994, p. A52).

The greatest burden of this movement toward loans has been on those from lower-income backgrounds. Although the nation's total amount of student aid has not decreased, and although growth in aid per FTE student has exceeded growth in tuition, this growth has been less and less focused on financial need. While grants based on financial need have grown modestly, loans have grown dramatically, especially in the form of unsubsidized, non-need-based loans, which go to students across the income range. What is more, there has also been growth in non-need-based grants, with a dramatic rise in state and institutional merit-based aid disproportionately serving students from middle- and upper-income backgrounds (see McPherson and Schapiro 1998). Together, these two trends make the rise in total aid a mixed blessing for lower-income students: there has been a significant decline in the proportion of overall aid based on financial need. According to the College Board (2000b), need-based aid nationally has fallen from roughly 80 percent of all aid a decade ago to less than 60 percent now.

Increasingly, aid for lower-income students comes in a form requiring repayment. This pattern continues those students' legacy of disadvantage relative to students whose families can afford to use savings and current income to pay for college attendance. Not surprisingly, grants tend to have more positive effects on high school graduates' college enrollment and choice than do loans, and lower-income students are more sensitive than other students in their enrollment decisions to aspects of prices and aid, including the grants/loans distinction (see Heller 1997; Campaigne and Hossler 1998; McPherson and Schapiro 1998; Cabrera et al. 2000). There is no evidence in the research literature that loan aid is as effective in improving lower-income students' access as is grant aid (e.g., see St. John and Noell 1989; St. John 1994a, 1994b). Therefore, as national policy has moved away from funding grants, it has moved away from funding the kind of aid most likely to ensure lower-income students' access, choice, and persistence.

The shift from grants to loans is thus not without troubling social implications. In this respect, it is not at all difficult to view the growth of federal loan programs through a dark lens. Their growth coincides with a troubled passage in student aid history. Yet it is important to remember the positive aspects of these programs as well. One analyst has estimated that a dollar of federal spending on the nondirect guaranteed loan programs may generate as much as $2.50 more funding from the private sector to fund students' higher education attendance (Mumper 1996). Envisioning a postsecondary system without these loan programs (and without their loss being substantially offset by more federal spending on grants or other forms of aid) probably means envisioning a system with significantly fewer postsecondary students and institutions.[16] As noted earlier here, cost/effectiveness assessments for student loans may be more favorable to the loans approach than purely effects-oriented assessments.

In 1991 economist and former college president David Breneman observed that the federal guaranteed student loan effort "grew like Topsy, seemingly lacking any inner compass, but adapting to the changing needs of students, lenders, and institutions. As such, it is an easy program to criticize, and probably no one starting from scratch would intentionally design what we have today. Nevertheless, for all its flaws, it is now central to the financing of higher education in this country" (1991, p. 386). That conclusion still applies more than a decade later, and it applies not only to the guaranteed loan programs but also to the other federal loan programs. Because of their ongoing centrality, the federal loan programs are probably not going to disappear or even be substantially cut any time in the near future. What seems most important now is responding appropriately to the lessons learned in the evolution of these massive, educationally critical efforts.

ACKNOWLEDGMENTS

The authors gratefully acknowledge the research assistance of James Eck and the helpful comments of Keith Jepsen and Edward St. John.

NOTES

1. The aid total is from the College Board (2000b) and includes aid from private sources partly subsidized by the federal government (e.g., aid provided through the subsidized Stafford guaranteed student loan program).

2. These loans have continued under different names and are currently called Perkins loans.

3. For a more detailed examination of the history of federal student loans, see Hearn (1998).

4. Morse (1977) noted two decades ago that, from the beginnings in 1958, federal officials consistently underestimated the demand for loans among college students. The pattern has continued to the present.

5. In the early years of the programs, this meant the scientific and engineering fields supported by the NDSL program, but more recently, with the initiation of federal income-contingency repayment options, the focus has been on traditionally low-paying but valued fields, such as teaching. There is no firm evidence, however, that providing such loans has transformed student borrowing, increased access, or affected students' career objectives (Burd 1998).

6. In 1989–90, the federal government supported five loan efforts: Perkins loans, Income Contingent loans, Subsidized Stafford loans, SLS loans, and PLUS loans. Ten years later, the government supported eight loan efforts: Perkins loans, subsidized Stafford loans under the Ford Direct Loans program, unsubsidized Stafford loans under the Ford

Direct Loans program, PLUS loans under the Ford Direct Loans program, subsidized Stafford loans under the Family Education Loans program, unsubsidized Stafford loans under the Family Education Loans program, SLS loans under the Family Education Loans program, and PLUS loans under the Family Education Loans program. While distinctions within this variegated portfolio become arguably clearer upon inspection, the array is unquestionably daunting to students and families as well as to student-aid officials and policymakers.

7. Indeed, the most often-cited and influential studies of the student loan programs have been those conducted by the Office of Management and Budget, the Congressional Budget Office, and the General Accounting Office, not those by the Department of Education.

8. Although less obvious, similar problems apply to the campus-based Perkins Loan program. Former American Council on Education official and NDSL director John Morse (1977) has recounted how management oversight posed a problem from the very beginnings of the NDSL program in the late 1950s, and Dean (1994) has noted that problems of quality control persist in the program because of poor incentives for evaluation and tight oversight.

9. Keith Jepsen, a veteran financial aid director, has noted that the extant data on student loans often substantially understate the volume of those loans because many private lenders and loans are not identified by the usual survey and program reporting techniques. Because of this, analyses of student debt levels are too frequently based on poor information (personal communication, December 19, 1995).

10. Notably, the debate over perhaps the single watershed policy innovation of the 1990s, direct student lending, was marked by bitter disputes among lobbyists and policymakers over the proper role of private-sector firms in aid delivery (Parsons 1997; Cook 1998; Hearn 2001b).

11. I am indebted for this insight to Keith Jepsen (personal communication, December 19, 1995).

12. Whether recent reforms in direct-lending, tax relief, and tax-credit programs serve as additional marginal adjustments or major reforms to federal aid policy remains to be seen, but for now the evidence seems to tilt more to the former explanation (Kane 1999).

13. For examples of analyses stressing one or more of these themes, see Mortenson (1990), McPherson and Schapiro (1991 and 1998), Dean (1994), Mumper (1996), and Cunningham and Parker (1999).

14. For one thing, criticisms of federal efforts have increased in a wide variety of areas, not solely in financial aid policy.

15. There is an implicit indictment of the "baby boom" generation in this observation: the parents of the 1980s and 1990s, many of whom attended college in the grant-rich environment of the 1970s, may be letting the burden of paying for college skip their own generation. That may be too harsh and too facile, however. Many of those parents are struggling economically, and many may be undertaking expensive education and training programs themselves. After all, the average age of postsecondary attenders has been rising in recent years, and many in their thirties, forties, and fifties attend (U.S. Department of Education 2001).

16. What is more, the absence of the programs would have multiplier effects not solely on institutions and students but also on local and national economies, as banks

and other financial institutions contract their loan volumes and most likely their staffing. There have been more beneficiaries of the loan programs over the years since 1958 than one might at first imagine.

REFERENCES

Advisory Committee on Student Financial Assistance. 2001. *Access denied: Restoring the nation's commitment to equal educational opportunity.* Washington, DC: Author.

Babyak, S., and J. Glickman. 2001. *Accountability for results work: College loan default rates continue to decline.* U.S. Department of Education Press Release, 19 September.

Breneman, D. W. 1991. Guaranteed student loans: Great success or dismal failure? In *ASHE reader on finance in higher education,* ed. D. W. Breneman, L. L. Leslie, and R. E. Anderson, 377–87. Needham Heights, MA: Ginn.

Burd, S. 1998. Few borrowers repay student loans through 'income contingent' system. *Chronicle of Higher Education,* 45 (5) (25 September).

Burd, S. 2000. Should borrowers fear a student-loan behemoth? Sallie Mae's massive growth may reshape the loan industry. *Chronicle of Higher Education,* 46 (49) (11 August).

Burd, S. 2001. Bringing market forces to the loan program. *Chronicle of Higher Education* 47 (21) (2 February).

Cabrera, A. F., P. T. Terenzini, and E. M. Bernal. 2001. *Leveling the playing field: Low-income students in postsecondary education.* Report from the College Board. Washington, DC: College Board.

Campaigne, D. A., and D. Hossler. 1998. How do loans affect the educational decisions of students? Access, aspirations, college choice, and persistence. In *Condemning students to debt: College loans and public policy,* ed. R. Fossey and M. Bateman, 85–104. New York: Teachers College Press.

College Board, The. 1993. *Trends in student aid: 1983 to 1993.* Washington, DC: Author.

College Board, The. 1995. *Trends in student aid: 1985 to 1995.* Washington, DC: Author.

College Board, The. 2000a. *Trends in college pricing.* Washington, DC: Author.

College Board, The. 2000b. *Trends in student aid.* Washington, DC: Author.

Cook, C. E. 1998. *Lobbying for higher education: How colleges and universities influence federal policy.* Nashville, TN: Vanderbilt University Press.

Cunningham, A. F., and T. Parker. 1999. *State of diffusion: Defining student aid in an era of multiple purposes.* Washington, DC: Institute for Higher Education Policy.

Dean, J. 1994. Enactment of the federal Direct Student Loan Program as a reflection of the education policy making process. In *National issues in education: Community service and student loans,* ed. J. Jennings, 157–78. Bloomington, IN: Phi Delta Kappa International.

DeLoughry, T. J. 1990. Seventeen changes in 4 years: Johns Hopkins grapples with new loan rules. *Chronicle of Higher Education* 37 (14) (December 5): p. A24.

Dresch, S. P. 1982. *Criteria for the evaluation of student loan alternatives: A report to the National Commission of Student Financial Assistance.* New Haven, CT: Institute for Demographic and Economic Studies.

Fife, J. D. 1995. Applying the goals of student financial aid. AAHE/ERIC Higher Education Research Report No. 10. Washington, DC: American Association for Higher Education.

Flint, T. A. 1991. Historical notes on regulation in the federal student assistance programs. *Journal of Student Financial Aid* 21 (1): 33–47.

Fossey, R. 1998. The dizzying growth of the federal student loan program: When will vertigo set in? In *Condemning students to debt: College loans and public policy,* ed. R. Fossey and M. Bateman, 7–18. New York: Teachers College Press.

Friedman, M. 1962. *Capitalism and freedom.* Chicago: University of Chicago Press.

Gillespie, D. A., and N. Carlson. 1983. *Trends in student aid: 1963 to 1983.* Washington, DC: College Board.

Gladieux, L. E. 1983. Future directions of student aid. In *Handbook of student financial aid,* ed. R. H. Fenske, R. P. Huff, and Associates, 399–433. San Francisco: Jossey-Bass.

Gladieux, L. E., ed. 1989. *Radical reform or incremental change? Student loan policy alternatives for the federal government.* Washington, DC: The College Board.

Gladieux, L. E., and T. R. Wolanin. 1976. *Congress and the colleges: The national politics of higher education.* Lexington, MA: D. C. Heath.

Hansen, J. S. 1987. *Student loans: Are they overburdening a generation?* New York: College Board.

Hartle, T. W. 1991. The evolution and prospects of financing alternatives for higher education. In *New ways of paying for college,* ed. A. M. Hauptman and R. H. Koff, 33–50. New York: American Council on Education and Macmillan.

Hartle, T. W. 1994. How people pay for college: A dramatic shift. *Chronicle of Higher Education* 41 (November 9): A52.

Hartman, R. W. 1971. Loans for students. In *Financing higher education: Alternatives for the federal government,* ed. M. Orwig, 177–99. Iowa City, IA: American College Testing Program.

Harvey, J., and J. Immerwahr. 1995. On Main Street and in the boardroom: Public perceptions of higher education. *Educational Record* 76 (4) (fall): 51–55.

Hearn, J. C. 1993. The paradox of growth in federal aid for college students: 1965–1990. In *Higher education: Handbook of theory and research,* vol. 9, ed. J. C. Smart, 94–153. New York: Agathon Press. Reprinted in *The finance of higher education: Theory, research, policy, and practice,* ed. M. B. Paulsen and J. C. Smart, 439–60 New York: Agathon Press (2001).

Hearn, J. C. 1998. The growing loan orientation in federal financial-aid policy: A historical perspective. In *Condemning students to debt: College loans and public policy,* ed. R. Fossey and M. Bateman, 47–75. New York: Teachers College Press.

Hearn, J. C. 2001a. Access to postsecondary education: Financing equity in an evolving context. In *The finance of higher education: Theory, research, policy, and practice,* ed. M. B. Paulsen and J. C. Smart, 439–60. New York: Agathon Press.

Hearn, J. C. 2001b. Epilogue to "The paradox of growth in federal aid for college students: 1965–1990." In *The finance of higher education: Theory, research, policy, and practice,* ed. M. B. Paulsen and J. C. Smart, 316–20. New York: Agathon Press.

Heller, D. E. 1997. Student price response in higher education: An update to Leslie and Brinkman. *Journal of Higher Education* 68 (6): 624–59.

Johnstone, D. B. 1999. Introduction. In *Financing a college education: How it works, how it's changing,* ed. J. King. Phoenix, AZ: American Council on Education and Oryx Press.

Kane, T. J. 1999. Reforming public subsidies for higher education. In *Financing college tuition: Government policies and educational priorities,* ed. M. H. Kosters, 53–75. Washington, DC: AEI Press.

Keppel, F. 1987. The Higher Education Acts contrasted, 1965–1986: Has federal policy come of age? *Harvard Educational Review* 57 (1): 49–67.

King, J. E. 1999. Crisis or convenience: Why are students borrowing more? In *Financing a college education: How it works, how it's changing,* ed. J. E. King. Phoenix, AZ: American Council on Education and Oryx Press.

Kramer, M. 1991a. Stresses in the student financial aid system. In *New ways of paying for college,* ed. A. M. Hauptman and R. H. Koff, 21–32. New York: American Council on Education-Macmillan.

Kramer, M. 1991b. New varieties of student loans. In *New ways of paying for college,* ed. A. M. Hauptman and R. H. Koff, 101–9. New York: American Council on Education-Macmillan.

Kramer, M., and W. D. Van Dusen. 1986. Living on credit. *Change* 18 (3) (May/June): 10–19.

Leslie, L. L. 1977. *Higher education opportunity: A decade of progress.* (ERIC/AAHE Higher Education Research Report No. 3). Washington, DC: American Association for Higher Education.

McPherson, M. S. 1988. On assessing the impact of federal student aid. *Economics of Education Review* 7 (1): 77–84.

McPherson, M. S., and M. O. Schapiro. 1991. *Keeping college affordable: Government and educational opportunity.* Washington, DC: Brookings Institution.

McPherson, M. S., and M. O. Schapiro. 1998. *The student aid game: Meeting need and rewarding talent in American higher education.* Princeton, NJ: Princeton University Press.

Merisotis, J. P. 1998. Federal student aid regulations: Next steps. In *Condemning students to debt: College loans and public policy,* ed. R. Fossey and M. Bateman, 76–84. New York: Teachers College Press.

Morse, J. W. 1977. How we got here from there: A personal reminiscence of the early days. In *Student loans: Problems and policy alternatives,* ed. L. Rice, 3–15. New York: College Board.

Mortenson, T. G. 1990. *The impact of increased loan utilization among low family income students.* Iowa City, IA: American College Testing Program.

Mumper, M. 1996. *Removing college price barriers: What government has done and why it hasn't worked.* Albany: State University of New York Press.

Parsons, M. D. 1997. *Power and politics: Federal higher education policymaking in the 1990s.* Albany: State University of New York Press.

Redd, K. E. 1999. The changing characteristics of undergraduate borrowers. In *Financing a college education: How it works, how it's changing,* ed. J. E. King. Phoenix, AZ: American Council on Education and Oryx Press.

Redd, K. E. 2001. *Why do students borrow so much? Recent national trends in student loan debt.* Washington, DC: Office of Educational Research and Improvement.

St. John, E. P. 1994a. Assessing tuition and student aid strategies: Using price response measures to simulate pricing alternatives. *Research in Higher Education* 35 (3): 301–35.

St. John, E. P. 1994b. *Prices, productivity and investment: Assessing financial strategies in higher education.* ASHE-ERIC Higher Education Report No. 3. Washington, DC: George Washington University, School of Education and Human Development.

St. John, E. P., and J. Noell. 1989. The effects of student financial aid on access to higher education: An analysis of progress with special consideration of minority enrollment. *Research in Higher Education* 30 (6): 563–81.

Spencer, A. C. 1999. The new politics of higher education. In *Financing a college education: How it works, how it's changing*, ed. J. E. King. Phoenix, AZ: American Council on Education and Oryx Press.

Tierney, M. 1980. The impact of institutional net price on student demand for public/private higher education. *Economics of Education Review* 2 (4): 363–83

U.S. Department of Education. 2000. *The condition of education*. Washington, DC: Author.

U.S. Department of Education. 2001. *The 2000 digest of education statistics*. Washington, DC: Author.

U.S. General Accounting Office (GAO). 1995. *High-risk series: Student financial aid.* GAO/HR-95-10. Washington, DC: Author.

U. S. General Accounting Office (GAO). 1997. *High-risk series: Student financial aid.* GAO/HR-97-11. Washington, DC: Author.

Wildavsky, A. 1979. *Speaking truth to power: The art and craft of policy analysis.* Boston: Little, Brown, and Company.

Wood, P. W. 1997. The harm done by excessive federal aid to students. *Chronicle of Higher Education*, 45 (35) (May 9): A56.

Woodhall, M. 1988. Designing a student loan programme for a developing country: The relevance of international experience. *Economics of Education Review* 7 (1): 153–61.

Zook, J. 1995. Congressional panel warned of growing Pell Grant fraud. *Chronicle of Higher Education* 41 (45) (July 21): A26.

# CHAPTER FOUR

# Federal Involvement in Higher Education Desegregation

## An Unfinished Agenda

## Clifton F. Conrad and David J. Weerts

Spanning several generations of debates, court cases, and compliance initiatives, the federal agenda to desegregate higher education remains unfinished. While a considerable distance has yet to be traveled, meaningful progress toward dismantling segregated statewide systems of higher education has been made—especially in the last decade. In particular, the leadership of the executive and judicial branches of the federal government has been instrumental in accelerating desegregation efforts. Guided by the U.S. Supreme Court's landmark ruling in *United States v. Fordice* (1992), many states and institutions—notably in the South—have implemented and continue to explore policies and practices aimed at eliminating dualism and reducing disparities between historically white and historically black institutions. Still, formidable barriers at the state and institutional level continue to stand in the way of completing the federal agenda to desegregate higher education.

The purpose of this chapter is to examine the federal government's involvement in seeking to eliminate the vestiges of segregation in higher education and to illuminate the challenges that stand in the way of desegregation. To that end, we begin by tracing the history of federal involvement—including both the judicial and executive branches—in promoting statewide desegregation. We then critique the federal legacy by examining both the strengths and limitations of federal leadership and involvement. In so doing, we argue that the federal government has been very influential in addressing issues surrounding liability both in the executive and judicial branches, but at the same time, it has not always been able to be a powerful vehicle by itself for bringing about change and reform at the state and institutional level—not least because meaningful change ultimately rests at those levels. Early in the new millennium some states are still grappling with designing desegregation policies and practices consonant with the aims of *Fordice*.

We conclude the chapter by identifying several major barriers through examining key desegregation challenges remaining at the state and institutional levels. We argue that—in light of the limitations of federal involvement and legal constraints surrounding practices such as affirmative action—the central remaining challenge is to encourage states and institutions to embrace desegregation. In particular, the political landscape at the state and institutional level and financial issues surrounding desegregation initiatives often stand in the way of finishing the agenda.

## The Legacy of Segregation and the Federal Impetus toward Desegregation

The end of the Civil War marked the beginning of opportunities for blacks to experience the full rights of U.S. citizenship. But these opportunities emerged only gradually and unevenly as a number of states—particularly in the South—were slow to grant blacks full privileges, including the right to an education. It would not be until the second Morrill Act of 1890 that the benefits of higher education would begin to be extended to blacks, allowing for the establishment of dual systems—composed of both white and black institutions—so long as the funds were equitably divided. Subsequently, statewide dual systems of higher education were established and remained undisturbed until 1954, when the U.S. Supreme Court ruled in *Brown v. the Board of Education of Topeka* that "separate but equal" educational facilities were unconstitutional (Conrad and Shrode 1990).

Although dismantling segregated higher education systems was implied in the *Brown* decision, meaningful steps toward desegregating higher education would have to wait until the 1960s when President Lyndon B. Johnson signed the Civil Rights Act of 1964. Title VI of the act restricted federal funding to schools and colleges that discriminated on the grounds of race, color, or national origin. Using his executive powers, Johnson charged the Office of Civil Rights (OCR) within the Department of Health, Education, and Welfare (HEW) with the responsibility of enforcing state compliance with Title VI standards for admission. Following its mandate, HEW eventually found ten states to be in violation of Title VI and requested plans from each of these states to address desegregation.

Despite federal orders, the mandate was largely ignored by most states. Frustrated by states' lack of compliance with desegregation orders, the NAACP Legal Defense Fund filed suit in 1970, alleging that federal funds had continued to be granted to institutions in violation of the law. In *Adams v. Richardson* (1972), Judge John Pratt from the U.S. District Court for the District of Columbia found in favor of the NAACP Legal Defense Fund. Subsequently, HEW obtained state plans for desegregation, but in 1977 Judge Pratt ruled that the plans were ineffective. Throughout the late 1970s and 1980s, HEW guided states in their desegregation efforts. By 1985 the federal government determined that fourteen states were officially desegregated.

At the same time, other states continued to struggle to comply with Pratt's orders, often falling short of making significant progress—especially in terms of black students matriculating at white institutions and black faculty being employed in white institutions. Perhaps most significant, program duplication and inequality between traditionally white and historically black institutions was conspicuous in many of these noncompliant states. While the *Adams* litigation was dismissed in 1990, the desegregation agenda gained new strength in 1992 with a landmark case that continues to shape contemporary efforts toward desegregating higher education: *United States v. Fordice.*

## The Fordice Case (1992)

Although a number of states complied with Judge Pratt's orders in the 1970s and 80s, others, including Mississippi, argued that nondiscriminatory practices, as identified in *Brown,* were sufficient to meet federal standards for desegregation. Not convinced that this standard was just and adequate, Jake Ayers and other black citizens from the State of Mississippi filed a suit in 1975 demanding a more equitable state system of higher education. Emphasizing disparities in educational opportunities between historically white institutions and historically black colleges and universities (HBCUs), the plaintiffs called for increased funding for the state's three HBCUs. Over a twelve-year span Mississippi responded by adopting institutional mission statements that they considered race-neutral and by developing differentiated missions for the eight public institutions in the system. Although admissions policies no longer explicitly discriminated by race, the institutions remained largely segregated: historically black institutions remained predominantly black and historically white institutions remained predominantly white (Weerts and Conrad 2002).

The district court in Mississippi finally heard the Ayers case in 1987, and while the court raised issues of discriminatory admissions policies, funding inequities, and program duplication within the state system, it ruled that the state's legal duty of desegregation did not extend to these areas. Instead, the court declared that states were only responsible for creating policies that were racially neutral, were developed in good faith, and did not contribute to making the institutions racially "identifiable." This interpretation of the law was subsequently upheld by the U.S. Court of Appeals for the 5th Circuit.

Not satisfied with the outcome, the federal government, through the U.S. Department of Justice, joined the plaintiffs and brought the case to the U.S. Supreme Court in what became known as *United States v. Fordice*. Relying on the findings introduced in the district court, the Supreme Court pointed to multiple practices in Mississippi that perpetuated segregation among the eight public institutions. While not limiting themselves to these areas, the Court focused on four areas that needed to be addressed to eliminate the vestiges of de jure segregation: admissions standards, program duplication, institutional mission assignments, and the continued operation of separate universities. Informed by guidance from the Court, these policy areas became the touchstones for designing desegregation strategies in Mississippi, Maryland, and nine other states. A number of states continue to explore desegregation policies and practices consonant with the four policy areas advanced in *Fordice*.

## Strengths of Federal Involvement to Desegregate Higher Education

In reflecting on federal involvement in desegregation over the last forty years, it is clear that the federal government has experienced considerable success as well as some failure in advancing its agenda. Still, while the journey to desegregate higher education has been long and challenging, meaningful progress has been made due in large part to the leadership of the executive and judicial branches of the federal government. The strengths of the federal involvement to desegregate higher education are amply illustrated by examining the role of both of these branches.

## Executive Leadership

At the executive level, President Lyndon B. Johnson played a critical role in advancing serious desegregation efforts in the 1960s. Foremost, he signed the Civil Rights Act of 1964—which achieved two critical aims. First, it enabled the federal government to bring lawsuits on behalf of black plaintiffs. Second, it restricted the spending of federal funds in segregated schools and colleges. The Civil Rights Act of 1964 created a clear and unmistakable desegregation mandate for America's colleges and universities (Brown 1999).

No less important, President Johnson's leadership paved the way for enforcement of desegregation in the higher education arena as he directed HEW to take the lead with the enforcement of Title VI standards for admission. A major strength of HEW involvement was that it was very thorough in defining parameters with which the administrative procedures for the Civil Rights Act of 1964 could be developed (Brown 1999). Still, HEW struggled to bring about meaningful reform, not least because most states—including Mississippi, Florida, and North Carolina—argued that they were already in compliance with the law (Williams 1988).

Even after the dismissal of *Adams,* HEW continued in its attempts to enforce state compliance with the desegregation mandate. By the end of the *Adams* litigation, HEW had already referred several state systems of higher education—including Tennessee, Alabama, Louisiana, and Mississippi—to the U.S. Department of Justice for litigation (Brown 1999). In a nutshell, HEW played a key role in keeping the desegregation mandate alive during a time of inadequate compliance initiatives and significantly diminished support from the judicial branch of government.

Following the lead of HEW, the Department of Justice was instrumental in pursuing the unresolved issues remaining from the dismissal of *Adams.* In particular, the department relentlessly pursued the desegregation agenda though the *Fordice* litigation. Joining the plaintiffs in the *Ayers* case, the Justice Department took a strong position in combating the argument that states were only responsible for creating higher education policies that were racially neutral, were developed in good faith, and did not contribute to making the institutions racially "identifiable." In *Fordice,* the Justice Department effectively and successfully demonstrated how vestiges of segregation continued to propel dual systems of higher education. Arguably, the leadership of the Justice Department in *Fordice* was responsible in large measure for bringing about a "sea change" in advancing desegregation effort by providing the legal and evidentiary foundation that persuaded the U.S. Supreme Court to develop a new standard for assessing liability in regard to segregation and desegregation in higher education.

## *Judicial Leadership*

Noting the success of the executive branch's leadership—again, most recently through the U.S. Department of Justice—the judicial branch of the federal government has also played a pivotal role in advancing higher education desegregation. As evidenced by the effects of *Fordice* in terms of inviting and eventually bringing about statewide desegregation resolutions and remedies, the U.S. Supreme Court has had a very substantial impact by clarifying statewide responsibility for eliminating the vestiges of segregation.

The Supreme Court's leadership in *Fordice* was paramount because it set a legal standard for evaluating whether a state has addressed its duty to dismantle de jure segregation in its higher education systems. In so doing, the *Fordice* opinion made clear that the lower courts misinterpreted the law and failed to apply the correct legal standard for Mississippi's system of higher education. The Court noted that present policies perpetuated segregation even though racial neutrality was expressed in institutional missions. Simply put, the Court declared that a number of factors more or less predetermined an individual's choice of institution—and that this predetermination was based on race.

In *Fordice* the Court concluded that "if policies traceable to the *de jure* system are still in force and have discriminatory effects, those policies too must be reformed to the extent practicable and consistent with sound educational practices." Stated another way, the Supreme Court through *Fordice* made clear its intent to eliminate policies and practices that made institutions racially identifiable and thus wittingly or unwittingly steered students to attend a particular college based on their race (Weerts and Conrad 2002). *United States v. Fordice* continues to stand as the judicial guidepost for desegregation efforts across the country (Brown 1999).

In summary, the progress of the higher education desegregation effort since the 1960s can be attributed in no small measure to the concerted efforts of the executive and judicial branches of the federal government. Beginning with the signing of the Civil Rights Act of 1964 and the efforts of the Department of Health, Education, and Welfare (HEW), the executive branch has been instrumental in marshalling efforts to eliminate the vestiges of segregation in higher education. Most significantly, the U.S. Department of Justice and the U.S. Supreme Court have more recently fueled a powerful effort to finish the federal agenda to desegregate higher education. The Office of Civil Rights—now housed in the Department of Education—has successfully worked with several states in the last several years, including Maryland, to meet the standards set down in *Fordice* and continues to work with the remaining states in completing the desegregation agenda.

## Limitations of Federal Desegregation Efforts

This chapter has thus far highlighted the successes of the federal government's involvement in advancing desegregation. As the history of desegregation shows, however, there clearly are limits to the federal government's leadership. The limitations of federal involvement in the desegregation of statewide systems of higher education are threefold. First, the *Fordice* case provided a template for states and institutions to explore policies and practices to desegregate, but this template has nonetheless left states with many questions about the appropriateness of specific courses of remedy. Second, the relationship between the federal courts and the U.S. Justice Department has, at times, been more adversarial than collaborative. Finally, the Office of Civil Rights has arguably had to negotiate trade-offs with some states that may eventually compromise desegregation touchstones as envisioned by the Supreme Court in *Fordice*. While the combination of these limitations has contributed to the sluggish pace of some states and institutions as they have gone about responding to the federal directive to desegregate, we discuss only the first limitation in depth here.

Conceptually, the Supreme Court template for desegregation following *Fordice* is anchored in two policy directives aimed at increasing the other-race presence in traditionally black and traditionally white institutions. One addresses dualism—namely, the unnecessary (nonessential) program duplication between historically white and historically black institutions. The second addresses unequalness—that is, states are expected to address historic disparities in mission, funding, programs, and facilities between historically white and historically black institutions.

Many scholars and policymakers acknowledge that the general template advanced in *Fordice* has been useful in informing desegregation initiatives but also argue that its interpretation and subsequent implications for implementation remain murky. To illustrate, the Court made it clear that more than racial neutrality and good faith efforts are needed to eliminate the effects of prior discriminatory systems but left it up to the states to achieve these ends using "sound educational policy." Some scholars have interpreted "sound educational policy" with an emphasis on intangible elements—such as the quality of education for blacks—not necessarily the racial balance between whites and blacks (Brown 1999). Interpreted slightly differently, the basis for evaluating policy may be focused on the *intention* to discriminate. Thus, "sound educational policy" arguably may allow for the preservation of HBCUs while requiring white institutions to integrate (Brown-Scott 1994).

Adding to the uncertainty following *Fordice* is confusion over federal guidelines for Title VI compliance. Brown (1999) argues that "a lack of consensus exists regarding the remedy necessary to overcome the continuing discriminatory effects on higher education institutions plagued with vestiges of *de jure* segregation. The confusion surrounding the construction of universal standards for Title VI compliance leaves higher education grappling to articulate what it means to be desegregated or to have dismantled dual educational structures. This ambiguity allows states to continue circumventing and misinterpreting the legal guidelines issued in *Fordice.*" Following this line of criticism, some scholars are critical that *Fordice* makes no official statements about whether additional funding is needed to achieve full dismantlement under the new judicial standards. They also point out that *Fordice* lacks an aggressive mandate for traditionally white colleges and universities' increasing their numbers of blacks and fails to create a long-term plan for continuous monitoring of the desegregation effort (Brown 1999). Anchored in these issues, some scholars claim that "*Fordice* raises more concerns than it resolves" (Stefkovich and Leas 1994). At the least, a major limitation of federal desegregation involvement is that important questions regarding remedy remain unanswered.

In light of these limitations—more precisely, constraints—concerning federal involvement in the desegregation of higher education, the next major phase toward collegiate desegregation will ultimately be left in the hands of states and institutions. Three major barriers to desegregation stand out. For one, at both at the state and institutional levels, the politics of desegregation has not infrequently interfered with advancing meaningful reform in state systems of higher education. For another, the policy of affirmative action has not been a significant tool in advancing desegregation because it stands at the crossroads of political and legal disagreement. For still another, states continue to struggle to secure state funding to meet the aims articulated in *Fordice*—a critical factor that is central to the success of desegregation.

## The Politics of Desegregation

Because the act of policymaking is deeply embedded in the political process, it is difficult to arrive at noncompromising solutions for many government initiatives and policies. Efforts to desegregate higher education are no different. As seen in the cases of *Adams* and *Fordice*, it is the breakdown of the political process that has led to litigation in states. As the Supreme Court declared in the desegregation case *Knight v. Alabama* (1994): "Many of the issues involved in this case essentially require political solutions. . . . The failure of politics has left this matter with the court" (Brown 1999). Still, the formation of policies and practices to advance desegregation are ultimately filtered through political means to more or less create "sound educational policy." As Brown (1999) put it, "the political dimensions of the policy making process are often played out between forces that advocate rational, systemic change and those that desire more incremental steps that maintain power and the status quo." These opposing forces are at work in many states and have resulted in desegregation plans that remain variously stalled in the political arena.

One striking example of a political standoff between factions can be seen in the debate over closing or merging black colleges with neighboring white institutions as a way to accomplish desegregation. Proponents of this policy argue that such a measure would be consonant with the *Fordice* mandate to address dualism and have the added benefit of promoting cost savings within the system. However, members of the black community often cite this option as an inappropriate remedy, pointing out the irony of closing the very institutions that sustained blacks during segregation as a way to combat its vestiges. Many black scholars and activists argue for the importance of black institutions as environments that preserve black culture and provide shelter, networks, and comfort for blacks (Brown and Hendrickson 1997). The debate over the future of black institutions is at the heart of the *Fordice* mandate to address dualism, which not least aims to increase the other-race presence in historically black colleges and traditionally white institutions. But whether closing or merging black colleges for the purposes of desegregation is "sound educational policy" has been subject to lively political debate—not the least in Mississippi, where one state plan proposed the closing of historically black Mississippi Valley State University.

Embedded in some of these political struggles are racial disputes related to desegregation. For example, claims of racial discrimination in Louisiana have plagued efforts to assemble a leadership team at a new community college in Baton Rouge aimed at advancing desegregation. In Mississippi, a proposal to expand the Gulf Coast campus of the University of Southern Mississippi has fueled great controversy as black critics argue that funds to be used for expansion are better spent enhancing the state's three HBCUs (Lords 2000).

Political obstacles at the board and system level have also existed. In attempts to increase the "other-race presence" at some institutions, there has sometimes been a lack of cooperation between four-year and two-year systems, thereby creating an obstacle to smooth student transfer between institutions (Conrad and Shrode 1990). Since governing and consolidated boards play an important role in promoting statewide desegregation efforts, states would be well advised to give fuller support to boards as they navigate the politics associated with desegregation.

## *Affirmative Action and Desegregation*

Much of the activity surrounding increased access for blacks in traditionally white institutions lies in the politically charged—and legally challenged—policy of affirmative action. Affirmative action initiatives have taken a variety of forms both inside and outside the walls of the academy. On the inside, such policies seek to promote access based on characteristics associated with the economically or academically disadvantaged—factors that would disproportionately benefit blacks as a whole. Outside of the institution, efforts continue to be made to diversify boards of trustees, state coordinating boards, and planning commissions (Weerts and Conrad 2002).

During the last six years affirmative action policy has struggled to gain a consistent ruling in the courts concerning race-based scholarships and admissions. Guided by the Supreme Court's 1978 *Bakke* decision, for nearly two decades many institutions have taken race into consideration for the purposes of advancing educational diversity in higher education. However, in the *Hopwood* decision (1996), the 5th U.S. Court of Appeals suspended the University of Texas Law School's affirmative action admissions program, ruling that the *Bakke* decision was invalid. The court rejected the legitimacy of diversity as a goal, asserting that "educational diversity is not recognized as a compelling state interest." In deciding not to hear the case, the Supreme Court allowed the ruling to stand (Greve 2001).

Since *Hopwood,* other institutions have come under legal attack for giving minority applicants a specific point "boost" or putting them on a separate track in the admissions process. In September 2001, the 11th Circuit Court ruled that that University of Georgia's admissions system of awarding a half point to black applicants in the admissions process was in violation of the Constitution (Gose and Schmidt 2001). In 2003, the Supreme Court ruled that the University of Michigan's undergraduate admissions policy's automatic distribution of 20 points (out of 150 possible) to every member of an underprivileged minority was unconstitutional because it was not narrowly tailored to achieve the compelling state interest of educational diversity that the university claimed justified the program (*Gratz v. Bollinger,* 2003).

Eradicating affirmative action policy has already gone into effect in some states like Florida, where Governor Jeb Bush barred the use of race-conscious admissions by public colleges in an executive order. Bush's decision was upheld in July 2000 by Judge Charles Adams, who held that "affirmative action is no longer needed to ensure equal access to higher education" (Selingo 2000).

The juxtaposition of *Fordice* and the recent court cases challenging affirmative action policies has left some states and institutions puzzled as to how to fully realize their legal responsibilities to desegregate as well as their strategies for increasing diversity. In particular, the ambiguity surrounding affirmative action policy has been a barrier to desegregation as outlined in *Fordice.* The desegregation mandate is focused on eliminating policies and practices that make institutions racially identifiable; and affirmative action policy, by promoting a diverse student body, can be highly compatible with advancing desegregation. The present legal disputes about affirmative action as a means to advance diversity undermine institutional efforts to move forward with their legal duty to eliminate the vestiges of segregation. Simply put, progress toward desegregation has been undercut because states and institutions are unclear about the legal implications of improving black access to historically white institutions through affirmative action.

## The Challenge of State Funding

Adding to the political and legal challenges faced by institutions attempting to desegregate is their constant struggle to obtain the necessary state resources to implement desegregation plans. A core expense of the effort lies in strengthening the institutional identities and uniqueness of HBCUs as a way to reduce program duplication and thereby eliminate unequalness and promote white matriculation. To achieve these goals, states are aiming to enhance missions, programs, and facilities of HBCUs. A central priority is to create high-demand, high-quality programs at the master's and doctoral level (Weerts and Conrad 2002).

But the current economy may interfere with the desegregation plans as public colleges face new reductions in state support. During the last budget cycle, governors of nine states instructed public universities to prepare for midyear cuts in state appropriations in the range of 1 to 7 percent. Many other states received the same warning signs of forthcoming reductions in support (Schmidt 2001).

To illustrate, the sluggish economy may significantly affect Mississippi's ability to deliver on its $503 million settlement plan to enhance Mississippi's HBCUs. The proposal calls for $246 million to support new academic programs, $75 million for construction projects, and $70 million for a publicly financed endowment over a 17–year period. The plan also calls for a $35 million privately financed endowment (Hebel 2002). State Senator Ronald D. Farris, a Republican, spoke out against the plan, saying that it would drain too many resources from the state's higher education system during tough budget times. Farris declared that lawmakers had to cut $60 million from college budgets in 2001, and the financial picture looks as bad, or worse, for next year, he added. "The money is not there," said Farris (Hebel 2002).

On the other side of the spectrum, opponents of the proposal argue that the settlement is not enough to adequately expand the roles of the state's three public historically black universities. In particular, critics argue that the proposal does not sufficiently improve college access for Mississippi's black students (Hebel 2002). Despite these criticisms, Mississippi senators have passed a resolution supporting the $503 million plan, which has since been approved by U.S. District Judge Neal B. Biggers Jr. (Gose 2002).

Like the plans themselves, financing higher education desegregation is mired in politics. Policymakers, scholars, and administrators have varying views on what should inform the dollar amounts to meet the aims of *Fordice*. As Senator Farris declared about the Mississippi settlement, "This settlement appears to be more about money than about desegregation. These expenditures, in my view, amount to mere reparations" (Hebel 2002). But others point to larger goals, such as enhancing the educational attainment for blacks, as the definitive measure for resources allocated to the desegregation effort (Brown 1999). Clearly, the issue of funding will continue to be debated as the remaining segregated states attempt to comply with *Fordice*.

## Conclusion

The path to desegregation can be portrayed as a winding road that leads to a faraway and uncertain destination. On a path littered with more than century-old remnants of discrimination, obstacles still remain on the way to completing the journey. Nonetheless, the very considerable movement down this path, especially in the last decade and a half, has been fueled in no small measure by the strong involvement of the federal government. Executive branch leadership, initially through the Department of Health, Education, and Welfare (HEW) and the U.S. Department of Justice, and most recently the Office of Civil Rights in the U.S. Department of Education as well, has been crucial in moving the desegregation agenda forward. The U.S. Supreme Court—in *Fordice*—has set a standard by which states are held liable for perpetuating dual and unequal systems of higher education.

Still, the federal government's success in desegregating higher education is mixed. Notwithstanding strong leadership in the executive and judicial branches, questions still remain about the appropriate course of remedy to achieve desegregation. In light of constraints on the federal government, it will ultimately be up to states and institutions to finish the agenda. Challenged by the political process, continuing ambiguity surrounding affirmative action, and financial struggles, state policymakers and college and university representatives have their own barriers to overcome as they seek to follow the desegregation template advanced by the federal government. In the end, the extent to which federal efforts to desegregate higher education throughout the nation are fully realized will be left in the hands of states and institutions—and the public officials and institutional leaders who are responsible for, and committed to, maintaining fidelity to advancing desegregation.

REFERENCES

Brown, M. C. 1999. *The quest to define collegiate desegregation.* Westport, CT: Bergin and Garvey.

Brown, M. C., and R. M. Hendrickson. 1997. Public historically black colleges at the crossroads. *Journal for a Just and Caring Education* 3 (1): 95–113.

Brown-Scott, W. 1994. Race consciousness in higher education: Does "sound educational policy" support the continued existence of historically black colleges? *Emory Law Journal* 43 (1): 1–81.

Conrad, C. F., and P. E. Shrode. 1990. The long road: Desegregating higher education. *NEA Higher Education Journal* 6 (1): 35–45.

Gose, B. 2002. Federal judge approves settlement of desegregation lawsuit in Mississippi. *Chronicle of Higher Education* 48 (March 1): A22.

Gose B., and P. Schmidt. 2001. Ruling against affirmative action could alter legal debate and admissions practices. *Chronicle of Higher Education* 48 (September 7): A36.

*Gratz v. Bollinger,* 123 S.C+. 2411, 2003.

Greve, M. 2001. Affirmative action is on the rocks, thanks to college leaders. *Chronicle of Higher Education* 47 (April 20): B11.

Hebel, S. 2002. Judge says he will sign Miss. desegregation settlement if lawmakers finance it. *Chronicle of Higher Education* 48 (January 18): A24.

Lords, E. 2000. Racial disputes stymie efforts to remedy desegregation in Louisiana and Mississippi. *Chronicle of Higher Education* 46 (April 28): A38.

Schmidt, P. 2001. Downturn in economy threatens state spending on colleges. *Chronicle of Higher Education* 48 (October 19): A22.

Selingo, J. 2000. Judge upholds Florida plan to end affirmative action. *Chronicle of Higher Education* 46 (July 21): A23.

Stefkovich, J., and T. Leas. 1994. A legal history of desegregation in higher education. *Journal of Negro Education* 63 (3): 406–20.

Weerts, D. J., and C. F. Conrad. 2002. Desegregating higher education. In *Higher education in the United States: An encyclopedia.* Santa Barbara, CA: ABC-CLIO Publishers.

Williams, J. B., III. 1988. Title VI regulation of higher education. In *Desegregating America's colleges and universities: Title VI regulation of higher education,* ed. J. B. Williams III, 3–53. New York: Teachers College, Columbia University.

# Part II / The Changing
## Context in the States

$\text{T}$he authors in Part II address issues related to the role of states in higher education. States directly fund public colleges and universities, develop master plans that guide the development of public systems of higher education, and provide grants for students based on merit and/or financial need. The new policy environment has influenced each of these state functions.

In the new policy context, the states' share of the burden for funding institutions has declined, while the students and their families pay a larger share of education costs as a result of rising tuition. William Zumeta addresses this new financial context and suggests strategies for rethinking public finance in the states. A professor of public policy at the University of Washington, Zumeta examines the new policy environment in the states from the perspective of theory concerning the policy process. He recognizes that the policy process is political but is concerned about the underlying rationale used in state policy. He critically examines the new context and suggests adaptations that policymakers can make to expand access within a more fiscally constrained financial environment.

While the federal courts required states to address the legacy of desegregation, the agenda was left unfinished (Conrad and Weerts, chapter 4). Christopher Brown II (Pennsylvania State University), along with Jason Butler and Saran Donahoo (both at University of Illinois) consider how states can address desegregation and affirmative action in the new conservative policy environment. Brown, Butler, and Donahoo focus on the legal aspects of desegregation and diversity in the state institutions of higher education. They consider the issues from a perspective that values social justice and diversity, but they also consider the roles of evidence and legal constraint.

The new merit-based student grant programs substantially complicate efforts to maintain equal access for students who prepare for college. Edward P. St. John and Choong-Geun Chung (Indiana University) address the underlying legal question pertaining to inequitable distribution of state grants in the Michigan Merit Scholarship Program and illustrate the roles of policy analysis in this new policy context.

While legislators seldom explicitly consider theories of student choice when they vote to create new programs, these programs are constructed within a policy environment that rests on legal issues that relate to student choice processes. In Michigan, the state court is considering the legality of using a state achievement test as the basis for awarding merit aid. St. John and Chung reexamine the assumptions made in the Michigan Merit Scholarship Program, using a balanced model for access that considers the roles of both finances and academic preparation. They present analyses of alternative remedies that would maintain an emphasis on merit but would result in a more equitable distribution of aid.

The authors in this section recognize that states are the arenas in which the privatization battle is being waged. The old rationale for public funding focused more on institutional subsidies than on the issues related to equal access. However, with the erosion in institutional support, this is an opportune time to reconsider this position. With students and families paying a larger share of educational costs, states must focus on equalizing access to higher education for students who prepare academically. Without this minimal level of commitment, according to the U.S. Advisory Committee on Student Financial Assistance, the inequalities in educational and economic opportunity will expand because a growing number of low-income and lower-middle-income students lack the ability to pay for college. Thus, while privatization may be inevitable, given the new financial context discussed by Zumeta, lobbyists need to consider equity along with the narrower and more immediate interests of their campuses.

In combination, these analyses provide insight into the complexity of a major new challenge facing states: how can equal opportunity be maintained in the face of an increasing emphasis on privatization of public higher education? The chapters also illustrate that researchers who are interested in education policy and change face two types of choices about their research: they can either examine the issues from a distanced vantage, describing policy developments and their outcomes; or they can provide analyses that are intended to inform policy development. Both types of analyses can have an influence on policy, but in different ways. Moreover, researchers also face choices in taking an advocacy position. These choices are complex because neither theory nor ideology is neutral relative to the social equity issues that are now paramount in educational policy.

# CHAPTER FIVE

# State Higher Education Financing
## Demand Imperatives Meet Structural, Cyclical, and Political Constraints

## William Zumeta

Higher education in 2003 faces a variety of opportunities as well as major challenges. Most of the key trends, ranging from a tighter linkage than ever before between advanced education and individual and societal economic prospects, to an increase in numbers of underprepared high school graduates, present both. In brief, higher education faces the odd paradox of being simultaneously highly sought after by key societal elements, and sharply constrained in its ability to gain effective political support and thereby adequate financial sustenance—at least from its traditional sources—to realize its own aspirations and those society holds for it. This chapter will explore this conundrum in some depth and consider the merits and problems inherent in various routes out of it.

Perhaps the most important pertinent development in recent years is the economic shift that has forged a new nexus between higher education and economic outcomes. Although the relationship between a society's level of education and its pace of economic development and growth has long been recognized (Denison 1962; Schultz 1960), with the advent of the "postindustrial" fast-moving, globalized, and technologically driven—in short, knowledge-based—economy in the last quarter century or so, the linkage has tightened considerably (Marshall and Tucker 1992). From the perspective of state policymakers, the strong correlation between the proportion of a state's population enrolled in college and its rate of economic growth depicted in Figure 5.1 is powerful. Equally important is the evidence of a stronger-than-ever connection between an individual's level of education and his or her economic success in the labor market. According to the National Center for Education

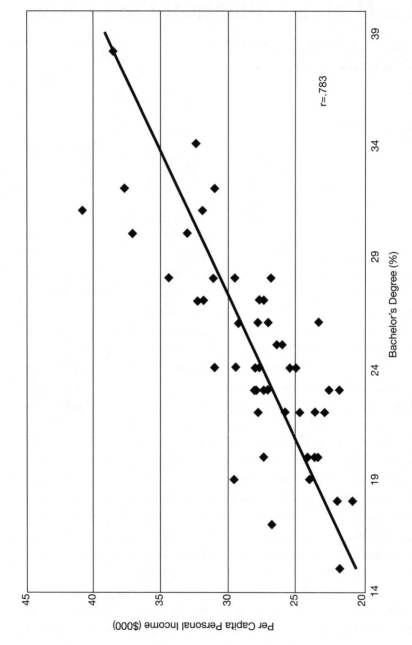

*Figure 5.1.* State Per Capita Personal Income by Proportion of Population Age 25 and Over with Bachelor's Degree, 2000. (Adapted from Mortenson 2002, 15)

Statistics (1997, cited in Kane 1999, p. 1), the "college wage premium" in terms of earnings of college graduates compared to high school graduates (here male workers aged 25–34) jumped from 19 percent in 1980 to 52 percent in 1995.[1] This is a far cry from the mid-1970s, when economists were questioning whether the American populace might be "overeducated" (Freeman 1976).

These economic forces, together with outreach efforts made by colleges and universities during the recent demographic dip in numbers of high school graduates, have increased the appetite for higher education among individuals beyond the traditional college age and their employers. Such "nontraditional" students, who often enroll part-time, have sought a variety of new accommodations and services that make the higher education enterprise more complex and, at least on a per-full-time-student basis, arguably more expensive. At the same time, the tighter connections between higher education and employment-related needs and aspirations have fueled a debate that increasingly questions the social need or desirability of the traditional large public subsidies for the enterprise (Johnstone 1999). On the other hand, many argue that the increased essentiality of higher education to individuals' life chances in modern society makes it all the more necessary that public policy ensure equity of access across an increasingly diverse population.

Another key challenge facing higher education is demographic. The long-awaited students of the "baby boom echo" are now appearing on the doorsteps of colleges and universities, ending the long period in the 1980s and 1990s when all but the most wealthy and attractive schools had to scramble to fill seats. Now schools must find ways to convince their supporters—whether legislators, students, parents, or donors—to provide resources to fuel the necessary expansion of capacity. As will be made clear in this chapter, this presents a major challenge. An increased proportion of high school graduates in the near future will be minorities and students of modest means (Callan 2002), which means higher education has the chance to better serve one of its key missions: to broaden the social distribution of opportunities. Yet serving these groups of students is likely to be more costly per student than was the traditional clientele since they tend to be less well prepared academically and more likely to need financial aid.

In addition, technological change, in particular information technology (IT), creates the opportunity for exciting improvements in students' access to educational materials and in the variety of vehicles for teaching and learning, and this makes it possible to reach people whose access to higher education was formerly restricted by distance and life commitments that keep them at work or home most of the time. Moreover, given the pervasiveness of IT in students' lives and in the modern workplace, colleges and universities have little choice but to infuse their teaching with it. The emerging competition that traditional colleges and universities face from the for-profit education sector is already using it. Yet the capital infrastructure, equipment, staffing, and faculty training costs of this change are very significant, although still imperfectly understood (Green 1997; Rumble 1997).

Another "challenging opportunity" for higher education is posed by the demand for academe to provide more direct and visible service to society. Beyond educating students and advancing knowledge, colleges and universities are increasingly called upon to harness their expertise to attack social problems like inadequate elementary and secondary education, urban decay, environmental degradation, and the like. Many institutions have responded with more applied research, consulting services and, increasingly, "service learning" programs that seek to integrate student service to the surrounding communities with academic learning. To the extent that these programs are explicitly funded, this is no doubt a largely positive development that can both enhance academe's social contributions and increase its public support.[2] Yet adequate funding does not always follow the greater demands. Also, at some point we might begin to worry about excessive redirection of attention from institutions' primary missions of knowledge creation and transmission.

A challenge linked to all of the above comes in the realm of fiscal accountability. If taxpayers and their elected agents, students and parents, and donors are to be willing to provide substantial additional resources to higher education, it is quite clear that such largess will be accompanied by similar demands for accountability for demonstrable results as are being visited upon other sectors of society (Zumeta 1998). These demands present some special problems for higher education and may create costs of their own, but in some form or another they will have to be met (Zumeta 2001).

Finally, there is the challenge to maintain quality. This is nothing new, but it seems harder than ever now as the world and the knowledge and skills needed to prepare students for it change at a breathtaking pace. Faculties clearly need continued training and renewal by a steady inflow of new blood in the face of such rapid change. Equipment needs associated with sustaining quality, notably in the realm of IT but also in many scientific and technical fields, are greater and more expensive than in the past. Accountability demands related to quality impose their own costs. Thus, simply maintaining, much less improving, academic quality is more costly than ever.

This chapter provides an analysis of the juxtaposition of these challenges and exciting opportunities for service to society with the increasingly clear reality of basic constraints in the traditional sources of funding for higher education. After laying out this conundrum, I will outline its unfortunate consequences and some policy alternatives for both institutions and states to escape from the box it presents, along with the associated claims and rationales. Get out of this box we must, for advanced education is clearly crucial to the economic and thus to the social and political fortunes of states and the nation in the emerging age of knowledge and global technological competition.

## Embedded Fiscal Constraints Facing Higher Education

Some of the fiscal challenges facing higher education are suggested above. It is crucially important to understand that these confront a fundamentally weak fiscal support structure, particularly for the public academic sector (Duderstadt and Womack 2003). State support for higher education—which includes core operating support for public institutions, a total of some $5 billion annually in state funding for student scholarships and grants, direct aid to private colleges and universities in some states, and funding for state governance operations—has fallen steadily as a percentage of personal income across all fifty states for more than twenty years (see Figure 5.2). Even counting tuition revenue, which has been growing rapidly, total funding for higher education per student has increased only sluggishly since the mid-1980s (Callan 2002, p. 9).[3]

While some have attributed much of this decline in support to the rise of political and cultural elements critical of higher education, a more compelling explanation lies in the structure of state budgets and the growth of powerful claims by elements with stronger positions in this structure. Within state general fund budgets, support for higher education competes with other major claimants, including elementary and secondary education, corrections, Medicaid and other health care expenditures, public welfare, and social services.[4] Most of these functions are strictly caseload-driven in that when pupils arrive at the schoolhouse door, or prisoners have been sentenced, or clients qualify under federal rules for Medicaid, states have to provide the necessary funds. In these cases, the state contribution is often mandated by federal law (Medicaid),

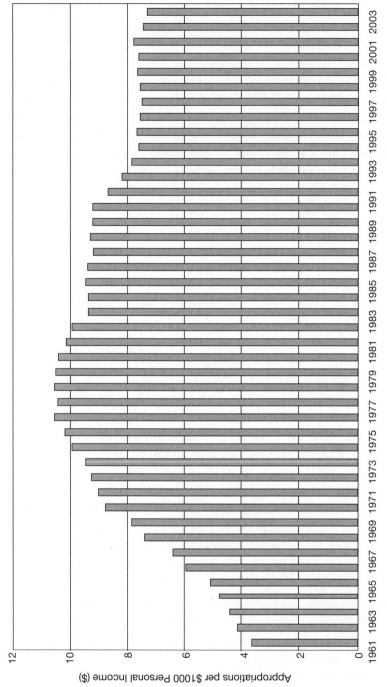

*Figure 5.2.* Appropriations of State Tax Funds for Operating Expenses of Higher Education per $1000 of Personal Income, FY 1961 to FY 2003. (Adapted from Mortenson 2003, 8)

court rulings (prisons), or longstanding practice often enshrined in state constitution or statute (K–12 education). And indeed, in recent years the numbers of school-age children, prisoners, and Medicaid clients have been growing. In the health care field costs per client have also escalated rapidly, so that this component has overtaken higher education as the second-largest piece (after K–12 education) of state general fund spending (National Governors Association 2001, p. 4).

In short, most of the major state budgetary claimants have a mandatory or near-mandatory character. Higher education, on the other hand, is seen as discretionary in that its "caseloads" (enrollments) can be reduced or its planned growth postponed—or students can be asked to pay more—to help balance the state's budget in times of need or when other fields have higher policy priority. For example, the 1990s saw states place a high priority on K–12 education reform, and this effort attracted considerable discretionary investment in many states (Liebschutz, Schneider, and Boyd 1997).

To fully understand the depth of the structural fiscal problems facing higher education, it is necessary to trace how higher education has fared in different stages of the economic cycle. State revenues and thus budget expenditures are powerfully driven by economic conditions. As Figure 5.3 shows, during periods of economic slowdown such as those in the early years of the 1980s, 1990s, and 2000s, state budgets grew little if at all. Once reserve funds are exhausted—which happens quickly, since large reserves are targets for tax cutters—states have to find places to cut substantial sums in order to meet norms of budget balance as demands from recession-sensitive budget components such as welfare, low-income health care, and criminal justice burgeon.[5]

Higher education, as explained above, is the largest broadly discretionary item in state general fund budgets, so it is the most vulnerable target for budget cutting. Moreover, unlike most of the other major state budget components, higher education has other substantial sources of funds that policymakers feel can be tapped if institutions need to cope with deep budget cuts. These include tuition increases,[6] private donations, and grants and contracts. Figure 5.5 shows that higher education suffered the most among major state general fund budget components during the recession of the early 1990s and its aftermath of state fiscal stress (see also Gold 1995). The result of the interplay of these forces has been sharp increases in tuition and fee rates during recessionary periods[7] (Figure 5.4). These tuition increases have contributed to a substantial shift in the burden of paying for higher education from states to

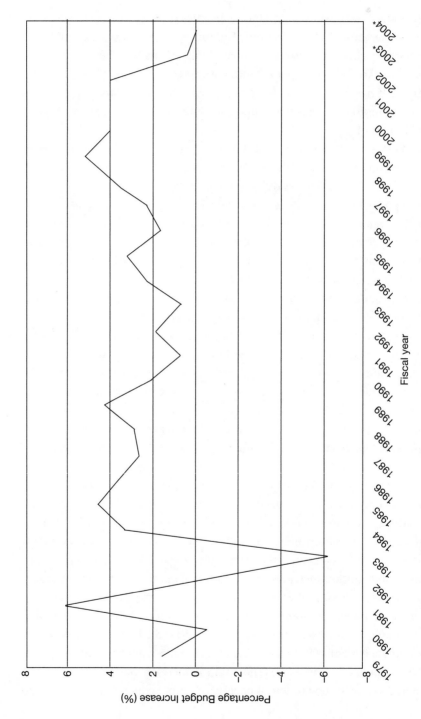

*Figure 5.3.* Annual Percentage Budget Increases, Fiscal 1979 to Fiscal 2004. Adjusted for inflation using state and local government implicit price deflator. FY 2003 is a change from FY 2002 to FY 2003 estimated. FY 2004 is a change from FY 2003 estimated to FY 2004 recommended by governor. (NGA and NASBO 2003, 4)

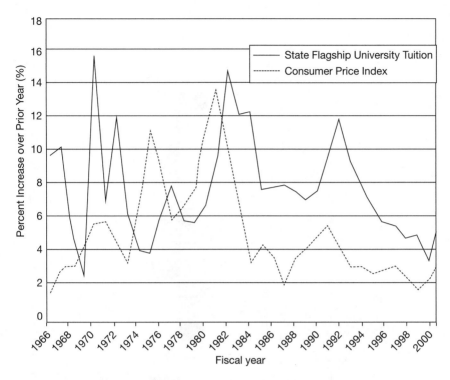

*Figure 5.4.* Annual Percentage Increases in State Flagship University Tuition and Consumer Price Index, 1966 to 2001. (Adapted from Mortenson 2001d, 14)

students and their parents. Figure 5.6 shows the substantial increase in the student/parent share of higher education funding over the past two decades, a trend that began during the recession of the early 1980s. (This graph does not capture the sharp upturn in the student and parent share during the recent years of state funding stagnation.)

Generally in the past, higher education has been able to recoup the financial losses it suffers during downturns with disproportionate gains in state support relative to other budget claimants during periods of prosperity. During the most recent "boom" period following the early 1990s recession, however, it took a number of years for state policymakers to feel comfortable enough with the stability of revenue growth and to recognize that other needs had been met sufficiently[8] to begin reinvesting in higher education. Only in fiscal years 1999, 2000, and 2001 did gains in state appropriations for higher education exceed the aggregate growth rate in general fund appropriations—and then only

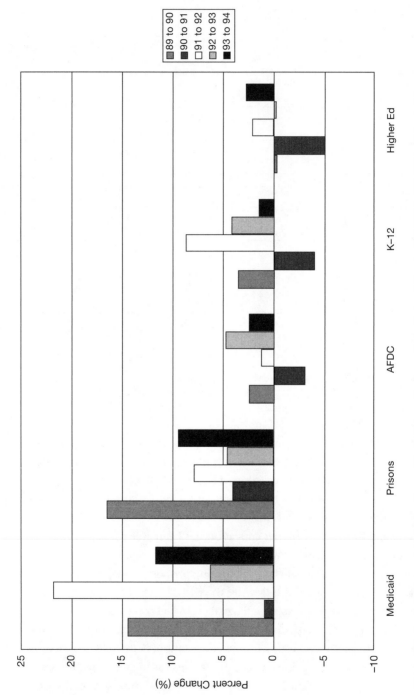

*Figure 5.5.* Annual Changes in Major Expenditure Categories from State General Funds, FY1990 to FY 1994. (Adapted from Mortenson 1994, 10)

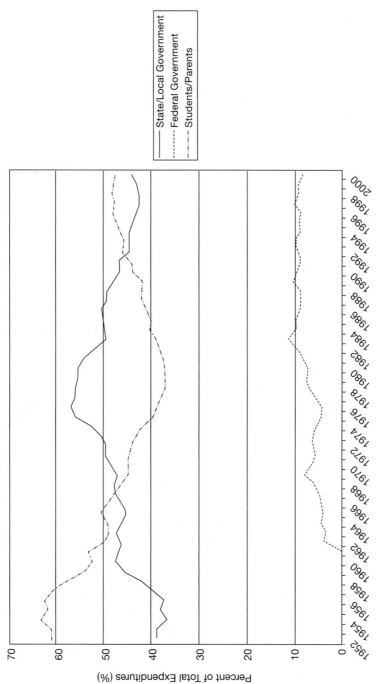

*Figure 5.6.* Distribution of Responsibilities for Financing Higher Education, 1952 to 2000. (Adapted from Mortenson 2001c, 16)

barely.[9] Thus, even in the longest unbroken period of prosperity in the nation's history, higher education did not catch up very much in relation to its long stagnation in real funding per student. This is one powerful sign that a new era is upon higher education that will require much more fundamental rethinking than simply planning to wait out the latest economic slowdown.

## Emerging Consequences of Fiscal Constraints

As the young college-eligible population swells with the coming of age of the baby boom echo cohort and as employers and workers increasingly seek higher education access, it is clear that in many states the capacity to provide desired educational opportunities will be stretched. In the next section some policy options for dealing with the capacity crunch are surveyed, but in any case there remains concern that capacity may not be able to keep pace with demand so that participation rates in higher education may begin to fall. Such a shortfall would tend to slow economic growth and could easily work to disproportionately dampen the aspirations of newly emerging groups of would-be students. These are serious consequences indeed in a world where knowledge and the ability to use it are essential to both individual success and the economic prospects of states and the nation.

As shown above, higher education's state funding has been constrained for at least two decades. Federal funding—mainly in the form of student aid, since public colleges and universities in the U.S. are creatures of the states—has been erratic in its growth patterns and has, since around 1980, come increasingly in the form of loans and loan guarantees rather than grants. Thus, the substantial shift in responsibilities for financing higher education away from government and toward students and their families has been a real one: students have not been able to shift most of the increased cost burdens they have faced onto federal grant programs; loans must be repaid by the borrower. One consequence of the shift in financing responsibilities has been increased student debt (Fossey and Bateman 1998). Thus far, the evidence that students' debt burdens have had a strong effect on their choices about graduate study and careers is mixed.[10] At some point, however, it seems that the specter of large debts must further erode the competitiveness of lower-paying but socially vital service-oriented careers such as teaching, public service, and even scientific research.[11] It is known that first-generation college students and those from underrepresented groups are more reluctant than others to take on debt, which may well play a role in dampening their participation and graduation rates.

These rates need all the help they can get. Trends in college participation and graduation rates by socioeconomic status (family income) and ethnicity show large and persistent gaps favoring more affluent students and whites and Asians, with African Americans, Hispanics, and Native Americans trailing far behind.[12] For example, in the 1996–2000 period, the proportion of dependent 18- to 24-year-olds enrolled in college ranged from around 80 percent for those from families with incomes above $75,000 per year to less than 35 percent for those with incomes below $25,000 (Mortenson 2001a, p. 1). In terms of chances of baccalaureate attainment by age 24, the gap was even larger, with the rates ranging from 52 percent for the top income quartile down to 7 percent for the lowest income group. The second-lowest income quartile had a B.A. attainment rate of 14 percent in 1997 (Mortenson 2001b, p. 8). The main change in these rates over the past several decades has been that while the highest income youths have made large gains since 1980, those in the lower groups have gained very little ground.

These largely flat trend lines in low-income access and achievement in the face of considerable variations in federal and state aid to students over the years do not provide strong evidence that financial aid has had a large impact. Kane (1999) and Ellwood and Kane (2000) argue convincingly that much of the persistent socioeconomic and ethnic gaps are results of differential precollegiate opportunities in schools, homes, and communities. Financial aid for college thus comes too late to address the roots of the inequalities for many. Yet it is also clear that low-income and minority students react strongly to tuition prices and financial aid (Kane 1999, pp. 101–14; Thompson and Zumeta 2001).

State aid to students has grown considerably in recent years and now approaches $5 billion annually , but this aid is quite concentrated in a small number of states and is negligible in many (De Salvatore and Hughes 2002). In addition, the most rapid growth sectors in state aid recently have not been need-based aid, which can materially affect participation rates of students of modest means, but rather "merit-based" aid and aid to students pursuing particular high-demand professions (Heller and Marin 2002). These forms of assistance are much less likely to help low-income students to attend college.

While higher education price and aid policies are not the whole answer to inequalities in educational attainment in U.S. society, progress of the underserved will surely be stymied if these policies are not conducive to the enrollment of students of modest means once they are qualified. Thus, developments like those described here that tend to push prices up and threaten funding for student aid will surely be detrimental to the key policy goal of broadening access to higher education.

Finally, a major concern with the slow growth in funding per student is that it must eventually affect quality. Absent major shifts in the technology of production of high quality educational services—that is, given the apparently inevitable labor-intensive nature of the enterprise,[13] underfunding eventually has to result in fewer faculty (and other) resources per student and further deterioration in academe's ability to compete for top professional talent. This must surely impact the quality of education available to students.

## Policy Options for Institutions and States

Given the clear importance of higher education in the modern economy and the profound forces of change at work in their environments, institutions and states cannot afford to sit still and allow the types of negative consequences just described to wash over them. Most will seek to respond in some way. I will survey the most likely types of responses by institutions first and then turn to the choices facing state policymakers, pointing out some of the advantages and problems with each strategy.

### What Colleges and Universities Can Do

Once an organization recognizes that decreased revenue flows from traditional sources are not temporary and once initial efficiency steps have been exhausted, we may expect two types of behavior in response to the changed context. One class of responses seeks to address the organization's cost structure; the other, its flows of revenues. In higher education, the primary approach taken in recent years to cut costs has been to reduce the share of full-time, tenure-track faculty in the ranks by using more graduate student, part-time, and temporary faculty who are generally available at much lower cost per course. These faculty are normally hired strictly to teach. Up to a point, such faculty may provide valuable flexibility and even important perspectives from the field that are not as readily provided by full-time scholars. But problems arise when such limited-commitment faculty make up a substantial proportion of a department's teaching force. Their limited stability and their commitment primarily to course teaching makes it difficult for departments to maintain curricular coherence and to get necessary tasks done like curriculum planning, student advising, and interfacing with other institutional units and outside constituents (not to mention doing scholarly research). Evidence that the limits of the strategy of heavier dependence on part-time and limited-term faculty may have been reached is suggested by the fact that the use of such faculty appears to have leveled off in the past few years, following many years of growth (U.S. Department of Education 2002, p. 271). Prospects for further cost savings from this source thus seem likely to be limited.

During the 1980s and early nineties, when numbers of students of traditional college age were decreasing in much of the country, colleges and universities showed considerable enterprise in making their offerings more attractive and accessible to new groups of students. Key to their strategy was offering courses in the evening and generally at times more convenient for nontraditional students (Zumeta 1999a). Now that the main impetus is for cost savings in the face of burgeoning demand, institutions can go further down this path by seeking to accommodate some of the new demand within existing facilities by using them more intensively on weekends and in summers. There are now examples of institutions that are moving in these directions, but the pace of movement is surprisingly staid. One impediment may be faculty resistance to working at personally inconvenient times, so outside incentives may be necessary to accelerate this process.

Emerging instructional technologies, especially those involving the Internet and other modes for reaching students at a distance and asynchronously, create the opportunity for potentially revolutionary innovations in teaching and learning and the associated economics. If these technologies can be used in ways that educate students satisfactorily at lower faculty cost per student— that is, by substituting low-cost capital for higher-cost labor—then savings in per-student spending are possible. Thus far, though, it is not clear that instructional IT has worked this way at all. Not only is the equipment and associated staffing and faculty training (and continuous updating) expensive,[14] but faculty are still needed to design courses and to interact with students and their academic work. Indeed, so far the evidence generally suggests that distance-learning courses require more, not less, faculty time per student.[15] The availability of distance-learning opportunities may well provide access to more students, an important policy goal; but if true, this necessarily expands the size and cost of the instructional enterprise as well. It is possible that private, for-profit purveyors of postsecondary education will devise cheaper models of technology-based instruction that produce quality results and that their innovations will diffuse in some measure to the "traditional" higher education sector.[16] Yet it is likely that issues of how quality is defined and of the nature of faculty jobs in such a brave new world would be highly contested, with unpredictable outcomes in terms of public policies.

In sum, the most likely approaches to additional cost cutting in higher education are fraught with problems and uncertainties. Experimentation in this arena is surely to be encouraged though. Indeed, institutions that are not working to stay abreast of the emerging technologies and competitive forces in the new higher education marketplace could quickly find themselves in danger of obsolescence even in their traditional market niches.

On the revenue side, colleges and universities are increasingly looking to a range of steps that are sometimes collected under the umbrella heading of *privatization* strategies. The general argument is made that if public authorities will not provide adequate funds to sustain quality institutions and their growth to meet new student demands, then colleges and universities should seek more private resources—including increased revenues from tuition—to pursue these noble ends. Plainly, various types of institutions have differential prospects for successful privatization, and there are basic differences between the public and independent higher education sectors. Many schools that are highly dependent on annual student revenues—under-endowed private colleges and public colleges where even state appropriations may be closely tied to enrollments—often do not have the market power (surplus applicants) to raise tuition prices substantially without defeating their purpose by decreasing enrollments. Others with some market power may not wish to pay the price in terms of harmful impacts on financially needy or underrepresented students or on their competitiveness for students with strong academic backgrounds whom they wish to attract.

Elite colleges and research universities with ample supplies of surplus qualified applicants, on the other hand, may have room for further substantial increases in tuition and other student charges, although this sector has generally increased charges most rapidly over the last two decades. Public research universities are more constrained in these calculations by considerations of maintaining political support, but even private institutions have to pay heed to public and congressional concerns about excessive price increases.[17] As of mid-2003, there were clear signals from both the Bush administration and

Congress that the federal government would place increasing pressure on higher education to restrain tuition increases (Burd 2003).

Higher education might seek to blunt the effects of this price control pressure by turning to a more united and explicit advocacy of a *high tuition–high aid* approach to its financing. Under such a financing model, tuition in the more heavily subsidized public sector would move sharply upward toward a full average-cost-per-student level, while need-based aid would follow closely, thus theoretically not harming financially needy students. Meanwhile, more affluent students would be paying substantially more into institutions' coffers. There is evidence that enrollments of affluent students would be little affected by higher prices;[18] in other words, the existing subsidies built into public college tuition rates are largely a windfall to them. This makes the approach potentially attractive in an era of constrained resources for higher education subsidies, especially if most institutions in a school's competitive set adopt it simultaneously. It is less attractive to institutions, of course, if they have to fund most of the higher aid demands from their increased tuition revenue than if they are able to transfer some of the costs to state or federal student aid programs. Thus, we will return to these very issues in the next section on public policy options.

Institutions of higher education can also try to privatize more of their revenue streams by more aggressively seeking private funds from donations and quasi-commercial ventures such as technology licensing or equity investments in spin-off companies. No doubt some institutions can do more in the realm of private giving, but in the aggregate, higher education has vastly expanded its efforts in this direction in the past twenty years or so—in large measure to help offset the long stagnation in public funding—and it is questionable how much more rapidly private giving can be expected to grow in an increasingly competitive environment for the charitable dollar.[19]

Some research universities have succeeded, generally after years of investments, in producing significant revenue streams from technology transfer activities, but in all but a handful of cases, the net revenues are quite modest (Blumenstyk 2002). It is possible that some of the newer biotechnology and software-related spin-offs will be more lucrative, but excessive focus on technology transfer activities carries the risk of skewing faculty and institutional priorities and even compromising intellectual autonomy.[20] Moreover, the benefits of such activity are not likely to be much available to institutions outside the research university sector. Other types of institutions, including community colleges, can broaden their revenue streams somewhat by pursuing training and applied research contracts with private firms, and these may have some indirect benefits for students. But this type of activity mainly serves purposes other than the primary educational mission of these institutions. It does relatively little to increase capacity to educate more students.

Clearly, the list of attractive revenue-broadening options available to institutions acting on their own is not long or without significant problems. Public institutions in particular, but private colleges too in some ways, will need help from public policies if they are to respond effectively to reduced availability of public subsidies.

## *What States Can Do*

The high tuition–high aid financing approach sketched above has surfaced in state policy discussions off and on for more than two decades (Blaydon 1978; Griswold and Marine 1996). It has resurfaced with new impetus in the last few years, however, as the fundamental nature of higher education's funding crisis has become clearer. From the perspective of state policymakers, the approach has some attractions but also some serious problems. On the positive side, the promise of providing more of higher education's funding needs from sources other than state taxes is certainly attractive. Not only would the pocketbooks of more affluent students and families be tapped but, more attractive politically, in most cases higher tuition charges would count in the calculation of students' financial need for federal financial aid. Thus, the federal student aid programs could theoretically help to finance state colleges and universities, in effect replacing some state appropriations.[21] Of course, if many states took this tack in a substantial way, the demands on the federal aid programs would escalate sharply, which might provoke a counter-reaction in Congress.[22]

The difficulties with the high tuition–high aid approach are formidable, however. First, many states have deeply entrenched traditions of low or moderate tuition in their public institutions—a few have even enshrined low-tuition goals in the state constitution—and these will be vigorously and emotionally supported by advocates. They may be able to mobilize considerable and potent political support from middle- and upper-income voters who have counted on modest tuition at their state's public institutions in making their financial plans over many years for children's or grandchildren's education. Low-tuition advocates will also point out that low-income and minority students are particularly sensitive to the "sticker price" of higher education, not fully comprehending the complexities and uncertainties of the financial aid system, a view that has considerable support (Kane 1999, esp. chap 2).

The financial advantages for states of more tuition-based financing of public higher education would no doubt be mitigated by demands for substantially greater state funding of student aid. Most states have student aid programs, and they generally use similar formulas for determining student need as do the federal programs: higher tuition charges generate more need. The demand to "hold harmless" low-income students and probably many in the moderate-income group would be great, and the debate over where to draw the lines as to how much increased need to meet via state funding could be highly charged. Finally, a great fear of access advocates is that, during times of revenue stagnation that states inevitably face periodically, student aid for the needy would have less political clout than sustaining appropriations for institutions. Thus, high tuition–high aid could well become high tuition–*low* aid with disastrous consequences for equitable access.

Since capital costs represent a very important part of the cost of expanding higher education capacity, states will be looking for ways to economize on these. Perhaps the most basic strategy available to states is to create incentives for colleges and universities to make more intensive use of existing facilities so that the need for new buildings and the like is minimized. State policymakers can use "carrots" or "sticks" in pursuing this goal. They could try to mandate use of classrooms more hours through the week, on weekends, and in summers and refuse to fund new buildings (the "stick" approach). This approach will not go far though, if students are unwilling to attend classes at the targeted times without other policy changes. Thus, states might fund pilot projects and supportive investments, including marketing efforts, designed to demonstrate the feasibility of expanded weeks (e.g., for students who work full-time during the week) and a different approach to summer school classes that better integrates these into degree curricula (the "carrot" approach). The latter is likely to require a complex and carefully designed change process for faculty, who are accustomed to using summers for research (as well as for family vacations when children are out of school) and for students, who use them to work to provide savings to pay bills for the ensuing academic year. Institutions themselves often schedule revenue-producing conferences and special programs during the summer months as well as major maintenance activities. These are not easy matters to change, but given the long-term constraints on resources for higher education and the inertia that often persists at the institution level, it seems a useful role for state policymakers to try to catalyze structural changes that could reduce the capital costs of enrollment expansion.

Similarly, states may wish to provide resources and incentives for institutions to innovate in the delivery of higher education services to students via distance learning. Distance learning may not only make higher education accessible to students who would not otherwise participate but could also, if carefully designed, work to reduce capital needs by offering some instruction to many enrolled students with less use of classrooms. Some of the pioneers in this field have found that many students appreciate a mix of some intensive on-campus instruction[23] with the opportunity to take some courses or parts thereof without traveling to campus. Over time, this type of instructional mix might significantly reduce demand for new classrooms and other student facilities on campus, since fewer would be there at any given time. Use of technology to reduce the need for faculty seems more problematic as was mentioned earlier, but it probably behooves states to support and monitor experiments in all these areas to see both how learning outcomes and completion rates compare and whether substantial savings in capital and other costs are achievable. It is important to note, however, that the investments in instructional technology and associated support, training, and upgrading costs have to be weighed against any savings in bricks and mortar.

Elsewhere I have written extensively about approaches to, and prospects for, states to respond to increased demand for higher education by inducing more students to enroll in private (independent) colleges and universities (Thompson and Zumeta 2001; Zumeta 1996; 1999b). Where demand is growing substantially and such private sector capacity exists and is willing to expand, states have several policy tools at their disposal for inducing such shifts. Most basically, states can, if they choose, use public institution tuition policy to serve two complementary purposes: increasing non-state revenue to public institutions by increasing their tuition prices, while at the same time enhancing the competitive position of private institutions so they attract a larger share of the growing enrollment load.[24] Also widely applicable is the manipulation of state student aid programs' appropriations and formulas to make attendance at private institutions more financially attractive.[25] In short, the state may come out ahead if it can induce a substantial number of students over the next ten years to attend private colleges for an additional $2,000 or $3,000 per year added to their state scholarships if the alternative is bearing the full cost of expansion of public sector facilities and faculties to teach them. Both program design and political issues are tricky, however.[26] How can the state avoid paying the enhanced scholarship dollars to thousands who would have attended private institutions in any case? And how can the powerful pressures from public higher education constituents to continue to claim the lion's share of state-funded scholarship funds be resisted, particularly if their own tuition prices are increasing?

Another policy tool available to many states can avoid some of these difficulties. This is direct state aid to private colleges provided in return for enrollment of state-resident students. While in some states the constitution or basic political values (or private institution resistance) make direct state payments to private colleges in return for services delivered unthinkable, the author found in national surveys that about half the states had at least some form of direct appropriations or contract arrangements with private colleges and universities (Zumeta 1992; 1996). Some of these supported capital projects or research programs, but several provided per-student payments to private schools for enrollment of certain kinds of students (often medical or other health professions students)[27] or, in a few cases, for any state-resident undergraduate. Where private colleges and universities were available and willing, such payments could be calibrated so as to enroll sufficient numbers to preclude some of the need for costly public sector expansion to serve undergraduates. States lacking appropriate private sector capacity could even consider purchasing spaces in institutions (public or private) in other states, although policymakers may be reluctant to see state dollars "migrating" out of state.

Another part of the private postsecondary education sector also merits attention here. In the rapidly evolving new world of information technology, new forms of education providers have emerged and appear to be thriving and growing. Many of these providers are for-profits offering, via the Internet, employee training, or business or technical degree programs to people who will use them directly in their work or for changing careers. But also emerging are partnerships involving universities or groups of them and for-profit firms that offer a broader range of content. Over time, these offerings might come to include more of what colleges and universities have traditionally offered on campus. Financing models vary, but the for-profits are plainly seeking eventually to cover their costs and make profits on these courses, implying that students will pay the full cost. States could conceivably sit back and watch this market develop and conclude that expansion of public higher education was less necessary than in the past because much of the need was being met privately.

At a minimum, state policymakers will want to closely monitor market developments in the world of private postsecondary education. Perhaps eventually public system expansion can be thought of more in terms of filling gaps in the market's offerings than of seeking to be comprehensive, as in the past. Yet it seems unlikely that the private for-profit education industry will ever supply programs requiring high-cost laboratory facilities, high-quality Ph.D. programs, or the kinds of personalized educational experiences many students will likely continue to seek on residential campuses. And even if for-profits did come to supply an important segment of study programs in business, vocational fields, and some other subjects, states would still face claims for student subsidies to ensure access for the full range of citizens. Also, in an environment of greater private-public competition in postsecondary education, the state role in consumer protection and quality assurance will surely be more prominent and more complex. Certainly, it is too early to say how all this will play out for the states' role in higher education and on what timetable; but there may well be considerable fiscal implications, and policymakers will surely need to keep the proverbial ear close to the ground as educational technology and markets evolve.

Finally, to return to more familiar territory and a shorter time horizon, where states face large-scale growth in enrollment demand that for one reason or another they choose to respond to by expanding capacity in public institutions, many may want to look to two-year colleges to meet more of this need than they have in the past. States vary widely in the extent of development of their two-year college systems, and several with relatively undeveloped systems have moved to expand them in recent years (e.g., Indiana, Kentucky, and Louisiana). Community and technical colleges are well suited to meet many of the demands of the modern economy for workers with some postsecondary education but less than a four-year degree, while at the same time also providing opportunities for transfer to baccalaureate institutions for those who desire them.

These colleges have generally responded well to local needs and demands, especially in the realm of economic development. Their lower-cost plants support their broad geographical distribution in many states, which facilitates student access. Access has also been promoted because states and localities, which often share the costs of two-year public colleges, have been willing to offer enrollment at much lower tuition rates than for four-year schools while still generally spending less in public funds per student. All these features make two-year colleges an attractive place to expand the public higher education system in a time of growing enrollment demand and limited public funds. Theoretically at least, room for more two-year college transfers to move on to baccalaureate colleges could be created by making the latter institutions more specialized in the "upper division" of college work (roughly the last two years of a traditional four-year degree program). Systemically, having a greater proportion of students begin at the lower-cost two-year schools should reduce the total cost of educating each student.[28]

Of course, this type of macro-system planning is easier to talk about than to pull off. Many four-year colleges resist the idea of giving up all or most of their freshman and sophomore classes. (What will it do to the football team and traditional student campus life?) There is ample evidence that students who commence studies at two-year schools are less likely to complete four-year degrees, and take longer when they do succeed, because of the personal and bureaucratic complexities of changing institutions and articulating curricula. These are not small problems. Inducing large institutions and systems to work together efficiently is a major challenge, but the pressures to do so are likely to be stronger than ever before.

## The Federal Backdrop

Federal policies are relevant to state finance of higher education in limited but important ways. Most important are federal support for research and development and student aid. R & D funds not only support academic research projects and graduate students, but the substantial indirect cost allowances on federal grants are a major source of largely discretionary income to research universities.[29] If R & D funding were threatened with stagnation by federal budget problems, this would seriously affect research universities, many of which—especially those in the public sector—are already financially hard-pressed.

Federal funding for student aid totals some $60 billion per year (excluding tax credits) and, unlike R & D funding, is very broadly distributed across the higher education system. If renewed federal budget problems and politics threaten the usual growth patterns in the student aid programs just at the time when more students seek to use them (Burd 2003), it will be that much more difficult for states to ensure student access to higher education. They will be under more pressure to increase their own aid programs[30] and will have much more difficulty using any strategy involving substantial public sector tuition increases to help pay for increases in enrollment capacity. Presumably, the federal government is no longer in any fiscal position or political disposition to finance boosts in its student aid to cover substantial increases in student need for aid that would result from implementation of high tuition–high aid policies. The brief window of opportunity that might have existed to facilitate such a state strategy seems now to have closed.

## Conclusion

In this chapter I have sought to sketch the challenging picture that is before higher education leaders and state policymakers as they face, simultaneously, an era of great social demand for higher education, and powerful constraints on traditional sources of finance. Decision makers will need to be creative and innovative in thinking about how to tap more effectively both old and new sources of support and, very likely, how to achieve more with fewer resources per student. They will also need to be closely attentive to rapid changes in technology, student needs, and market dynamics. State policymakers in particular will need to increase their efforts at "market intelligence," consumer protection, and quality oversight. The most urgent public policy imperatives for all, however, will continue to be access and equity: how can we ensure places in a quality postsecondary education enterprise for all who can benefit, regardless of their economic status? These are worthy challenges indeed for higher education leadership in the early morning of the twenty-first century.

NOTES

1. Individuals with graduate degrees have seen their relative economic advantage increase the most in recent years, and of course, a college degree is normally a prerequisite for entrance into graduate school.

2. Campus-based community service projects can sometimes become controversial, however, when they get involved in issues where views and interests among the public are mixed.

3. Since higher education remains a labor-intensive "industry" where quality is defined largely by faculty-student interaction, there has been little or no productivity gain to help offset the effects of funding stagnation.

4. Transportation expenditures, dominated by highways, are another large expenditure category but are generally funded primarily from "special fund" revenue sources such as fuel taxes.

5. The fiscal threats posed by surging costs are particularly worrisome in the current period of economic sluggishness following the recession of 2001. Medicaid costs are sky-rocketing again after a few years of more modest escalation (National Governors Association 2003), although some federal fiscal help has recently been enacted (Walters 2003). In welfare, since the federal Personal Responsibility and Work Opportunity Reconciliation Act (PRWORA) went into effect in 1997, states are formally relieved of their legal responsibility under federal law to provide part of the funding for new welfare cases because welfare is no longer a legal entitlement of destitute families. Under this welfare regime, federal aid to states for welfare is provided in the form of a block grants tied to federal subvention levels of the mid-1990s. While this aid was more than adequate during the economic boom years when the welfare rolls were falling, now states have no guarantee of federal help with caseload pressures that are building with the recent stagnation.

6. Tuition increases are generally the largest, readiest, and most discretionary source of additional income that institutions and states can tap to help offset cutbacks in state appropriations. Yet they understandably produce mixed reactions in legislatures, which are also responsive to outcries from students and parents and may be concerned about deterrent effects on access for low-income and underrepresented students. On balance, policymakers have generally permitted relatively large tuition hikes during recession periods (see Figure 5.4).

7. Independent (private nonprofit) colleges and universities also suffer during recessions because economic slowdowns generally reduce private donations and returns on endowment income (Van Der Werf 2002). Thus, these institutions also turn to larger-than-normal tuition increases during recessionary times just when students and families may be least able to pay more.

8. These included infrastructure funding, funding for K–12 education reforms, and tax cuts as well as new efforts to control criminal justice, health, and welfare spending.

9. State appropriations to higher education grew at a rate of about 7 percent per year nationwide during these three years (Schmidt 2000, pp. A34–35, citing figures compiled by the National Conference of State Legislatures).

10. For a thorough literature review see Millett (2003).

11. On the impact of economic considerations on the choices of the most talented young Americans with potential for careers in science, see Zumeta and Raveling (2001).

12. Recent data show some signs of modest positive trends in minority enrollments (Harvey 2001).

13. I will comment below on the prospects for changes in this premise given the emergence of new instructional technologies.

14. It should be noted that these costs should be compared with the costs of more buildings and the like in the traditional delivery model.

15. Delivery via distance learning also seems to be associated with higher dropout rates, raising questions about the premise that the quality of educational services as perceived by the student is comparable.

16. This could occur either by the design of instructional materials requiring less faculty interaction with students or by the creation of a faculty "star" system, where a few outstanding faculty provided some content via taped lectures or the like, while the personal contact with students and their work was provided by much lower-priced individuals functioning somewhat like traditional teaching assistants responsible for course sections.

17. Congress supplies vital research dollars to both private and public universities, and private colleges are quite sensitive to the levels of federal and state aid made available to their students. In a few states legislatures provide state appropriations directly to private colleges and universities (Zumeta 1996), which gives policymakers additional potential leverage over pricing policies.

18. Such students might well move around among institutions as prices shifted (Hilmer 2001), but the evidence is clear that affluent students are not very price sensitive in terms of their propensity to enroll somewhere (McPherson and Schapiro 1991). This is one reason that public policy involvement is likely to be needed to make such a regime workable.

19. The stock market boom of the 1990s provided handsome payoffs indeed for those schools with substantial endowments, but the era of supercharged market returns seems likely to be over for a while. In any case, most colleges and universities have very modest endowments.

20. For example, in a few cases companies have essentially purchased, for large donations, special access to a department's research products prior to publication and some ability to delay publication. The department also guarantees that much of its research activity over a period of years will be devoted to topics of interest to the company. See Blumenstyk (1998; 2001) for coverage of two prominent examples at Washington University and the University of California, Berkeley. University equity investments in companies spun off from faculty research raise potential questions of conflict of interest as do heavy faculty involvement therein. For extensive analysis of the benefits and problems of university "technology transfer" and related policies, see Bok (2003).

21. See McPherson and Schapiro (1991) for a discussion of how this would work.

22. The current recession-induced jumps in tuition rates seem to be producing just such a response in Washington.

23. Note that for working students, the on-campus modules might well be scheduled on weekends.

24. State policymakers do not always have direct control over public colleges and universities' tuition charges, but they can exert powerful influence through control of their state appropriations. Of course, any sharp increase in tuition should be accompanied by appropriate provision for increased need-based student aid.

25. Most of the states have such student aid programs for which state resident students who attend both private and public colleges are eligible (De Salvatore and Hughes 2001).

26. For a fuller analysis of these see Zumeta (1999b).

27. A few states have used this method to purchase spaces for students in private university medical schools to avoid the need for establishing an additional public medical school.

28. Many states are going one more step to streamline the public education system by encouraging students to begin taking college courses while still in high school.

29. These allowances are designed to reimburse universities for the portion of their costs for buildings, libraries, computing, administration, and myriad support services that are broadly attributable to these institutions' heavy commitment to funded research but are not readily identifiable with individual projects.

30. These are large in some states but quite small in many (De Salvatore and Hughes 2001).

REFERENCES

Blaydon, C. C. 1978. State policy options. In *Public policy and private higher education,* ed. D. W. Breneman and C. E. Finn, 353–88. Washington, DC: Brookings Institution.

Blumenstyk, G. 1998. Berkeley pact with a Swiss company takes technology transfer to a new level. *Chronicle of Higher Education* 45 (16) (December 11): A56.

Blumenstyk, G. 2001. A vilified corporate partnership produces little change (except better facilities). *Chronicle of Higher Education* 47 (41) (June 22): 24.

Blumenstyk, G. 2002. Income from university licenses on patents exceeded $1billion. *Chronicle of Higher Education* (March 22): A31.

Bok, D. 2003. *Universities in the marketplace.* Princeton, NJ: Princeton University Press.

Burd, S. 2003. Bush's next target? *Chronicle of Higher Education* 49 (44) (July 11): A18–20.

Callan, P. M. 2002. *Coping with recession: Public policy, economic downturns and higher education.* National Center Report #02-2. Washington, DC: National Center for Public Policy and Higher Education.

Denison, E. F. 1962. *The sources of economic growth in the United States and the alternatives before us.* Supplementary Paper No. 13. New York: Committee for Economic Development.

De Salvatore, K., and L. Hughes. 2001. *National Association of State and Student Grant and Aid Programs 31st Annual Survey Report: 1999–2000 Academic Year.* Albany: New York State Higher Education Services Corporation for NASSGAP.

De Salvatore, K., and L. Hughes. 2002. *National Association of State and Student Grant & Aid Programs 32nd Annual Survey Report: 2000–2001 Academic Year.* Albany: New York State Higher Education Services Corporation for NASSGAP.

Duderstadt, J. J., and F. W. Womack. 2003. *The future of the public university in America: Beyond the crossroads.* Baltimore: Johns Hopkins University Press.

Ellwood, D. T., and T. J. Kane. 2000. Who is getting a college education? Family background and the growing gaps in enrollment. In *Securing the future: Investing in children from birth to college,* ed. S. Danziger, S. and J. Waldfogel, 264–82. New York: Russell Sage Foundation.

Fossey, R., and M. Bateman, eds. 1998. *Condemning students to debt: College loans and public policy.* New York: Teachers College Press.

Freeman, R. B. 1976. *The overeducated American.* New York: Academic Press.

Gold, S. D., ed. 1995. *The fiscal crisis of the states: Lessons for the future.* Washington, DC: Georgetown University Press.

Green, K. C. 1997. Think twice and businesslike about distance education. *AAHE Bulletin* (October): 3–6.

Griswold, C. P., and G. M. Marine. 1996. Political influences on state policy: Higher tuition, higher aid, and the real world. *Review of Higher Education* 19 (4): 361–89.

Harvey, W. B. 2001. *Minorities in higher education 2000–2001: Eighteenth Annual Status Report.* Washington, DC: American Council on Education.

Heller, D. E., and P. Marin, eds. 2002. *Who should we help? The negative social consequences of merit scholarships.* Cambridge, MA: Civil Rights Project, Harvard University.

Hilmer, M. J. 2001. Redistributive fee increases, net attendance costs, and the distribution of students at the public university. *Economics of Education Review* 20: 551–62.

Johnstone, D. B. 1999. Financing higher education: Who should pay?" In *American higher education in the 21st century: Social, political and economic challenges,* ed. P. G. Atlbach, R. O. Berdahl, and P. J. Gumport, 347–69. Baltimore: Johns Hopkins University Press.

Kane, T. J. 1999. *The price of admission: Rethinking how Americans pay for college.* Washington, DC: Brookings Institution.

Liebschutz, D. S., J. S. Schneider, and D. J. Boyd. 1997. Governors; FY 1998 education budgets focus on property tax cuts and enrollment changes. *State Revenue Report* no. 43. Center for the Study of States, State University of New York, Albany, May.

Marshall, R., and M. Tucker. 1992. *Thinking for a living: Education and the wealth of nations.* New York: Basic Books.

McPherson, M. S., and M. O. Schapiro. 1991. *Keeping college affordable: Government and educational opportunity.* Washington, DC: Brookings Institution.

Millett, C. 2003. How undergraduate loan debt affects application and enrollment in graduate or first professional school. *Journal of Higher Education* 74 (4): 386–427.

Mortenson, T. 1994. State appropriations for FY94 and FY95: Better for higher education but still not a high state priority. *Postsecondary Education Opportunity* (February).

Mortenson, T. 2001a. College participation by family income, gender and race/ethnicity for dependent 18 to 24 year olds. *Postsecondary Education Opportunity* (December): 1–8.

Mortenson, T. 2001b. Family income and higher education opportunity 1970–2000. *Postsecondary Education Opportunity* (October): 1–9.

Mortenson, T. 2001c. Higher education refinancing measured by the national income and product accounts 1952 to 2000. *Postsecondary Education Opportunity* (November): 12–16.

Mortenson, T. 2001d. Undergraduate tuition and fees at state flagship universities 1965 to 2001. *Postsecondary Education Opportunity* (April): 9–16.

Mortenson, T. 2002. State per capita personal income in the human capital economy 1973–2001. *Postsecondary Education Opportunity* (October): 10–16.

Mortenson, T. 2003. A nation at risk, again. *Postsecondary Education Opportunity* (May): 1–10.

National Governors Association and National Association of State Budget Officers. 2001, 2003. *The fiscal survey of states.* Washington, DC: Author.

Rumble, G. 1997. *The costs and economics of open and distance learning.* London: Kogan Page.

Schmidt, P. 2000. State higher-education funds rise over all, but growth slows in much of nation. *Chronicle of Higher Education* (December 15): A34–35.

Schultz, T. W. 1960. Capital formation by education. *Journal of Political Economy* 86: 571–83.

Thompson, F., and W. Zumeta. 2001. Effects of key state policies on private colleges and universities: Sustaining private-sector capacity in the face of the higher education access challenge. *Economics of Education Review* 20: 517–31.

U.S. Department of Education. National Center for Education Statistics. 1997. *The condition of education: 1997.* NCES 97-388. Washington, DC: NCES.

U.S. Department of Education. National Center for Education Statistics. 2002. *Digest of education statistics 2001.* NCES 2002-130. Washington, DC: NCES.

Van Der Werf, M. 2002. Recession and reality set in at private colleges. *Chronicle of Higher Education* 48 (25) (March 1): A26–28.

Walters, J. 2003. Feds bearing gifts. *Governing* (July): 14.

Zumeta, W. 1992. State policies and private higher education: policies, correlates, and linkages. *Journal of Higher Education* 63 (4): 363–417.

Zumeta, W. 1996. Meeting the demand for higher education without breaking the bank: A framework for the design of state higher education policies for an era of increasing demand. *Journal of Higher Education* 67 (4): 367–425.

Zumeta, W. 1998. Public university accountability to the state in the late twentieth century: Time for a rethinking? *Policy Studies Review* 15 (4): 5–22.

Zumeta, W. 1999a. *How did they do it? The surprising enrollment success of private, nonprofit higher education from 1980 to 1995.* IHELG Monograph 99-9. Houston, TX: Institute for Higher Education Law and Governance. University of Houston Law Center.

Zumeta, W.. 1999b. Utilizing private higher education for public purposes: Design challenges facing efforts to help meet higher education access demands through the private sector. In *The substance of public policy,* ed. S. Nagel, 192–230. Commack, NY: Nova Science Publishers, Inc.

Zumeta, W. 2001. Public policy and accountability in higher education: Lessons from the past and present for the new millennium. In *The states and public higher education policy: Affordability, access and accountability,* ed. Donald E. Heller, 155–97. Baltimore: Johns Hopkins University Press.

Zumeta, W., and J. Raveling. 2001. The best and the brightest for science. In *Innovation policy in the knowledge-based economy,* ed. M. Feldman and A. Link, 121–61. Boston: Kluwer Academic Publishers.

# CHAPTER SIX

# Desegregation and Diversity

Finding New Ways to Meet the Challenge

## M. Christopher Brown II, Jason L. Butler, and Saran Donahoo

Collegiate desegregation continues to be a much-debated issue across the nation. Discourse on the topic has expanded to include campus diversity. While education is a responsibility reserved for the states, the failure of state-level efforts to address segregation issues has necessitated federal involvement in the desegregation of our educational institutions. In order to reduce the need for federal involvement, numerous court cases and government policies have been introduced. These have proved schizophrenic—at first seeking to ensure desegregation by any method, and now concentrating on delimiting the scope of the same initiatives.

While none of these recent efforts have been successful in eliminating the mandate or need for such programs, court cases in California and Michigan make it clear that these programs and policies are under attack. Scholars and policymakers contend that desegregation programs are outdated and unnecessary. Nevertheless, the issues of low minority enrollments, inadequate funding of minority programs, and the continued perpetuation of racially discriminatory ideologies and practices by college administrators, professors, and students serve as evidence of the continuing need for desegregation and diversity activity. Despite the various misnomers associated with them, diversity programs are not indicative of preferential treatment, proxies of a quota system, or purveyors of "reverse discrimination." Rather, these initiatives are necessary tools designed to promote institutional diversity, provide equal opportunity, and prevent discrimination.

Since the *Adams* decision, the federal government has played a direct role in desegregation of state systems of higher education. The history of segregation and court-ordered remedies has been widely reviewed (e.g., Brown, 1999; Conrad and Weerts, chapter 4 in this volume). This chapter focuses on the state role in promoting diversity, given the new policy context. We review the recent regression and dissolution of desegregation policy, discuss the position of opponents to diversity that underlie these developments, reflect on the consequences of these positions, and identify issues that merit consideration in states.

## Regression and Dissolution

This era of collegiate desegregation began in the late 1970s with *Regents of University of California v. Bakke* (1978) and continues to affect diversity programs today. Confusion, dissension, and debate characterize this period, as desegregation efforts are now encumbered and restricted by recent court decisions and changing public priorities. *Bakke*, serving as the antithesis to *Florida ex rel. Hawkins* (1956) caused an earthquake in the collegiate desegregation arena. Rather than encourage colleges and universities, *Bakke* and many of the post-Bakke decisions have made it difficult for institutions to develop diversity programs that are both effective and acceptable under new legal standards.

In *Regents of University of California v. Bakke*, Alan Bakke, a white male seeking admission to the University of California at Davis Medical School, charged the institution with practicing reverse discrimination after he was twice rejected. At the time this lawsuit was filed, the UC Davis Medical School operated a special admissions program in which disadvantaged members of underrepresented minority groups were chosen to fill sixteen out of the one hundred places allotted to each year's entering class. As such, the U.S. Supreme Court upheld the earlier decision made by the California Supreme Court, in part, ruling that this specific program is unconstitutional because it violates the Equal Protection Clause of the Fourteenth Amendment by establishing a quota system. However, the Supreme Court also reversed part of the lower court's decision finding that it is acceptable to consider race in the admissions' process. Providing a swing vote in the decision, Justice Lewis Powell argued against the program while simultaneously adopting the view that "obtaining the educational benefits of an ethnically diverse student body" justified taking race and ethnicity into account (Justiz, Wilson, and Bjork 1994, p. 87). As such, the Court's decision in *Bakke* eliminated the use of quota systems to increase institutional diversity without dismantling diversity programs. Despite this effort, *Bakke* did not resolve the larger question surrounding the place of diversity programs in higher education. Indeed, rather than bring resolution to this issue, the *Bakke* decision both fueled the debate over collegiate desegregation efforts and encouraged more challenges to diversity programs and civil rights legislation.

Since the *Bakke* decision, a variety of legal challenges have attempted to procure a more definitive judgment of collegiate diversity programs. Although not a higher education case, *Wygant v. Jackson Board of Education* (1986) established the "strict scrutiny" test to determine the constitutionality of diversity programs. In this case, the Board of Education in Jackson, Michigan, was troubled by demands to ease racial tensions. In an effort to alleviate its problems, the board added a provision to its collective bargaining agreement that would protect many minority teachers in the event of a layoff. The provision stated that no more minority teachers than the percentage on staff could be laid off during times of fiscal stress. When layoffs occurred, some of the minority teachers who remained on staff had less seniority than some of the teachers who were let go because their employment was not protected by the board's provision. Some of the teachers who lost their jobs brought suit against the board, arguing that the provision violated the Equal Protection Clause of the Fourteenth Amendment. Similar to its ruling in *Bakke,* the Supreme Court's decision in *Wygant* only settled part of the diversity programs debate. While the Court held that the layoff provision did violate the Fourteenth Amendment, it also stated that a public employer's diversity program does not have to be based on evidence that the employer has a history of discrimination. In an attempt to provide more clarity regarding which diversity programs are constitutionally permissible, the Court also established the "strict scrutiny" test. Contending that the use of race is legal as stated in *Bakke,* the test in *Wygant* required that such programs both support a compelling interest of the state and be narrowly tailored to address and satisfy a particular interest. Although this ruling did not end diversity programs altogether, it did eliminate the general use of historic discrimination as justification for such programs. The fact that discrimination has occurred in the past is no longer a legally acceptable reason for establishing or maintaining a diversity program.

In another important ruling, the *strict scrutiny* test established in *Wygant* was used to make a determination in the case of *Richmond v. Croson* (1989). In 1983 the City of Richmond passed an ordinance requiring construction contractors whose businesses are not minority owned to subcontract at least 30 percent of their contract amount to one or more businesses located anywhere in the nation where U.S. citizens of a racial or ethnic minority group own and control at least 51 percent of the enterprise. Applying *Bakke* and *Wygant,* the Supreme Court ruled that this ordinance established a quota, which was unconstitutional under the Equal Protection Clause of the Fourteenth Amendment. The city failed the *strict scrutiny* test provided in *Wygant,* since there was no evidence that the program established in the ordinance was in the city's compelling interests and because it failed to narrowly tailor the ordinance to rectify a particular discrimination problem. Indeed, the Court also took special exception to the fact that the City of Richmond could not provide any evidence that discrimination existed in its construction industry. Although the Court upheld diversity as a justifiable goal in *Bakke,* the *Croson* decision suggests that it is unclear what businesses, states, and other organizations are allowed to do in order to accomplish this goal. *Croson* further indicates that even if the program itself can survive legal challenge, the Court may still require specific evidence of discrimination to allow it to continue.

Unlike the *Bakke, Wygant,* and *Croson* cases, the program at issue in *Kirwan v. Podberesky* (1992) did not involve a quota system. The program disputed in this case was the Benjamin Banneker Scholarship at the University of Maryland at College Park. This scholarship provided assistance to selected students of African American descent who were admitted to the university. Accepted to the institution in the fall of 1989, a Hispanic student named Daniel Podberesky challenged the program because he did not fit the racial criteria and therefore was not considered for an award. In its ruling, the Fourth Circuit Court of Appeals reversed the earlier decision made by the District Court of Maryland ruling that this scholarship program failed the first element of the *strict scrutiny* test, since the university did not prove that it served a compelling state interest. In order to meet this interest, the Fourth Circuit asserted that the university must provide strong evidence demonstrating that this action was necessary. Rather than order that the program be discontinued, the Fourth Circuit remanded the case back to the District Court of Maryland for further review, giving the university the opportunity to produce evidence illustrating a need for the program. Reexamined as *Podberesky v. Kirwan* (1993/1994), the District Court of Maryland reviewed evidence provided by the university and concluded that the scholarship satisfied both elements of the *strict scrutiny* test. However, on appeal, the Fourth Circuit reversed the lower court's decision on the basis that the university failed to show that its scholarship program was narrowly tailored. In addition, the Fourth Circuit enjoined the University of

Maryland from using it. The final resolution not only ended the Benjamin Banneker Scholarship but also suggested that it is virtually impossible for an institution with even the worst history of segregation to craft a program that will withstand legal challenge.

Like *Podberesky, Hopwood v. State of Texas* (1994) also applied the *strict scrutiny* test. In this case, Cheryl Hopwood and three other white students filed suit against the State of Texas, the University of Texas Board of Regents, the University of Texas School of Law, and other affiliated defendants. Hopwood and her co-plaintiffs alleged that the defendants violated both the Equal Protection Clause of the Fourteenth Amendment and Title VI of the Civil Rights Act of 1964 by operating a quota system that gave preferential treatment to African American and Mexican American law school applicants. In deciding the case, the Western District Court of Texas ruled that the admissions policy of the University of Texas School of Law was, in effect, a quota system. Nevertheless, the university was allowed to continue its policy until a final determination could be reached. However, this decision did not stand. In 1996 the Fifth Circuit Court of Appeals reviewed the lower court's decision and held that the University of Texas School of Law had violated both the Fourteenth Amendment and the Civil Rights Act of 1964. In addition, the Fifth Circuit also ruled that the law school must eliminate race from its admissions decisions. Rather than assuage the debate over diversity programs, these rulings appear to have renewed public interest. These decisions mandated the end of even basic consideration of race in admissions at the University of Texas School of Law while also declining to rule on the constitutionality of such policies *per se* (as a whole), making the future of higher education diversity programs even more uncertain. This is supported by the fact that in the years since the initial *Hopwood* decision, a few states have successfully eliminated the use of diversity programs altogether.

Attempts to create a standard collegiate desegregation policy throughout the states have yet to succeed. Voters in California and Washington, however, have seriously attempted to end this debate. Voters in California passed Proposition 209, now Article I, Section 31 of the California State Constitution, ending diversity programs throughout that state in 1996 (Krauthammer 2001). In a similar fashion, voters in Washington passed Initiative 200 in 1998, achieving the same result (*Washington State I-200*, 2000). This legislation and the *Hopwood* decision ended legal support for diversity programs in California, Washington, and Texas, respectively ("Ruling" 2001). Even so, the state university systems in these states have adopted various methods in an attempt to maintain their pre-1996 minority enrollments. The University of California system now gives more value to the SAT II, the essay portion of the exam, than to the SAT I, the traditional aptitude portion of the test. This has been especially helpful to non-native English speakers who choose to take the exam in their first language (Krauthammer 2001). In the fall of 1999, following the passage of Initiative 200, the University of Washington experienced a 32 percent decrease in minority enrollment (McCormick 2000). The university responded by drafting a privately funded but legally questionable $65.6 million scholarship program designed to attract more minority undergraduates to the institution (Rivera 2000). In Texas, traditional diversity programs have been replaced with a policy that guarantees students who graduate in the top ten percent of their high school class admission to any public institution ("Ruling" 2001). As these programs suggest, the diversity debate rages on in these states in spite of recent legal mandates.

Unlike efforts in California and Washington, 1997 and 1998 attempts to enact legislation ending diversity programs in Michigan both failed (Kosseff 1997; Spahn 1998). Diversity programs continue to be a source of controversy throughout the state. *Gratz v. Bollinger* (2001), filed in 1997 by white undergraduates who were rejected by the University of Michigan College of Literature, Science, and the Arts (LSA), and *Grutter v. Bollinger* (2001), filed in 1997 by white applicants rejected by the University of Michigan Law School, contend that the admissions programs used by the University of Michigan violated both the Equal Protection Clause of the Fourteenth Amendment and Title VI of the Civil Rights Act of 1964. In the *Gratz* ruling, issued on February 26, 2001, the Southern Division of the Eastern District Court of Michigan found that the use of race in admissions by the College of LSA was not an effective way to remedy either past or present discrimination. Although the University of Michigan offered evidence justifying its admissions program, the court held that it did not support the use of the current race-conscious admissions process. A month later the same court provided a similar decision in the *Grutter* case, ruling that the University of Michigan Law School's admissions program violated both the Fourteenth Amendment and Title VI of the Civil Rights Act. Recent Supreme Court rulings in the two Michigan cases, however, bode well for diversity in higher education. The *Grutter* decision (2003) did not fully resolve this issue, although there now is a basis for maintaining diversity.

The ambiguity of these latest judicial decisions, combined with the elimination of diversity programs in California, Texas, and Washington, has led to chaos in the realm of collegiate desegregation, which has, as a result, become an increasingly perplexing and confusing issue for both public and private institutions. While Title VI of the Civil Rights Act of 1964 outlaws discrimination and mandates diversity efforts, it does not define what discrimination based on race or national origin means. Unlike elementary and secondary schools, which are often required to adhere to a court order or administrative directive, diversity programs in selective universities and professional schools operate on the basis of voluntary compliance. Courts unquestionably have the power to impose race-conscious remedies in cases where a university or school has been found guilty of intentional segregation, but lawsuits and findings of this kind are rare for selective universities outside the South. Although several of the more recent cases charge higher education diversity programs with doing more than the law allows, many states in the South continue to avoid making even the slightest attempt to comply.

Unlike *Bakke, Hopwood,* and many other widely debated collegiate desegregation cases, *United States v. Fordice* (1992) was not an attempt to dismantle an existing diversity program. Centered on higher education in the state of Mississippi, *Fordice* provided an opinion on the current constitutionality of the formerly *de jure* segregated state higher education system. Like many other Supreme Court decisions, the key premise of *Fordice* was the quality of guidance it provided to the states, prospective plaintiffs, lawyers for the parties, and trial and appellate judges with regard to the standards they should use to determine if a former *de jure* segregated state system of higher education remained unconstitutional (Stefkovich and Leas 1994). The initial opinion in this case provided prescriptive information for similarly situated states and institutions. In its initial findings, *Fordice* stated that litigants and courts should endeavor to identify vestiges of a prior *de jure* segregated system of higher education and determine their continuing constitutional significance. A "vestige" is a state policy or practice of omission or commission adopted during the *de jure* segregation era that continues to effect racial segregation. As such, vestiges purport racial segregation in student enrollment in state university systems. However, like Title VI, *Fordice* failed to expressly identify either how vestiges contributed to the continuation of segregation in Mississippi's state higher education system or to outline the basis on which such contributions may be characterized as significant (Stefkovich and Leas 1994).

Furthermore, the Court's initial ruling in *Fordice* also indicated that Mississippi might be able to resolve this issue by demonstrating educational policy necessity, thus leaving some or all of the vestige in place. Similar to its treatment of vestige, the Court did not provide a description of what such a policy might include. However, *Fordice* stated that lack of funds needed to sufficiently promote collegiate desegregation was not in and of itself an acceptable excuse (Stefkovich and Leas 1994).

Another problematic finding in *Fordice* was the fact that all higher education institutions created during the *de jure* era are regarded as vestiges of segregation. Historically black colleges and universities tend to view this element of the decision as a direct threat to their survival. However, it is important to note that the Court's use of the term *vestige* applies equally to both black and white higher education institutions of the *de jure* era. As such, both types of colleges and universities face the possibility of being revamped or closed (Altbach and Lomotey 1991; Stefkovich and Leas 1994).

## Opposition to Diversity Programs

When attempting to convince the nation to eliminate diversity programs, opponents advance four main arguments, contending that diversity programs: (a) are quota systems, (b) confer preferential treatment, (c) cause reverse discrimination, and (d) do not uphold the standards of a meritocratic society. However, opponents fail to acknowledge the history of this nation that necessitated the development of diversity programs in the first place. Accepting and acknowledging past history would force opponents to concede that racial bias and discrimination continue to exist in today's society. Rather than reorganize their argument to fairly and accurately assess the place diversity programs occupy in U.S. history and society, opponents simply choose to ignore the actions, policies, and beliefs that created and contributed to the problems that exist today.

The argument that diversity programs create *quota systems* (Brimelow 1993; Yam 1998) is both inaccurate and misleading. It has been used in an attempt to thwart diversity programs since their initial development. Diversity programs were not designed to institute quotas at their inception. In reality however, the efforts toward change meant that quota systems could be used if businesses failed to voluntarily comply with the established rules and regulations. In addition, the *Bakke* decision specifically made quotas illegal. If diversity programs were, in fact, quota systems, they would have ended in 1978 as a result of the Supreme Court's ruling in *Bakke*. The fact that this decision by itself did not provide the legal impetus needed to dismantle all diversity programs in higher education suggests that they do not fit the Court's definition of a quota system. Although opponents would like to believe that diversity programs force colleges and universities to admit a certain number of under-represented students every year, this is simply not the case.

Furthermore, opponents of diversity programs also promote a fallacy by accusing them of fostering *preferential treatment* (Connerly 2000; D'Souza 1995; Montgomery 2000; Williams 1997). Although this term generally suggests that some groups of students are treated better than others, the opposition has redefined it to suggest that less-qualified and ill-prepared students of certain racial and ethnic backgrounds are more likely than others to gain access to, and benefits in, higher education. Addressing this concern, President Clinton stated, "Diversity . . . does not mean the unjustified preference of the unqualified over the qualified, or discrimination of any kind, including reverse discrimination" (Dunn and Zandarski 1998, p. 2). Exploring the impact of diversity programs, Coelen, Berger, and Crosson (2001) found that New England's minority college students are just as qualified as their white classmates. In their seminal study, Bowen and Bok (1998) found that African Americans who enrolled in college in 1976 achieved considerable success with more than 30 percent of them earning professional or doctorate degrees and approximately 43 percent occupying civic leadership positions. The fact that these students completed their undergraduate degrees and went on to be successful, active citizens after college disproves the contention that diversity programs provide preferences or access to unqualified applicants. By accusing diversity programs of conferring preferential treatment, opponents deny the role of white-skin privilege in making these programs necessary. Whether they recognize it or not, white Americans enjoy certain advantages and opportunities due to the color of their skin. Robert Jensen, a journalist for the *Baltimore Sun,* states that "whites, whether overtly racist or not, benefit from living in a mostly white-run world that has been built on the land and the backs of non-white people" (quoted in Dunn and Zandarski 1998, p. 2). While diversity programs do not create a completely balanced school or social structure, they serve to eliminate some of the barriers to equitable participation by all persons without respect to race or other subjective categories.

Another erroneous allegation aimed at diversity programs is that they lead to reverse discrimination (Pincus 2001). The term *reverse discrimination* is in itself a misnomer. Regardless of whether it is directed at blacks or whites, discrimination only works one way—to unfairly or unjustly exclude certain groups or individuals. By adapting the term *reverse discrimination* and applying it to diversity programs, opponents invoke the perceived threat to white privilege by assuming they have something to lose by treating other groups equally. Although it has not been addressed as such by the courts, the accusation of reverse discrimination also assumes that higher education is indeed an entitlement, since the term presupposes that whites lose rights that they have long taken for granted. However, it is important to note that even though diversity programs have given greater access to minority students, they have not diminished the higher education participation of white students. As such, the underlying principle behind the notion of reverse discrimination is clearly unfounded.

In addition to the previous assumptions, opponents of diversity programs also accuse them of *endangering the meritocracy,* that is, the nation's tradition of awarding social benefits on the basis of merit (Connerly 2000; D'Souza 1995; Williams 1997). It is important to note that the meritocratic society that opponents are attempting to protect is defined in terms that are most beneficial to the nation's white middle and upper classes. This allegation further assumes that diversity programs allow minority students access to higher education solely on the basis of race. Both of these assumptions invalidate the merit argument. The belief that these programs give access to unqualified applicants solely because of their race is also flawed since the purpose of diversity programs is to give all qualified applicants the same opportunities. Minority applicants must often exhibit qualifications that exceed those of their white counterparts to even be considered. Rather than make race the only criteria for admission, these programs seek to prevent race from being used to the *detriment* of applicants. Indeed, these programs reinforce the merit system by opening and extending it to members of all races and ethnicities.

## Eliminating Collegiate Desegregation and Diversity Programs

Efforts remain underway to dismantle diversity programs in California, Washington, and Texas. These repercussions may include lower numbers of minorities being admitted to selective higher education institutions. A decrease in acknowledging diversity in higher education may also lead to a prohibition of new ideas. Today, education is viewed as society's major vehicle for individual, familial and collective progress. Nevertheless, there are historically and predominantly white institutions that still have not fully opened their doors to significant numbers of racial minority students. Both inside and outside the realm of higher education, there has been a widespread attack on the civic gains made by African American since the 1950s. We see this attack in federal and state governments backtracking on diversity programs and moving away from the rigorous enforcement of anti-discrimination laws (Feagin, Vera, and Imani 1996). We notice it in the weakening or abandonment of college and university programs for diverse students. We observe the erosion of support through the recent sale of hundreds of thousands of copies of books questioning diversity programs, anti-discrimination laws, and even the intelligence of African Americans and other people of color.

In recent years it has become increasingly clear that the social policy has moved away from its longstanding commitment to "liberty and justice for all." Both educational and societal desegregation have mostly been defined and implemented by white policymakers, many of whom have weak or no commitment to effecting longstanding racial change. At the same time, college administrators and professors are not welcoming minority students and are ultimately discouraging them from achieving academic excellence. Furthermore, once admitted to predominantly white institutions, minority students must endure an alienated and hostile environment as a result of racial discrimination. The poor racial climates at these institutions make academic success difficult and may force many African Americans to attend historically black colleges and universities (HBCUs) to ensure that they will have the opportunity to learn in an atmosphere that is more considerate of racial issues. Psychologist Jacqueline Fleming (1984) completed a study of 2,500 black students in fifteen colleges and universities. She found that black students who went to black colleges averaged better academic gains than those at white colleges because they had greater social support (Feagin, Vera, and Imani 1996). Far from promoting the end of diversity programs, this fact suggests that existing efforts simply are not enough. Although it is good that students are given the option of attending an HBCU, the availability of these institutions is not enough to justify ending diversity programs. Moreover, Fleming's findings indicate that programs designed to give minority students access to predominantly white colleges and universities do not do enough to ensure that they will be academically successful once they enroll. These findings suggest that even more dramatic changes must be made to the U.S. educational system.

Another consequence of the debate surrounding diversity programs in higher education is that it implies that cultures and ethnicities that do not dominate American society may become less important over time. As a college education is recast as a necessity for social and economic success, many may refuse to admit or acknowledge the role and impact of racial bias and discrimination. Instead, some opponents have even gone so far as to argue that race is no longer an issue or factor influencing college access. This is likely to further deteriorate college and universities' interest in rectifying the affects of racial discrimination. After all, they do not have to address the problem if it does not exist.

In addition to absolving higher education institutions of the need to address racial concerns, denying the problems associated with race has also imbedded subtle forms of discrimination more deeply into every thread of American life. Diversity programs directly combat this effect by acknowledging the significant role race has in society and attempting to alleviate some of its negative present and historical effects. These programs also foster the nation's development by allowing all of its citizens the opportunity to participate in the manner they choose regardless of racial or ethnic background. Without diversity programs to promote equal opportunity, our nation will suffer greatly by forcing a significant portion of the population to exist on the periphery of society. Limiting the ability of racial and ethnic minorities to participate in higher education decreases their ability to have a positive impact on the nation. Thus, by ignoring the effects of racial discrimination, America is only hurting itself.

## Desegregation and Diversity Policy Issues

Currently, the fate of diversity programs and even Title VI in general remains uncertain. Disguising their arguments in seemingly race-neutral rhetoric, opponents of these mandates continue to garner support for dismantling them. The fact that racist ideologies and practices continue to exist in today's society suggests that, at least in some respects, these programs have failed. Although well-intentioned, these programs have been ineffective in combating and addressing *institutionalized racism,* that is, the type of racism that does not rely on or even support the overt actions that are generally associated with racial discrimination. Institutionalized racism is the acceptance of certain socially constructed norms and beliefs as biological and unalterable facts. Examples include the assumption that all welfare recipients are lazy black women in the inner city who deliberately continue to have children so they can avoid working, and the stereotype that all young black and Latino men are gang-banging, drug-dealing criminals. Laws designed to prohibit discriminatory acts against individuals based on race have done little to deconstruct institutionalized racism. As a result, people of color continue to be confronted by racist ideologies in employment, education, housing, and other elements of society. In spite of *Brown v. Board of Education* (1954), people of color, especially blacks and Latinos, continue to be denied the same educational opportunities as whites and should not, therefore, be judged according to the same standards as whites whose lives are often characterized by an abundance of opportunities. After years of legal challenges and changes, our society is far from being truly equal and just. Blatant discrimination has been replaced by more subtle forms that cannot be recognized as easily. In spite of their limited scope, because racism and discrimination persist in today's society, diversity programs have "not outlived [their] usefulness" (Smith 1998, p. 27).

As we have seen, there are no easy solutions to America's race problems. The development of effective remedies will require people of color as well as educators, professors, and administrators to come together. In recent years many educators, parents, community members, and politicians have been relieved to see an end to the desegregation orders that heavily influenced decisions about educational and fiscal policies. Conversely, critics and civil rights advocates argue that the current trend toward dismantling court-ordered desegregation in many school districts is a step backward toward segregated schooling. Recent studies (Frankenberg and Lee 2002; Orfield et al. 1997; Orfield and Yun 1999) indicate that school segregation and the creation of school districts with numerous poor students, which have increased throughout the 1990s, are also affecting Latinos. Latino students are increasingly isolated from whites and are more highly concentrated in high-poverty schools than are any other group of students (Peckham 1997). Because these schools do a poor job of preparing students to go on to higher education, this atrocity has led to the demise of equal educational opportunities for minorities in predominately white collegiate institutions.

The government has a compelling interest in bringing minorities onto campuses, particularly if these students would not otherwise have access to higher education. However, because these scholarship programs are based on race, they invoke the Equal Protection Clause of the Fourteenth Amendment. As the reviewed cases suggest, both the Supreme Court and the lower courts are reluctant to support the use of such programs unless they are provided with specific and extensive evidence that they are needed at each individual institution. As a result, it is unlikely that such programs could serve as a nationwide vehicle for promoting collegiate desegregation. To resolve legal issues and avoid legal challenges, scholarship programs should be redesigned to serve the needs of students from low-income families. While many students of color fall into this category, an economic designation is not likely to cause the same type of controversy as race-based programs. Currently, only 4 percent of the 1.3 million minority students attending undergraduate universities receive race-exclusive private and institutional financial assistance (Peckham 1997). The cost and impact of phasing out these programs would be minimal if scholarship programs targeting the financially needy replaced them. Economically disadvantaged minorities would automatically qualify for these scholarships, while those minorities who have never been economically disadvantaged—but are often the recipients of such benefits nevertheless—would not. In addition, programs based on economics would also provide financially disadvantaged white students with the same support and opportunities. Although this restructuring would not eliminate the need for other diversity programs, it would provide a delivery method for this type of financial assistance that is not likely to face legal challenge.

## Conclusion

The quest for collegiate desegregation and compliance with Title VI is not complete despite recent changes in enrollment and recruitment at higher education institutions. The effectiveness of diversity programs at colleges and universities tends to wax and wane based on interpretive legal support and changes in the national climate. Over the years, the wearing away of legal support has limited the impact of diversity programs on collegiate desegregation. Diversity programs do not mandate quotas, nor do they effectuate reverse discrimination. Instead, these policies and programs are specifically designed to desegregate historically white institutions by providing access to students of color (and other similarly situated persons). Success in desegregation and diversity practices may very well equate to success in schooling outcomes and societal civic participation.

REFERENCES

Altbach, P. G., and K. Lomotey. 1991. *The racial crisis in American higher education.* Albany: State University of New York Press.

Bowen, W. G., and D. Bok. 1998. *The shape of the river: Long-term consequences of considering race in college and university admissions.* Princeton, NJ: Princeton University Press.

Brimelow, P. 1993. When quotas replace merit, everybody suffers. *Forbes.* Accessed 2 October 2002 from www.vdare.com/pb/when_quotas.htm.

Brown, M. C., II. 1999. *The quest to define collegiate desegregation: Black colleges, Title VI compliance and post-Adams litigation.* Westport, CT: Bergin and Garvey.

Coelen, S. P., J. B. Berger, and P. H. Crosson. 2001. *Diversity among equals: Equal opportunity and the state of affirmative admissions in New England.* Quincy, MA: Nellie Mae Education Foundation.

Connerly, W. 2000. A vision for America, beyond race. *Intellectual ammunition.* Accessed 2 October 2002 from www.heartland.org/ia/novdec00/connerly.htm.

D'Souza, D. 1995. The "cruel compassion" of affirmative action. *Chronicle of Higher Education* 15 September. Accessed 2 October 2002 from chronicle.com/che-data/articles.dir/articles-42.dir/issue-03.dir/03b00101.htm.

Dunn, B. J., and A. M. Zandarski. 1998. *The evolution of affirmative action: Background of the debate.* Lansing: Michigan Legislative Service Bureau, Legislative Research Division.

Feagin, J. R., H. Vera., and N. Imani. 1996. *The agony of education: Black students at white colleges and universities.* New York: Routledge.

Fleming, J. 1984. *Blacks in college.* San Francisco: Jossey-Bass.

Frankenberg, E., and C. Lee. 2002. *Race in American public schools: Rapidly resegregating school districts.* Cambridge, MA: Civil Rights Project, Harvard University.

Justiz, M. J., R. Wilson, and L. G. Bjork, eds. 1994. *Minorities in higher education.* Phoenix, AZ: Oryx Press.

Kosseff, J. 1997. State rep. proposes Prop. 209 legislation. *Michigan Daily,* 23 October. Accessed 22 October 2001 from www.pub.umich.edu/daily/1997/oct/10-23-97/news/news3.html.

Krauthammer, C. 2001. Affirmative action fails again. *Washington Post,* 13 July, A21. Accessed 1 October 2001 from aad.english.ucsb.edu/docs/krauthammer.html.

McCormick, R. 2000. Race and the university: Why social justice leads to academic excellence. *Seattle Times,* 19 March. Accessed 21 October 2001 from aad.english.ucsb.edu/docs/mccormick.html.

Montgomery, A. 2000. A "poison" divides us. *Salon.com,* 27 March. Accessed 2 October 2002 from dir.salon.com/politics2000/feature/2000/03/27/connerly/index.html.

Orfield, G., Bachmeier, D. R. James, and T. Eide. 1997. *Deepening segregation in American public schools.* Cambridge, MA: Civil Rights Project, Harvard University.

Orfield, G., and J. T. Yun. 1999. *Resegregation in American schools.* Cambridge, MA: Civil Rights Project, Harvard University. Accessed 30 September 2002 from www.law.harvard.edu/civilrights/publications/resegregation99/resegregation99.html.

Peckham, V. 1997. Scholarships and the race-based cases. *Foundation News & Commentary* 38 (November/December): 34–37.

Pincus, F. L. 2001/2002. The social construction of reverse discrimination: The impact of affirmative action on whites. *Journal of Intergroup Relations,* 38 (winter): 33–44. Accessed 2 October 2002 from www.adversity.net/Pro_AA/docs/Pincus_JIR.htm.

Rivera, R. 2000. UW unveils plan for scholarships. *Seattle Times,* 21 October. Accessed 21 October 2001 from aad.english.ucsb.edu/docs/unveils.html.

Ruling that ended Texas affirmative action upheld. 2001. *USA Today,* 25 June. Accessed 1 October 2001 from www.usatoday.com/news/court/june01/2001-06-25-hopwood.htm.

Smith, J. C., Jr. 1998. Open letter to the President on race and diversity programs. *Howard Law Journal,* 42 (fall): 27–58.

Spahn, M. 1998. Anti-preference initiative launched. *Michigan Daily,* 18 March. Accessed 22 October 2001 from http://www.pub.umich.edu/daily/1998/mar/03-18-98/news/news1.html.

Stefkovich, J. A., and T. Leas. 1994. A legal history of desegregation in higher education. *Journal of Negro Education* 63 (3): 406–20.

Williams, J. B., III. 1988. Title VI regulation of higher education. In *Desegregating America's colleges and universities: Title VI regulation of higher education,* ed. J. B. Williams III, 3–53. New York: Teachers College, Columbia University.

Williams, J. B. 1997. *Race discrimination in higher education.* New York: Praeger.

Yam, J. I. 1998. Equality and affirmative action. *The World We Live In.* Accessed 2 October 2002 from www.johnyam.com/wor00015.html.

# CHAPTER SEVEN

# Merit and Equity

Rethinking Award Criteria in the Michigan Merit
Scholarship Program

## Edward P. St. John and Choong-Geun Chung

The State of Michigan implemented the Michigan Merit Scholarship Program, making awards to students in the first cohort (students in the high school class of 2000) based on scores on high school tests administered by the Michigan Educational Assessment Program (MEAP). The American Civil Liberties Union (ACLU), the National Association for the Advancement of Colored People (NAACP), and other groups brought suit against the State of Michigan based on the inequity in award distribution. Analyses for the plaintiffs demonstrated that the original method of awarding merit aid results in a distribution of student aid that is inequitable across racial/ethnic groups (Heller 2001). Based in part on these analyses, the court ruled that there was reason to go to trial. We conducted reviews and analysis aimed at informing the development of a fair and just remedy to the suit. This chapter presents the model for the redesign of the program presented in our initial report prepared for the plaintiffs, examines analyses of alternative methods for awarding Merit Scholarships, and describes the remedy proposed by the plaintiffs in the case.

## Background on the Equity Problem

The MEAP was originally implemented as a method of assessing the quality of schools in Michigan and of holding schools accountable for the achievement of the students they enroll. When the federal government began to push testing as a form of accountability, the expressed intent was to shift the focus of public policy from equalizing inputs to schools, to improving the outcomes of schools (Finn 1990). Thus, the intent of the expansion in the use of standardized testing was to improve schools, not to limit opportunity for students who do not attend high-quality schools. This distinction is important when we consider the use of these tests in rewarding merit grants.

After two decades of experience with accountability-driven school reform, it is possible to build an initial understanding of the effects of this movement. As generally applied, the implementation of standards and testing across the states has been accompanied by a modest reduction in high school graduation rates since 1980 and a substantial increase in college enrollment rates by high school graduates (St. John 2003). Although trends alone do not indicate that the changes in policy influenced the changes in educational outcomes, these trends indicate that more students graduating from high school are probably better prepared for college entry. However, many low-income college-qualified students cannot afford to attend college (Advisory Committee on Student Financial Assistance 2002), which is why equity is important in the awarding of state grants and scholarships. Thus, there is at least *prima facie* evidence that improving education standards, coupled with the use of standardized tests for accountability, can improve college preparation of students who graduate from high school even if it is does not equalize opportunity to complete high school or to enroll after preparing for college.

While standards and testing had some positive effects on academic preparation, some uses of standardized testing actually constrain educational opportunity for diverse groups. For example, requiring passage of high-stakes tests for high school graduation has been found to be associated with lower graduation rates by low-income students (Jacob 2001) and by special-needs students (Manset and Washburn 2003). With the concentration of children who are minorities and from low-income families in urban schools, there may be reason to rethink the current uses of MEAP tests in the Michigan Merit Scholarship Program. In the current policy environment, states should be careful to promote uses of standards and testing that improve academic preparation but should remain cautious about applications of these practices that restrict educational opportunities and increase inequities. However, more research is needed on the impact of testing and standards to reach definitive conclusions (Miron and St. John 2003).

The method the State of Michigan used to award the Merit Scholarships appears to restrict opportunity for diverse groups in ways that penalize students for attending poor-quality schools. Indeed, when the fact that many college-qualified low-income students cannot afford to attend is taken into account, the Michigan Merit Scholarship Program appears to discriminate against low-income students. In fact, earlier analyses indicate that African Americans and other minority groups were under-represented among scholarship recipients (Heller 2001), providing a further illustration of the problem with the current approach.

When the MEAP tests are used as a statewide ranking of students, as is the case with the current award criteria in the Michigan Merit Scholarship Program, the award method essentially holds low-income minority students accountable for attending low-quality schools rather than holding schools accountable and encouraging schools to improve. Therefore, it is desirable to modify the uses of MEAP tests in ways that provide an incentive for schools to make improvements in the academic preparation of students but that do not discriminate against any particular group of students.

## Rethinking Merit Aid

To understand how financial aid can influence both academic preparation and enrollment, a Balanced Access Model is needed, one that considers the role of academic preparation as well as of financial aid (Figure 7.1). The Balanced Access Model reconstructs the National Center of Education Statistics' academic pipeline, which emphasizes the steps of planning to attend, academic preparation, taking entrance exams, and applying for college (e.g., NCES 1997). It is also consistent with other, more balanced research on the college enrollment process (e.g., Hossler, Schmit, and Vesper 1999). In addition to acknowledging the role of this academic pipeline process, the Balanced Access Model expands the logic of the NCES model to include the role of family finances, consistent with the definition of financial access (i.e., the ability to afford continuous enrollment in public colleges).

The Balanced Access Model also recognizes that tuition and financial aid have both direct and indirect influences on enrollment decisions, consonant with the new definition of financial access. Consistent with more recent research on the role of finances (St. John, Cabrera, Nora, and Asker 2000), the Balanced Access Model[1] specifically recognizes the following linkages between family finances, financial aid, and college enrollment:

- Family income influences their concern about college costs and their ability to pay for college (perceptions of unmet need) (Linkage 1).

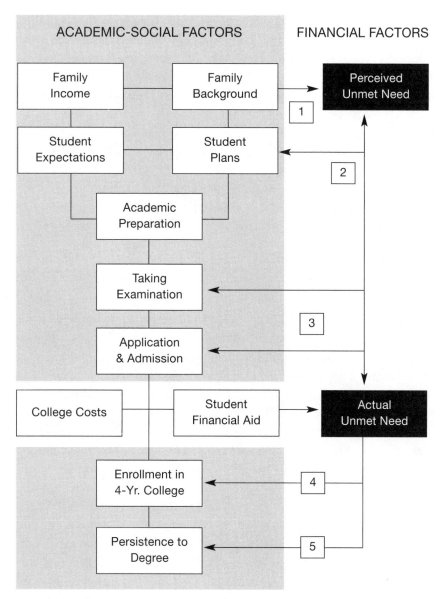

*Figure 7.1.* A Balanced Access Model (St. John 2002)

- Family concerns about finances—including their concerns about their costs after student grants (i.e., perceptions of unmet need)—can influence college plans and courses taken in high school (Linkage 2).
- Family concerns about college costs can influence students' decisions to take college entrance examinations and to apply for college (academic preparation) (Linkage 3).
- Family perceptions of financial problems can also influence student decisions to enroll in college and can especially constrain opportunity to enroll in a four-year college[2] (Linkage 4).
- Family perceptions of financial problems, along with their costs after student aid (net prices), can influence students' ability to afford continuous enrollment (persistence) in, or to transfer to, four-year colleges (Linkage 5).

Thus, the Balanced Access Model offers a more complete way of viewing the influence of academic preparation and financial aid on access. It also considers how financial aid might influence academic preparation (a process that is related to concern about financing college). This way of conceptualizing the role of finances is consistent with economic research on human capital, which shows that students consider their potential earnings, their potential debt, and their foregone earnings when they make educational choices (Becker 1964; Paulsen 2001). By examining these linkages, it is possible to untangle how finances influence academic preparation, college enrollment, and persistence.

Recent analyses using the Balanced Access Model confirm that there are large numbers of low-income students who do not prepare for college (48 percent of the high school class of 1992) and that substantial numbers of those who do prepare academically cannot afford to attend college (ACSFA 2002; National Center for Education Statistics 1997; St. John 2002). The Advisory Committee on Student Financial Assistance (ACSFA), a congressional panel, estimates that more than four million low- and middle-income college-qualified students will be left behind for financial reasons in the first decade of the twenty-first century (ACSFA 2002). In this context, state grant programs have a vital role to play in promoting academic preparation and ensuring financial access for students who take the steps to prepare for college.

Indiana's Twenty-first Century Scholars Program has been identified as a model state program by the National Governor's Association (NGA). The NGA sponsored a national meeting on "Twenty-first Century Scholars: Indiana's Best

Practices for Student Financial Assistance" in August 2002. Students who are eligible for the federal Free & Reduced Lunch Program can enroll in Indiana's Twenty-first Century Scholars Program in eighth or ninth grade. They pledge to take the steps to prepare for college, including maintaining a 2.0 grade point average. The state provides support services to the students and their families and promises to provide grant aid equaling tuition at an Indiana public college.

The Balanced Access Model helps illustrate why the Twenty-first Century Scholars Program is a success. First, the Scholars program has an indirect effect on plans and preparation (Linkage 2) because it alleviates family concerns about college costs. Recent analyses indicated that more than three-quarters of the parents of low-income high school children are very concerned about college costs (ACSFA 2002; NCES 1997). Second, participation in the Scholars program can have an influence on preparation—taking the right courses in high school—by students who plan to attend (Linkage 3). Ensuring that students will receive adequate student grant aid if they prepare for college can encourage more low-income students to prepare, a phenomenon illustrated in the Indiana study, a state that has implemented new policies requiring high schools to provide college preparatory curricula (St. John, Musoba, Simmons, and Chung 2002). The Scholars program sets an attainable goal, requiring students to maintain a 2.0 GPA in college preparatory classes. As part of the pledge they take when enrolling in the Scholars program, these students commit to applying for college and student financial aid. A recent follow-up study reveals that students enrolled in the program were more likely to take the steps to prepare for college and to apply than were other students, controlling for other variables that influence this process (St. John, Musoba, Simmons, Chung, Schmit, and Peng 2002). Third, the Scholars program has a direct effect on students' decisions to enroll in college (Linkage 4). The evaluation study found students who enrolled in this program were more likely to enroll in public and private four-year colleges and public two-year colleges than students who were not in the program, controlling for other variables that influence access (St. John, Musoba, Simmons, and Chung 2002). Finally, the Scholars program equalizes the opportunity to persist. Scholars who attended public colleges in Indiana were 2.0 times more likely to persist during their freshman year than the typical student, controlling for the variables that influence persistence (St. John, Musoba, Simmons, and Chung 2002).

The best way for the State of Michigan to ensure that the Michigan Merit Scholarship Program ensures equity is to encourage students who have financial need to take the steps to prepare for college. If the program were re-designed, it should include the following features:

- A pledge process that encourages low-income students to take the steps to prepare for college and that ensures they will receive a merit award if they complete those steps.
- An explicit commitment to take the courses required for entrance into a four-year college, with a requirement that students apply for college and student aid.
- A threshold of merit achievement that is attainable by students who might not otherwise take the steps to prepare for college.
- A sufficient commitment to grant aid (on top of other state and federal grants) to ensure that public colleges are affordable to low-income students in the state.

This conceptual model was presented originally in a paper we prepared for the plaintiffs in *White v. Engler,* discussed extensively in the deposition for the case, and included in the plaintiffs' remedy proposal. The key element of the plaintiffs' proposal was to develop a workable set of award criteria for the program.

## Alternative Award Criteria

The plaintiffs argued that the State of Michigan should use an alternative approach to awarding Michigan Merit Scholarships, one that is compatible with the design features outlined above. We argued that ideally the program would have a pledge process for students eligible for the federal Free & Reduced Lunch Program, but our initial analyses were limited to alternative ways of constructing the merit index. In the final remedy, however, a strategy was developed that allowed for an integration of merit and need. Below we describe the conceptual framework we used to assess alternative award criteria and summarize three stages in our analysis of alternative remedies.

### The Merit-Aware Index

An alternative method for awarding merit aid involves creating a merit index that adjusts the award criteria to the quality of the high schools students attend. The idea of the merit index that adjusts standardized tests for high school quality was proposed as a more equitable approach for college admission (Goggin 1999). The development of a merit index involves adjusting test scores and other merit criteria for the averages for the high schools students attend, then using these rankings in admissions decisions. This approach helps achieve greater racial balance because schools remain segregated in spite of court decisions in desegregation cases (Fossey 1998, 2003).

Empirical tests of this method to date have focused on adjusting standardized test scores to refine admission policies. Initial analyses indicate that a merit index yields a more ethnically diverse population of admitted students than does the strict application of a standardized test such as the SAT (St. John, Simmons, and Musoba 2002). Further, a merit index that adjusts SAT scores for high school contexts predicts college success about as well as the SAT (St. John, Hu, Simmons, and Musoba 2001).

While the extant research confirmed that the merit-index approach achieved the goals of rewarding merit in admissions while increasing diversity and equity, the method had not yet been extended to awarding merit aid. Conceptually, it had been previously argued that the same logic applied to merit aid (St. John, Simmons, and Musoba 2002), but the Michigan case presented special problems relative to the implementation of a merit index. Specifically, the legislation creating the program required that an "assessment test" be used that included consideration of the state tests (Plaintiffs' Settlement Proposal). There was a range of interests among the plaintiffs that encouraged a broader assessment framework, but ultimately the proposal was constrained by the legislation.[3] A three-stage approach to the analysis process eventuated.

## *Stage 1: The alternative method of using MEAP-Merit Index*

There are a variety of ways to construct a MEAP-Merit Index that would adjust the rankings of students within their schools. Using school-based rankings—for either GPA or a combination of GPA and test scores—provides an adjustment for school context that does not penalize students for attending troubled schools. As a preliminary test of the merit-index approach, our initial paper used data files with the raw test scores and the award information to develop the following preliminary[4] simulations:

- Simulations of a MEAP-Merit Index using one or more tests, allowing students taking at least one test into the pool.
- Simulations of a MEAP-Merit Index using all four tests, constraining the pool for each school to the students who took MEAP tests in all four subjects.

- Simulations of a MEAP-Merit Index using all four tests plus a hold-harmless provision[5] for students passing all four tests.[6]

Each of the methods yielded a more diverse set of award recipients than the original award method. Each racial/ethnic group was closer to its percentage of the population when the MEAP-Merit Index was used, even with the hold-harmless provision. Thus, it is clear that the use of a MEAP-Merit Index would improve equity in the awards structure. Key findings were:

- While the merit index approach created greater equity in awards for Hispanic, Native American, and multiracial students, the most substantial gains (in both percentages and total numbers) were made by African Americans.
- A MEAP-Merit Index that used one test included a higher percentage of minority students in the recipient group than did the index that used all four tests.
- When the hold-harmless provisions were used, the total percentage of minority recipients was lower than in other analyses because whites were over-represented in the 2000 recipient group.
- When the percentage of students receiving awards increased within each approach to the MEAP-Merit Index (i.e., one test, four tests, four tests with hold harmless), the number of students in all racial/ethnic groups receiving the awards increased.

Thus, these initial analyses confirmed that it was possible to modify the award index using only MEAP scores. Therefore, there was good reason to consider the alternative of further enhancing the MEAP-Merit Index. The principle disadvantage of the MEAP tests is not entirely overcome by using the MEAP-Merit Index. Many students simply do not take the tests, so a substantial percentage of potential scholars are left out if the award process is used. Enhancing the MEAP-Merit Index to include grade point averages and other measures of student achievement would be appropriate.

There are several approaches that the State of Michigan could use to improve equity in the awarding of scholarships through the Michigan Merit Scholarship Program, but the initial analyses were limited to the MEAP-Merit approach because there were no data on grade point averages. Our initial report emphasized the following options:

1. *Top Priority:* Redesign the Michigan Merit Scholarship Program to provide a balanced approach to the awarding of merit aid, recognizing the roles student aid plays in promoting academic preparation and financial access. This approach would maximize the impact of the program on access and educational improvement.

2. *Second Priority:* If a total program redesign is not possible, then the state should shift to the use of a merit index that uses high school GPA to rank students within high schools, possibly in combination with MEAP scores. This approach to merit would provide the most inclusive approach to awarding merit aid.

3. *Third Priority:* A merit index using MEAP tests only is technically possible. Although it would yield a more diverse group of awardees than the current method, it is not recommended since this approach is not as inclusive as the other methods.

## Stage 2: Analysis of a GPA-Merit Index

Based on this initial report, the litigants agreed to collect data from a sample of 20 percent of the state's high schools.[7] A random sample of 20 percent of the high schools was drawn within each type of locale in the state as a means of ensuring representation of diverse types of schools.[8] For each senior, high schools were asked to provide information on ethnicity, cumulative GPA, and the MEAP scores. This data was adequate to test the alternative of using a GPA-Merit Index.

While the sample mirrored the geographical distribution of high schools across the state, the responding high schools were not evenly distributed. The highest response rates were from high schools in cities and small towns, the types of schools that would benefit the most from alternative methods. A total of 8 urban high schools were sampled, and all responded; whereas 11 of the 14 high schools in small towns responded. In contrast, lowest response rates were from mid-sized cities (4 of 10 responses) and rural areas inside of large metropolitan areas (13 of 25 responses), the areas that benefited the most from the original award criteria. A total of 14,356 students were included in the sample. The overall response rate (61.6 percent) was adequate, but it was necessary to adjust for the inconsistencies in reporting.

Our method of adapting to these uneven response rates across local types was to compare awards using the original criteria for the MEAP[9] to awards using the GPA-Merit Index[10] using the sample population. This provided a means of judging whether the use of the GPA ranking would improve diversity of awards compared to the original award criteria.

When the original award criteria were used on the sample population, we found a similar inequality in the distribution of awards as in the earlier analyses:

- American Indians represented 0.5 percent of the sample and 0.5 percent of the population that qualified under the original criteria.
- Asians represented 2.0 percent of the sample and 1.8 percent of the scholarship-qualified population.
- Blacks were 17.3 percent of the sample, but only 6.5 percent of the scholarship-qualified group.
- Whites were 77.9 percent of the sample and 89.9 percent of the scholarship-qualified group.
- Hispanics were 1.7 percent of the sample and 1.2 percent of the scholarship-qualified group.[11]

These results echo the findings from earlier analyses (e.g., Heller 2001), indicating disproportional qualification across groups, especially for African Americans and whites. We also conducted simulations of the award distribution if the GPA-Merit Index were used for scholarship qualification (i.e., class rank). This set of simulations considered awards for 20, 25, 30, and 35 percent of high school classes. Each of the analyses provided a more balanced award distribution. The summary of the analysis of the 35 percent award level follows:

- American Indians and Alaska Natives were 0.5 percent of the sample and 0.4 percent of the scholarship-qualified group.
- Asians were 2.0 percent of the sample and 2.0 percent of the scholarship-qualified group.
- Blacks were 17.3 percent of the population and 16.8 percent of the scholarship-qualified group.
- Whites were 77.9 percent of the sample and 79.1 percent of the scholarship-qualified group.
- Hispanics were 1.7 percent of the sample and 1.4 percent of the scholarship-qualified group.

The second stage analyses were provided to attorneys for the plaintiffs and the defense before the deposition. Both the paper outlining the proposed model and the two sets of analyses were addressed in the deposition. Subsequent to the deposition process[12] and the election,[13] discussions were initiated about the settlement. The final set of simulations was conducted in support of the plaintiffs' settlement proposal.

## *Stage 3: Constructing a New Index*

Another set of analyses was developed explicitly for the plaintiffs' settlement proposal. In a conference call organized to discuss the settlement options, a strategy for developing a proposal was agreed upon. A key component of the agreement was to include a need component with differential awards for qualified students with need and qualified students who did not have financial need. Don Heller (2003) developed the cost estimate for the revised program. Our role involved developing a new merit index that combined the MEAP and GPA.

The revised index equally weighted the GPA and the MEAP text. The steps in developing the refined index and applying the new index to the sample population were:

- Developing a MEAP ranking
    1. Individual student's MEAP performance was reported in a 1–4 scale (1 = exceeds state standards, 2 = meets state standards, 3 = basic endorsement, 4 = not endorsed) for the four test areas.
    2. We took the sum of four MEAP results as the MEAP component of the revised index. For example, a student who met the standard on all tests would score an 8.
    3. We developed a ranking of students based on their scores on this scale. Tied scores were assigned the same ranking. Smaller values had a higher ranking.
- Developing a GPA ranking
    1. Using the reported GPA, we ranked the students within the school. Larger values had a higher ranking.
    2. The same value was assigned when students had the same GPA.
- Computing the index: We used the simple mean of the two ranks as the student's index within their school. The index provided the average of the MEAP ranking and the GPA ranking.
- Identifying the top 45 percent: The top 45 percent in each school were considered qualified, while the remaining 55 percent were considered not qualified.

Consistent with prior simulations, this method provided a more balanced award group. However, only 10,540 in the sample had taken the MEAP tests, which means that the total scholarship-qualified group was somewhat smaller than it would have been if GPA only were used in the index. The results were:

- American Indians and Alaska Natives comprised 0.6 percent of the index sample[14] and 0.4 percent of the scholarship-qualified group.
- Asians were 1.7 percent of the index sample and 2.0 percent of the scholarship-qualified group.
- Blacks were 19.9 percent of the index sample and 18.8 percent of the scholarship-qualified group.
- Whites were 75.8 percent of the index sample and 77 percent of the scholarship-qualified group.
- Hispanics were 1.7 percent of the index sample and 1.6 percent of the scholarship-qualified group.

Like the prior versions of the index, this version would yield a better balance in award recipients than the original award criteria. Furthermore, since students would have to take the MEAP exam to be considered for an award, the new approach retained the incentive structure to comply with the new assessment environment.

## Conclusions and Implications

Recently the plaintiffs' proposal was rejected by the defense attorneys, so the case could still be litigated. The simulations illustrated that a more just distribution of merit aid could be achieved. Furthermore, if the remedy includes full awards for students with financial need and partial awards for students who do not have financial need, then the state will save money on the revised program (Heller 2003).

This type of revision in the Michigan Merit Scholarship Program would change its regressive nature in a fundamental way. The original award criteria fell short of providing an incentive for low-income students to prepare for college. Indeed, our research indicates that merit scholarship programs actually have a negative influence on high school graduation rates.[15] In contrast, programs that provide real incentives for low-income students, like Indiana's Twenty-first Century Scholars Program, can encourage low-income students to graduate from high school and apply for college (St. John, Musoba, Simmons,

Chung, Schmit, and Peng 2002). Making 45 percent of students in all high schools eligible should provide an attainable incentive for more students to take the steps necessary to prepare for college. If such a program is adopted, it will be essential to get the word out, providing information to students in all schools about the new award criteria.

In addition to having a direct influence on policy development in Michigan, these analyses have three more general implications. First, the breakdown in the consensus about affirmative action does not mean that the courts will ignore historical and legal foundations for litigation about equity and social justice. Depending on the outcome of the Supreme Court's review of the Michigan admissions case now before it, racial preferences may cease to be a primary means of achieving equity. However, when states distribute tax dollars in ways that favor some groups more than others, then the equity provision in the federal and state constitutions provides a foundation for litigation aimed at seeking a more just approach. This clearly is the case in Michigan and may be the case in other states that make excessive use of merit aid (Heller and Marin 2002). However, the same principle may apply to college finance in general. It is possible that inequalities in college funding can be litigated based on inequalities in admission and distribution of resources (St. John 1997), although this notion needs to be further developed. The new legal environment should encourage thoughtful analysis of the justice issue, rather than cause dismay among equity advocates.

Second, given the shifting state priorities on student grants from need to merit, it is time to rethink the role of merit and whether financial need should be used with merit indexes in the merit award process. The Michigan solution seems workable. It is critical to hold together a coalition of legislators and other policymakers to provide ongoing support for state grant programs. Historically, need-based grant programs have lacked strong constituents in many states. Merit programs bring new constituents—families that feel they are left out of program funding when need-based criteria are used. In the plaintiffs' proposal in Michigan, there was an implicit recognition of this tension. By maintaining a merit portion of the scholarship programs, it may be possible to retain the support of political conservatives for grant programs. However, by having higher scholarship awards for students with financial need, it is also possible to increase the impact on enrollment rates. Certainly, hybrid programs like the one being proposed in Michigan should be considered in the future by states that have merit scholarship programs.

Finally, this chapter illustrates that policy experts can play a constructive role in policy development. In our analyses for Michigan, we provided empirical analyses to support and test the plaintiffs' claims. We were in agreement philosophically with the civil rights position held by the plaintiffs, but our analyses were not an ideological treatment of data. We provided an objective analysis. Indeed, it is ironic that the revised merit index has similarity to the use of grade point averages, an approach used in states that have done away with affirmative action in college admissions. The challenge, we think, is to find a just and empirically sound approach to college admissions and student aid. While the politics of higher education policy is heavily influenced by competing ideologies at the present time, we think it is critical that analysts test out new approaches to policy development that can help policymakers find a new common ground.

NOTES

This chapter incorporates and builds on a report by the same title written for Pitt, Dowty, McGehee & Mirer, & Palmer, P. C. in *White, et al. v. Engler, et al.* The earlier paper was included as part of attachment 1 in the *Plaintiffs' Settlement Proposal.*

1. The Balanced Access Model was described earlier by St. John (2002). William Goggin helped conceptualize the logic for the Balanced Access Model.

2. The model also applies to access to two-year colleges, which functions in a similar fashion. However, the courses taken in high school (e.g., advanced math, science, and language) have a much more substantial influence on enrollment in four-year colleges than in two-year colleges.

3. At the time of the settlement process, there was a serious tax revenue shortfall in the state. If there was full litigation to overturn the program, then it was doubtful that a new program would be created and funded. Therefore, the focus in the settlement process was to find economical and equitable ways of providing merit aid.

4. Because of time constraints and data limitations, these analyses were preliminary when initially submitted. Further analyses using improved data sources (i.e., GPA only or GPA plus MEAP) were proposed for a refined index.

5. The hold-harmless provision would continue to provide Michigan Merit Scholarships to students who meet the current state requirements.

6. Because of differences between the data file with "raw" scores and the data file with "award information," it is not possible to construct an analysis of the MEAP merit index without the hold-harmless provision.

7. Most of the members of the plaintiffs' coalition favored GPA or need over the MEAP test. After conference calls to discuss alternatives, we developed a format for a data collection.

8. Rural and urban schools had the highest levels of poverty and were the most likely to benefit from award criteria that included appropriate equity consideration. However,

the suburban districts had the greatest representation in the program under the original award criteria. It was important that efforts be made to have all types of districts represented in the sample.

9. The original criteria included some alternative methods of qualification (using a specialized vocational test), but very few students met these criteria. Therefore, we did not request information on the alternative test to reduce confusion about the data collection. The MEAP only analysis is essentially similar to the original award criteria.

10. The GPA-Merit Index was essentially class rank.

11. The simulations also considered students of "unknown" ethnic origin and Native Hawaiian or other Pacific Islander. Both of these groups were extremely small.

12. Don Heller and Edward St. John were two of the three experts used on the case. Their testimony was central to the decision to settle. The third expert focused on the validity of the MEAP test, which was not a focal point of the settlement process.

13. A Democrat was elected governor in November 2002, a development that also influenced the willingness of the state to settle the case.

14. As noted in the text above, this sample groups was smaller than the sample when GPA only was used.

15. This finding is from a study published by the Lumina Foundation for Education in a research monograph (St. John, Chung, Musoba, Simmons, Wooden, & Mendez, 2004).

REFERENCES

Advisory Committee on Student Financial Assistance (ACSFA). 2002. *Empty promises: The myth of college access in America.* Washington, DC: Author.

Becker, G. S. 1964. *Human capital: A theoretical and empirical analysis with special reference to education.* New York: Columbia University Press.

Finn, C. E., Jr. 1990. The biggest reform of all. *Phi Delta Kappan* 71 (8) (January): 584–92.

Fossey, R. E. 1998. Desegregation is not enough: Facing the truth about urban schools. In *Race, the courts, and equal education: The limits of the law,* vol. 15, *Readings on Equal Education,* ed. R. E. Fossey, 5–20. New York: AMS Press.

Fossey, R. E. 2003. School desegregation is over in the inner cities: What do we do now? In *Reinterpreting urban school reform: Have urban schools failed, or has the reform movement failed urban schools?* ed. L. F. Miron and E. P. St. John, 15–32. Albany: State University of New York Press.

Goggin, W. J. 1999. A "merit-aware" model for college admissions and affirmative action. *Postsecondary Education Opportunity Newsletter* (May). The Mortenson Research Seminar on Public Policy Analysis of Opportunity for Postsecondary Education, pp. 6–12.

Heller, D. E. 2001. *White, et al. v. Elger, et al.:* Supplementary analysis of Merit Scholarship Program First Cohort (High School Class of 2000), photocopy, 12 April.

Heller, D. E. 2003. *White, et al. v. Engler, et al.* Cost model for revised Michigan Merit Award Scholarship Program. Attachment 2, in "White, *et al.* v. Engler, *et al.,* Plaintiffs' Settlement Proposal," Transmitted by Michael L. Pitt, Pitt, Dowty, McGehee, Mirer & Palmer, Royal, Oak, MI, 28 January.

Heller, D. E., and P. Marin, eds. 2002. *Who should we help? The negative social consequences of merit scholarships.* Cambridge, MA: The Civil Rights Project, Harvard University.

Hossler, D., J. Schmit, and N. Vesper. 1999. *Going to college: How social, economic, and educational factors influence the decision students make.* Baltimore: Johns Hopkins University Press.

Jacob, B. A. 2001. Getting tough? The impact of mandatory high school graduation exams on student achievement and dropout rates. *Educational Evaluation and Policy Analysis* 23 (2): 99–122.

Manset, G., and S. Washburn. 2003. Inclusive education in high stakes, high poverty environments: The case of students with learning disabilities in Indiana's urban high schools and the graduation qualifying examination. In *Reinterpreting urban school reform: Have urban schools failed, or has the reform movement failed urban schools?* ed. L. F. Miron and E. P. St. John. Albany: State University of New York Press.

Miron, L. F., and E. P. St. John, eds. 2003. *Reinterpreting urban school reform: Have urban schools failed, or has the reform movement failed urban schools?* Albany: State University of New York Press.

National Center for Education Statistics. 1997. *Access to postsecondary education for the 1992 high school graduates,* NCES 98–105. By L. Berkner and L. Chavez. Project officer: C. Dennis Carroll. Washington, DC: NCES.

Paulsen, M. B. 2001. The economics of human capital and investment in higher education. In *The finance of higher education: Theory, research, policy and practice,* ed. M. B. Paulsen and J. C. Smart, 55–94. New York: Agathon Press.

St. John, E. P. 1997. Desegregation at a crossroads: Critical reflections on possible new directions. In *Special issue: Rethinking college desegregation,* ed. D. Hossler and E. P. St. John. *Journal for a Just and Caring Education* 3 (1): 127–34.

St. John, E. P. 2002. *The access challenge: Rethinking the causes of the new inequality.* Policy Issue Report # 2002-01, Bloomington: Indiana Education Policy Center.

St. John, E. P. 2003. *Refinancing the college dream: Access, equal opportunity, and justice for taxpayers.* Baltimore: John Hopkins University Press.

St. John, E. P., A. F. Cabrera, A. Nora, and E. H. Asker. 2000. Economic influences on persistence reconsidered. In *Reworking the departure puzzle,* ed. J. M. Braxton. Nashville, TN: Vanderbilt University Press.

St. John, E. P., C. G. Chung, G. D. Musoba, A. B. Simmons, O. S. Wooden, and J. P. Mendez. 2004. *Expanding college access: The impact of state finance strategies.* Indianapolis, IN: Lumina Foundation for Education.

St. John, E. P., S. Hu, A. B. Simmons, and G. D. Musoba. 2001. Aptitude v. merit: What matters in persistence? *Review of Higher Education* 24 (2): 131–52.

St. John, E. P., G. D. Musoba, A. B. Simmons, and C. G. Chung. 2002. *Meeting the access challenge: Indiana's Twenty-first Century Scholars Program.* New Agenda Series, vol. 4, no. 4. Indianapolis, IN: Lumina Foundation for Education.

St. John, E. P., G. D. Musoba, A. B. Simmons, C. G. Chung, J. Schmit, and C. Y. J. Peng. 2002. *Meeting the access challenge: An examination of Indiana's Twenty-first Century Scholars Program.* Presented at the Association for the Study of Higher Education Annual Meeting, November 2002, Sacramento, CA.

St. John, E. P., A. B. Simmons, and G. D. Musoba. 2002. Merit-aware admissions in public universities: Increasing diversity. *Thought & Action* 27 (2): 35–46.

# Part III / Changing Institutional Rationales

In the new policy context, advocates for higher education are confronted by a new set of issues related to the rationales used to argue for taxpayer support for higher education. The authors in Part III address three issues central to the policy context. Don Hossler addresses the role of strategic enrollment management in generating tuition revenue in public universities, a necessary development in many public universities, given the erosion of taxpayer support. Mary Louise Trammell provides a case study of the policy process in Louisiana, focusing on the ways lobbyists and legislators reconstructed the human capital theory traditionally used to argue for public funds. James Farmer gives evidence related to the efficiency of Web-based distance education programs, a new approach to the delivery of higher education that is in favor in some states. In combination, these chapters reveal the fundamental shift in the rationales for public funding. The older plea for tax support based on the public good has broken down in favor of specific arguments on specific new developments.

Privatization of public higher education has influenced a fundamental shift in the strategies universities use to generate revenue, as illustrated by Don Hossler (chapter 8). This rationale is informed by Bowen's revenue theory and Slaughter and Leslie's reinterpretation of resource dependency theory. Revenue theory argues that in their pursuit of excellence, institutions raise all the revenue they need. Resource dependency theory argues that institutions substitute for the erosions of one revenue source by increasing revenue from other sources. Hossler illustrates that in pursuit of excellence, institutions are raising tuition and using student aid in strategic ways to promote enrollment.

In this new context, institutions often shift the rationales they use to argue for funding. The old official rationale was based on the human capital theory. Mary Louise Trammell (chapter 9) examines the official rationales used by lobbyists and legislators who were involved in the construction of a new research program in Louisiana. She examines the official discourse, using a review of testimony and other legal documents and policy reports, an approach used in prior studies. However, Trammell also examines interviews with university officials, which illustrates that the key participants in the process were aware that these new arguments were needed to influence the legislative process.

The notion of efficiency is still used to argue for public investment in higher education even though the new technologies have often raised expenditures rather than reduced costs per student. The most recent wave of technology seems to hold the potential for delivering postsecondary education at a lower cost. James Farmer (chapter 10) examines theory and evidence related to the efficiency of educational programs that use the new technologies to support distance education. His analysis implicitly assumes the rational model of policy formulation and development, that is, that the theory and evidence relative to efficiency are important in policy development.

In considering new strategies and rationales, it is more than a bit ironic that Don Hossler's chapter addresses the financial challenges facing public universities. The issues he addresses—tuition, student aid, and enrollment—are the same ones that face private universities. Trammell also provides a reconstructed rationale for funding that was developed by a coalition of public and private research universities. And while Farmer's analysis could be used to appeal for public funding, it could also be used to develop strategies for privately funded distance education programs. Clearly, the "public" aspect of higher education has dwindled in this period of privatization.

In the midst of the changes now underway in education policy, both researchers and policymakers are faced with situations that depart from the traditional logic of textbooks on educational policy. Conservative ideologies have influenced a change in the way higher education is financed in the United States. In this new context, policymakers use research to make their pleas for new programs, and lobbyists construct rationales that are consonant with various political interests. If researchers recognize these complexities, they should be better able to contribute to the policy development process.

# CHAPTER EIGHT

# Refinancing Public Universities
## Student Enrollments, Incentive-Based Budgeting, and Incremental Revenue

## Don Hossler

A major recurring theme in the history of higher education in the United States is the ongoing search for sufficient resources to enable institutions to fulfill their mission and achieve their ever-expanding aspirations. Frederick Rudolph's *History of American Higher Education* (1962) describes fully the strategies employed by colleges and universities to secure financial resources. He describes, for example, a toll for crossing the Charles River in Cambridge, a state-approved lottery dedicated to a private university, and college presidents accepting farm goods in lieu of tuition payments. John Thelin's *History of College Admissions* (1982) references the role student tuition and enrollment schemes have played in financing individual institutions. Thelin notes that recruitment for survival, rather than for selectivity, has been the norm of American collegiate admissions.

Only a small number of private colleges and universities have large endowments that would seem to make them impervious to the need for additional financial resources. However, even the wealthiest institutions in the country announce ever-larger fundraising campaigns to further increase their wealth. In the 1999–2000 education year, the nation's top eight fundraisers were private colleges. The leaders among this group were Stanford University ($580,473,838), Harvard University ($485,238,498), and Duke University ($407,952,525) (Chronicle of Higher Education 2002). In 2000–2001, Harvard University raised the most, $683 million; Stanford University followed with $469 million; and Columbia University was third with $358 million (Whelan 2002).

Increasingly, public universities are also making fundraising a high priority. The leaders among public universities in 1999–2000 included the University of Wisconsin–Madison ($280,182,467) (ninth in the nation after eight private institutions), the University of California at Los Angeles ($253,764,625), and the University of Michigan ($230,605,282) (Chronicle of Higher Education 2002). In 2000–2001, higher education institutions (public and private combined) in the United States raised a total of $24.2 billion, a 4.3 percent increase from the previous year. Among public institutions, Indiana University was at the top with $301 million, followed by the University of Wisconsin–Madison with $292 million; and University of California at San Francisco was third with $271 million at the end of the fiscal year for June 2001 (Whelan 2002). Increased fundraising and revenues associated with student enrollments have both become part of the refinancing strategies of public universities (Morgan 2002; National Center for Public Policy and Higher Education 2002; St. John and Simmons 2001). This chapter, however, focuses on the increasingly important role that undergraduate student enrollment plays in funding public universities.

During the last decades of the twentieth century and the beginning of the twenty-first century, societal and public policy trends have accentuated the search for funding, and this has led to an increasing importance being placed upon student enrollments. Mas-Colell, Whinston, and Green (1995) define a *commodity* as comparable goods or services that are available in the marketplace to be purchased. They describe a market economy as a setting in which commodities are available for purchase from more than one source and consumers have sufficient information to make comparisons. Increasingly, colleges and universities are competing for students and using marketing strategies to achieve their enrollment goals. These trends have helped to transform the college matriculation decision among potential students so that a college degree is becoming one more commodity to be purchased.

Increasingly, terms like *marketization* and *commodification* are being used in the popular and scholarly literature to refer to trends affecting colleges and universities (e.g., Clark 1998; Pusser 2002; Slaughter and Leslie 1997). Newman and Couturier (2001) posit that the strength and resiliency of the American higher education system is rooted in the competitive forces that both stimulate and allow public and private universities to seek out their competitive advantages. The authors note that merit-based awards for students, academic programs for nontraditional students, and the competition for developing on-line education programs are all rooted in the desire of institutions to attract more students—and more tuition revenue. Because of the increasing use at both private and public universities of campus-based financial aid programs that are funded out of education and general fund revenue, in essence a tuition discount, the more relevant term is not "tuition revenue," but instead "net tuition revenue."[1]

Slaughter and Leslie (1997), describe trends among universities in many Western industrialized countries that have resulted in public universities' relying upon applied contract work, student enrollments, and other market-oriented activities as a means of providing revenue. Newman and Couturier (2001) observe that the competition for federal grants and the funding from these grants has also become increasingly competitive. More and more, universities in the United States are looking for ways to turn the research efforts of their faculty into patents and venture capital activities that will provide sources of money for their campuses.

These competitive, market-oriented trends have been taking hold for many reasons. Public institutions of higher education in United States have always operated on a mixed funding model. Their funding sources come from federal, state, and local sources; from tuition and fees; and from private fundraising. This is very different than funding models that have been used until recently in the United Kingdom, the People's Republic of China, Russia, and other countries formerly part of the Soviet Union. In these countries and many others, all funding for universities came from the federal government. This funding model created few market-oriented incentives around funding associated with student enrollments.

During the debates over reauthorization of the Higher Education Act in 1972 (Gladieux and Wolanin 1976), there were serious proposals for giving federal funds directly to colleges and universities to assure low-cost tuition rather than attaching the funds to students through federal financial aid programs, the eventual model that prevailed. This decision and later decisions to create state financial aid programs helped to speed the development of the market-oriented model among public colleges and universities that emerged during the later half of the twentieth century in the United States. By attaching funding directly to students, either by the tuition they bring or by state funding formulas that are sensitive to the number of students enrolled at a college or university, incentives associated with student enrollments were created.

Compared to many industrialized countries, the United States has more colleges and universities and has always operated under more of a market model for college degrees. However, in the 1980s, when the number of traditional college-age students declined precipitously, colleges and universities started to use marketing strategies borrowed from the for-profit sector (Grabowski 1981). This use of marketing techniques among postsecondary educational institutions has accelerated since that time.

Further accentuating the shifts toward marketization and commodification has been the increasing public attention focused on college rankings and guidebooks. Several scholars have described many of the problems with relying too much attention to rankings (McDonough et al. 1998; Hossler and Foley 1996), but rankings have become part of the public discourse on higher education. Many of the same colleges and universities that decry their use still use them aggressively for marketing purposes. In addition, many of the variables used in determining an institution's rank are based on the characteristics of the students they enroll. The emergence of rankings has resulted in even more attention to student enrollments not only as a source of revenue but also as a source of prestige.

The rise in marketing, a focus on student enrollments, and the emergence of rankings have accentuated the shift toward the commodification and marketization of higher education. Indeed, these two trends go hand in hand. More aggressive marketing leads prospective students, parents, and family members to view the choice of a college or university in which to enroll as just one more commodity to be purchased. Tuition prices, tuition discounts in the form of financial aid, and rankings give the consumers of higher education, students and parents, the information to optimize their trade-off between price and quality. Accurate and complete information for consumers is one of the essential ingredients of capitalism. It enhances the ability of market economies to function.

During his lifetime, Howard Bowen was regarded as the preeminent economist of higher education in the United States. Bowen did not focus specifically on student enrollments, but his often-cited "Laws of Higher Education Finance" helped explain why the number and characteristics of students have become important to colleges and universities. In his 1980 book, *The Costs of Higher Education,* Bowen examines the aspirations of institutions as well as their sources of revenue and how they spend their money. He examines the financial well-being of colleges and universities by sector and considers the impact of these trends. Bowen's (1980) "Laws of Higher Education Finance" can be summarized thus: *Colleges and universities raise all the money they can, and spend all the money they raise in an unceasing question for power, influence, and prestige.*

In an era of a market economy for American colleges and universities, enrolled students have become an important source of power, influence, and prestige through the revenue they generate as well as their educational and demographic characteristics (high school rank, SAT scores, ethnic diversity, etc.). For many public universities, an increased number of out-of-state or international students can mean a dramatic increase in tuition revenue because many public universities charge nonresident tuition rates that are twice as high as in-state student tuition rates. Enhanced student diversity or an increase of 10 points in the average SAT in an entering class of new students can be important indicators of institutional quality to important external and internal audiences. Student enrollment has become part of the new economics of higher education.

New budgeting systems being employed at public universities have also led to a greater focus on undergraduate student enrollments. An increasing number of public universities have adopted incentive-based budgeting systems (IBB). In recent years, a number of public institutions have adopted variants of responsibility-centered budgeting. Public research universities in Illinois, Indiana, Michigan, Minnesota, Vermont, and Rhode Island have implemented such systems (Priest, Becker, Hossler, and St. John 2002). In most instances, an important part of the revenue distribution system is based on the number of undergraduate majors or the number of undergraduate credit hours generated. These new IBB systems being implemented create powerful incentives for senior campus administrators and for deans and department chairs of large academic units to pay close attention to the number of undergraduates enrolled because there is a transparent connection between the number of students enrolled and the revenue garnered by individual academic units.

These societal, public policy, and institutional trends have lead to a greater emphasis on student enrollments in public sector universities than ever before. A new focus on the revenue and prestige associated with undergraduate enrollments has also become an integral part of the new financing strategy of four-year public institutions. There was a time when most public universities operated on the enrollment strategy of "y'all come." Those days are long gone, and in its place are an array of sophisticated, data-driven enrollment strategies that are closely linked to revenue and prestige goals for public universities.

The remainder of this chapter outlines how undergraduate student enrollment and budgeting goals are being linked at many public institutions and how information and institutional analysis are increasingly being used in the public sector. Together, they constitute part of the new economy for public higher education. It should be noted that institutions of higher education do not exist to earn a profit. The historic mission of higher education in the United States is to educate students, create and transmit knowledge, and preserve culture. However, these goals are ubiquitous, difficult to measure, and often taken for granted. More easily measured goals in the new economy of public universities are goals such as increasing revenue, a more diverse student body, and enhanced academic indicators among the undergraduate student body. These indicators help to define the new economy for public universities and cannot be separated from efforts to refinance them.

## Linking Budgets, Prestige, and Enrollments

State appropriations for public four-year colleges and universities have been stable or declining during the past two decades. Between 1987 and 1995 the percentage of state budgets going to higher education fell by approximately 2.5 percent (Roherty 1997, pp. 6–7). Many public institutions have started to describe themselves as state-assisted rather than state-supported. Some public university presidents have even made the case for becoming private institutions. At the same time, public universities have been asked to educate more students. These trends have placed public universities in difficult financial situations and forced them to search for additional sources of revenue. Consequently, at many public colleges and universities, tuition as a percentage of the total budget has steadily risen in importance (St. John and Simmons 2001). Analyzing tuition alone, however, understates the importance of student enrollments as a source of revenue. Many state funding formulas provide added dollars for each additional state resident enrolled. However, most state funding formulas do not provide enough funding to fully cover the costs of educating a student. Thus, an increased number of students to educate creates additional financial problems for public institutions (St. John 2003).

As has already been noted, there is a renewed focus on rankings and other indicators of institutional quality. This focus on quality, however, is intertwined with other important societal trends. Public colleges and universities were established to educate the citizens of their states. In most states, this mission resulted in a relatively open-access mission, or at least a mission to serve large proportions of the citizens. Historically, highly selective state universities like campuses of the University of California and the University of Michigan were the exception rather than the rule. This places many public universities at a disadvantage because standardized test scores, high school class rank, and high school grade point averages are an important part of the formula for calculating college rankings. In the last two decades, however, population growth in some states and aspirations for greater prestige have resulted in a newly emerging group of selective public universities. Institutions such as the University of Texas, Texas A&M, the University of Florida, and the University of Georgia have become increasingly selective because of the large number of high school students graduating in these states. As more and more public universities increase their prestige through becoming more selective at the undergraduate level, this places greater pressure on all public institutions to increase their selectivity. The stewards of public institutions—the trustees, campus administrators, and the faculty—have a vested interest in maintaining or enhancing the perceived qualities of the institutions for which they are responsible.

In addition to selectivity, state policymakers, trustees, administrators, and faculty are committed to making sure that their public institutions are reflective of the diversity in their respective states. Increasingly, university administrators feel compelled to compete both to increase their number of top academic students and to enhance their diversity. These two trends are propelling ever greater numbers of public universities to pay more attention and to expend more money to be more successful in these areas. Public universities have a limited number of levers to help them achieve their enrollment goals related to revenue, diversity, and academic quality. These include special academic programs, admissions selectivity, recruitment strategies, and campus-based financial aid. These have become part of the new economy of public institutions of higher education.

In an era of incentive-based budgeting systems, university administrators are developing new ways to link fiscal planning to enrollment planning. The relationship between fiscal planning and enrollment planning is complex and nonlinear. Several questions need to be taken into consideration:

1. Are undergraduate student enrollments at capacity at the institutional level? Are all undergraduate degree programs at capacity?
2. What percentage of educational costs do undergraduate tuition and fees for in-state students cover?
3. What percentage of educational costs do tuition fees cover for nonresident students?

4. What is the current admissions selectivity profile of the undergraduate student body? How important is it for campus administrators to raise the academic profile?

5. What is the current diversity profile of the undergraduate student body? How important is it for campus administrators to alter the profile?

6. How extensive is the availability of endowed scholarships for undergraduates and how much latitude do campus or academic administrators of individual academic units (colleges, schools, or departments in large universities) have in awarding these scholarships?

The answers to these questions outline the range of strategies that can be employed to achieve their objectives in the new economy of public universities.

## Understanding Strategies in the New Economy

Institutional aspirations exert a powerful impact on both enrollment goals and revenue goals. The capacity of the campus to educate and (in the case of residential campus) to provide housing for students and the availability of endowed scholarships form a nexus with enrollment and revenue goals in this new enrollment-driven economy for public universities.

### *Institutional Capacity and Instructional Costs*

The number of students that a university can educate is a critical factor. If a university has both the classroom space and the faculty to increase enrollments, this can provide a relatively straightforward path to enhanced revenue. If the goal is to increase revenue without too much concern for selectivity or diversity, excess capacity can be a simple way to increase revenue. However, for many public institutions this is not likely. St. John (2003) has noted that most public universities have gone through a period of increased enrollments, but state support has not increased at a level proportionate with the increase in student enrollments (St. John 2003; Hovey 1999; Habel and Selingo 2001). Many public universities find themselves at or beyond enrollment capacity, thus increasing the number of enrolled students is not likely to be an easy answer to increasing revenue.

Many untrained observers of public higher education simply assume a simple relationship between student enrollment and increased revenue. The assumption is that because students pay tuition, enrolling more students in public universities results in more revenue. There are, however, two important factors that must be taken into consideration. State citizens at public universities pay relatively low tuition compared with their private-sector counterparts. Data derived from the IPEDS Peer Analysis System, 2002 reveal that average in-state tuition and fees were $3,506 for public four-year institutions, and $15,531 for private four-year institutions (U.S. Department of Education, 2002). Thus, adding additional students may do little to help the overall revenue of a public university. In addition, if a university is already at or near capacity with respect to student enrollments, adding additional students may require more faculty, classrooms, and office space, which can lead to spending more in additional instructional costs than the additional tuition revenue provides. For example, average instructional expenditures per enrolled student at degree-granting public institutions was $6,073 in the 1976–77 education year (in 1996–97 constant dollars). This number increased to $7,229 in 1996–97. However, instructional expenditures as a percentage of education and general expenditures have actually decreased from 39.0 percent in 1976–77, to 35.1 percent in 1996–97 education year (Snyder and Hoffman 2002).

Enrolling more nonresident students at a public university, however, can be a source of additional revenue for public universities. In some states, the tuition paid by students who attend a public university outside of their home state (nonresident students) is substantially higher. For example, resident students enrolled at the University of Hawaii pay less than $2,000 in annual tuition, while nonresident students pay more than $7,000 dollars. Similarly, in-state students from the State of Georgia pay $3,418 in tuition, and out-of-state students pay $11,314. Students residing within the State of Virginia pay $4,421 to attend, while students enrolled at the University of Virginia from other states pay $18,453. In these instances, there can be significant incentives for a public university to increase the number of nonresident students enrolled. In other states, the nonresident tuition is not much greater than that of residents. Tuition for students from the State of Alabama attending Alabama A&M pay $2,800, and the tuition costs for out-of-state students is $5,200. At William Patterson College of New Jersey, residents pay nearly $5,700 for tuition, and nonresidents pay $8,880 (U.S. Department of Education 2002). At these universities, there would be fewer incentives to increase nonresident enrollments.

Pursuing more nonresident students can raise difficult public policy debates at public universities, however. To what extent should a public university use publicly funded campuses to educate citizens from other states? Historically, in most states the answer to this question was "not very much." However, as state appropriations have fallen further behind increased instructional costs, more public universities have been able to increase tuition costs for nonresidents and increase the number of nonresident students enrolled. More than half of all students enrolled at the University of Vermont, for example, come from outside the state. Vermont uses a strategy of high tuition for both resident and nonresident students to compensate for a small level of state support. The number of nonresident students at the University of Colorado usually hovers near 50 percent. The out-of-state tuition paid by these students is a significant source of income. There is a trend among many public universities that have sufficient visibility and prestige to seek more out-of-state students in order to provide more tuition revenue. Evidence for this comes in the form of a recent job description for a senior enrollment management administrator for the system of universities that comprise the State University of New York. The job description included a requirement that candidates have demonstrated expertise in developing strategies to increase the enrollment of out-of-state students. Nevertheless, the ability of any individual public university to enroll more nonresident students to provide more tuition revenue can vary widely, depending on the reputation of individual campuses, the political climate of each state, and the policies of the boards of trustees of public universities.

### Increasing Diversity and Academic Quality

Revenue is not the only valued commodity derived from student enrollments. The diversity of the enrolled student body and the academic quality (as measured by SAT or ACT scores, class rank, and/or grade point average of entering students) are also highly valued by most public universities. Several strategies can be employed to enhance quality. However, it is important to keep in mind that the word *quality* is a relative term. For a regional public university that admits 90 percent of all applicants, increasing the number of students with a B+ average, or the number of students with a score of 1000 on the SAT, can be perceived as increasing quality. For a selective public flagship university, students with these characteristics might be viewed as marginal or even inadmissible. The mission of public universities can also differ widely from state to state. For example, campuses of the University of California are intended for students in the top 12 percent of their graduating classes. The trustee-established admission policy of Indiana University requires that all in-state students in the top 50 percent of their graduating class be admitted. At one time, the University of Kansas was required to admit all high school graduates from the State of Kansas. In each of these contexts, enhancing quality can mean very different things.

If a campus has too many students, becoming more selective by accepting fewer students can be a relatively easy way to enhance quality. Unfortunately, improving quality is seldom this simple. I have served as a consultant at some public universities where nonresident students, who paid significantly higher tuition rates, were generally not as academically qualified as resident students. In this case becoming more selective can result in less tuition revenue. At other public universities, out-of-state students tend to be stronger students, thus in these cases increasing the number of nonresident students can enhance both tuition revenue and traditional indicators of quality.

Similar sets of issues are associated with increasing the proportion of students of color at public universities. The demographic characteristics of the population base exert a strong impact on the percentage of enrolled students of color on any public university. For example, Hossler and St. John (1995), found that among regional public historically black colleges and universities in the southeast, the proportion of African American students in surrounding counties to a large extent determined the proportion of African American students enrolled at these regional institutions. Similarly, the proportion of minority students enrolled at public flagship universities in public Big Ten universities closely approximates the overall percentage of citizens of color in the state in which the university is located (Hossler 1999). Therefore, a greater emphasis on increasing the number of students enrolled from other states may conflict with efforts to increase student diversity. This is particularly true if a public university is at or near its total enrollment capacity.

Although equal opportunity continues to be part of the American ethos and is an often-stated public policy goal, this goal has yet to be achieved. Unfortunately, social scientists continue to find positive statistical relationships between minority status and lower socioeconomic status. It is also true that lower socioeconomic status is correlated with lower standardized test scores and other indicators of success in primary and secondary schools (Reich 2000). These realities can make it more difficult for colleges and universities to achieve their twin goals of greater diversity and higher levels of quality, especially if standardized tests are used as the primary measure of academic quality. The purpose of this chapter is not to critique or endorse the use of standardized tests, but to highlight the extent to which private and public universities emphasize test scores in their admissions decision and how this can disadvantage low-income students. Such policies are likely to exclude a disproportionate number of students of color. Thus, admissions standards can also influence the ability of a public university to diversify its enrollment. In addition, the fact that students of color are more likely to come from lower-income family groups means that federal, state, and campus-based financial aid programs will be important tools for enhancing diversity. I will return to this issue later in this chapter.

In the market model that dominates higher education in the United States, students of color and high-ability students are highly sought after, and both public and private universities compete for them. Campus-based financial aid has become essential in the efforts to recruit more high-ability students and more students of color. Increasingly, campus-based financial aid has become an integral part of the new economy of public universities.

The use of campus-based financial aid to enhance quality and diversity raises a complex set of issues, however. Federal and state lawsuits have challenged the legality of use of preferential financial aid policies to increase student diversity. The use of financial aid to reward academic talent is also controversial at many public universities. Historically, most public universities were established to serve state citizens and provide access for those citizens who could not afford to attend private colleges and universities. Because high-ability students are more likely to come from economically advantaged families, providing these students with non-need-based financial aid runs counter to the founding ethos of many public universities. Equally important, campus-based financial aid often comes from general tuition revenue, thus placing these goals in tension with the goal of increasing revenue. The more education and general fund revenue that is invested into campus-based financial aid, the less there is available from net tuition revenue.

## Using Campus-Based Financial Aid to Achieve Enrollment Objectives

It is a myth that all private universities have large endowments from which to offer campus-based financial aid. However, they are more likely to have substantial amounts of their endowments set aside for campus-based scholarships than are public universities. An analysis of data from the *2001 Digest of Education Statistics* reveals that between 1980–81 and 1997–97, the average public university devoted approximately 4.3 percent of its budget to scholarships and financial aid. During this same time period, private institutions devoted 11.4 percent of their budgets. Whether scholarships are funded by education and general fund revenue or from endowment is a significant issue in the new economy of public universities. Scholarships funded by education and general fund revenue are essentially a tuition discount. This means that any university using its own education and general fund resources to pay for scholarships has fewer dollars to pay faculty and staff salaries, maintain buildings, or provide support services for students. Enhancing student diversity or student quality may be an important goal, but using campus dollars always means taking away dollars from other important campus priorities.

In recent years, however, important policy shifts have started to take place in public sector institutions. The *2001 Survey of Undergraduate Financial Aid Policies* (NASFAA and The College Board 2001), documents the increase in merit-based, campus-funded financial aid at public colleges and universities. This increase in merit-based aid inevitably comes at the expense of need-based aid. This is true even if campuses are also increasing their need-based aid funds. Only if a university has sufficient funds to fully meet all unmet need of undergraduate students can campus funds be diverted to merit-based aid without detracting from equity, access, and, frequently, diversity-oriented enrollment goals. The 2001 survey points out that public universities, however, are more likely to have increased non-need-based financial aid rather than need-based aid. This point emphasizes the dilemma public universities confront as they attempt to optimize student enrollments to achieve the goals of enhanced tuition revenue, diversity, quality, and equal access for all state residents. Despite the rapid increase in tuition at public universities and the growing acceptance of the high tuition–high aid concept in the public sector, it appears that many public institutions have not devoted significant amounts of campus-based aid to students with financial need. This may be because of the historic low tuition at public universities; they have not yet perceived the need to devote significant amounts of money to need-based financial aid. These trends raise difficult questions related to the mission of public universities, their changing circumstances, and the new economy of public universities.

The growing use of campus-funded scholarships at public institutions raises a complex set of issues. For two decades policy scholars have suggested that state policymakers could more effectively and equitably use public funds by letting tuition levels at public institutions rise and investing more state dollars in need-based state financial aid programs (Hearn and Longanecker 1985). Proposals for high tuition–high aid models in the public sector have generated a good deal of discussion and debate, but few states or public systems have pursued this policy option.

The situation is at least somewhat different for endowed scholarships, however. It can be argued that raising endowed funds for scholarships does have opportunity costs, because the development professionals might otherwise be able to convince donors to give funds for buildings, endowed faculty chairs, or other important purposes. Nevertheless, once a scholarship is endowed, there are clear benefits for universities to award them because they cannot garner the revenue from an endowed scholarship unless it is awarded. Hence, every endowed scholarship that helps to enhance quality or diversity helps increase net tuition revenue and achieves other important university goals (such as equity and access). Traditionally, public universities have not had a large number of endowed scholarships. In recent years, however, many public universities have made raising funds for scholarships an important part of their fundraising campaigns. For example, the Ohio State University recently completed a $1 billion endowment campaign in which a major part of this campaign was dedicated to undergraduate scholarships (Ganley 1998, p. A58). Only endowed scholarships enable public universities to avoid choosing between optimizing their tuition revenue and striving to optimize diversity and academic selectivity.

## Sorting Through Competing Priorities

The new economy for public universities has produced a high premium on student enrollments to enhance revenue, diversity, and quality. For many public universities, there are costs and trade-offs associated with the pursuit of any one of these goals. The challenge for senior public university administrators is to determine how they want to balance these competing goals. Figure 8.1, places these three goals at three points of a triangle. For university administrators, their goals, aspirations, and plans force them to hold in tension all of these goals simultaneously. Because of the costs associated with recruiting a more diverse student body or becoming more academically selective (if traditional measures of quality are used), pursuing either of these goals is likely to adversely affect net tuition revenue. As the distance along the points of the triangle suggests, the closer a public university moves exclusively toward traditional measures of academic quality or diversity, the greater the distance from the point associated with net tuition. For most public universities, the more

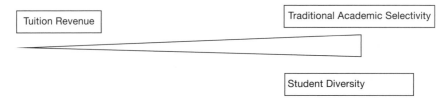

*Figure 8.1.* Balancing the Competing Goals of Student Enrollments

they focus net tuition revenue, the more difficult it will be to achieve their quality and diversity goals. Pursuing academic selectivity or diversity are not mutually exclusive goals but neither do they represent the same goals, especially if traditional indicators such as standardized test scores are used as the primary measure of academic quality. Unfortunately, as a nation we have not yet achieved the societal equity goals we espouse; and because a disproportionate number of minority students are from low-income families, a disproportionate number of students of color may be less likely to score well on traditional indicators of academic quality.

Most universities try to simultaneously achieve revenue, diversity, and quality goals. Thus, rather than moving exclusively along the perimeter of the triangle toward any one goal, university administrators operate within the interior of the triangle in an attempt to simultaneously find an optimal location to satisfice on all three of these goals: tuition revenue, diversity, and quality. I use Herb Simon's (1997) term *satisfice* intentionally because no university can reach its ideal goals in each of these areas. Ultimately, universities have to settle for "good enough." It has been my experience, however, that many universities lack the information environment and the analytical capacity to fully understand how they can optimize their goals in all three areas. The new economy of public universities requires close working relationships between senior enrollment officers and chief financial officers and a strong institutional research function.

As public universities have started to use education and general fund revenue to fund campus-based scholarships, this requires more coordination between enrollment management and financial offices. The following questions become a key part of campus discourse in the new economy:

1. How much money will be available for campus-based scholarships?
2. What kind of return on investment in the form of net tuition revenue can the campus expect?

*Table 8.1    Simulated Effects of Merit Aid Scholarships on In-State Students*

| Proposed Discount/Group | $1,000 | $2,000 | $4,500 | $6,000 |
|---|---|---|---|---|
| SAT Scores | 1100–1250 | 1251–1300 | 1301–1450 | 1451 & above |
| *Before award changes* | | | | |
| Yield | 28.7% | 26.4% | 18.5% | 9.7% |
| Admits in group | 1198 | 1325 | 324 | 279 |
| Matrics in group | 344 | 350 | 60 | 27 |
| Net tuition revenue | | | | |
| (NTR) (000s) | 4,037 | 3,705 | 579 | 258 |
| *After award changes* | | | | |
| Simulated matrics | 354 to 356 | 350 to 359 | 67 to 68 | 39 to 40 |
| Matric change* | 10 to 12 | 8 to 9 | 7 to 8 | 13 to 12 |
| Percent change | 0 | 1.4 to 1.1 | 15.0 to 13.3 | 48.1 to 44.4 |
| Simulated NTR (000s) | 4,026 | 3723 to 3713 | 547 to 538 | 264 to 257 |
| NTR change (000s) | –11 | 18 to 7 | –33 to –41 | 6 to –1 |
| Std. dev. NTR change (000s) | 1 | 1 | 1 | 1 |
| Change in NTR per | | | | |
| matric (000s) | 0 | .1 to 0 | –.5 to –.6 | .2 to 0 |
| Change in SAT of class | 0 | –.1 | .2 to –.6 | –.5 to .8 |
| Change in HSRank of class | 0 | 0 | 0 to .1 | 1.6 to 1.5 |
| Average old grants** | 1,234 | 2,383 | 3,319 | 3,429 |
| Average new grants*** | 1267 | 2,482 | 3826 to 3829 | 5049 to 5052 |
| Total expenditure: proposed | | | | |
| grants (000) | 436 | 881 to 879 | 819 | 348 to 344 |

* Matric change = Change in the number of students enrolling
** Average old grant = The average grant awarded to similar students last year
*** Average new grant = The average grant awarded for the coming year

3.   What can the campus expect in terms of quality and diversity indicators in each entering class?

The focus on these questions has also resulted in the adoption of financial aid techniques first used at private colleges and universities to determine the impact of campus-based scholarships on the enrollment decisions of students. Public universities are using their own institutional research staff or hiring consultants to employ a growing array of statistical techniques to calculate the effects of scholarships on student enrollment decisions frequently measured by yield (the number of admitted students in any population of interest who matriculate). These same models are also used to calculate the impact of campus-based financial aid on net tuition revenue. Table 8.1 is illustrative of the kind of data that can be produced by linking enrollment planning, financial planning, and institutional research functions. This table helps policymakers to estimate the impact of targeted scholarships on specific populations.

The example in Table 8.1 focuses on merit aid scholarships for high-ability students. It enables policymakers to engage in a form of trade-off analysis. A president who aspires to increase the quality of the student body can ask, "What kind of scholarship award will be required to increase the number of students enrolling with an SAT score above 1450?" It also enables the chief financial officer to remind other policymakers that an increase in financial aid expenditures would reduce the dollars available for salary increases by 0.5 percent. This kind of analysis can help shape the discourse about the "big three" enrollment goals in the new economy of public universities: net tuition revenue, diversity, and quality. It can be invaluable to help shape realistic and satisficing revenue and enrollment goals. It can also avoid setting foolish and unrealistic goals.

In the end, this kind of analysis brings us back to Bowen's (1980) revenue theory: Colleges and universities raise all the money they can, and spend all the money they raise in an unceasing question for power, influence, and prestige. The success of a public university in achieving these goals will have an impact on their revenue stream and their ability to garner power, influence, or prestige. These are not the only resources that are important in the new economy in which public universities function, but they have become key resources for many public universities.

NOTE

1. The phrase net tuition revenue (NTR) is usually used within the context of undergraduate tuition and campus-based financial aid. NTR is calculated by subtracting all campus-based financial aid that is funded from general fund revenues from total tuition dollars derived from students paying tuition. The percentage of total tuition revenues being devoted to general fund campus-based financial aid is often referred to as the financial aid discount rate.

REFERENCES

Bowen, Howard. 1980. *The cost of higher education: How much do colleges and universities spend per student and how much should they spend?* San Francisco: Jossey-Bass.

Chronicle of Higher Education. 2002. *Almanac.* Available online at *chronicle.com/weekly /almanac/2001/nation/0103102.htm.*

Clark, Burton R. 1998. *Creating entrepreneurial universities: Organizational pathways to transformation.* Oxford, UK: Pergamon Press.

Ganley, Susan. 1998. Developments in 6 capital campaigns. *Chronicle of Higher Education* 45 (9): A58.

Gladieux, Lawrence E., and Thomas R. Wolanin. 1976. *Congress and the colleges: The national politics of higher education.* Lexington, MA: D. C. Heath.

Grabowski, Stephen W. 1981. *Marketing in higher education.* AAHE/ERIC Higher Education Report, no. 5. Washington, DC: American Association of Higher Education.

Habel, Sara, and Jeffrey Selingo. 2001. For public colleges, a decade of generous state budgets is over. *Chronicle of Higher Education* 47 (32): A10.

Hearn, James C., and David Longanecker. 1985. Enrollment effects of alternative postsecondary pricing policies. *Journal of Higher Education* 56: 735–50.

Hossler, Don. 1999. *Report to the trustees on minority student enrollment at Indiana University.* Bloomington: Indiana University.

Hossler, D., and E. M. Foley. 1996. Reducing the noise in the college choice process: The use of college guidebooks and ratings. In *Evaluating and responding to college guide and rating books.* New Directions in Higher Education, No. 88, ed. R. Dan Walleri and Marsha K. Moss San Francisco: Jossey-Bass.

Hossler, Don, and Edward P. St. John. 1995. *An analysis of the factors that influence student choice at HBCUs: Three studies of external and internal factors affecting white enrollments.* Prepared for the University of Alabama, Office of Counsel.

Hovey, Harold A. 1999. *State spending for higher education in the next decade: The battle to sustain current support.* The National Center for Public Policy and Higher Education #99-3. San Jose, California.

Mas-Colell, Adreu, Michael D. Whinston, and Jerry P. Green. 1995. *Microeconomic Theory.* Oxford University Press.

McDonough, Patricia M., Anthony Lising Antonio, MaryBeth Walpole, and Leonor Xochitl Perez. 1998. College rankings: Democratized knowledge for whom? *Research in Higher Education* 39 (5): 513–38.

Morgan, Richard. 2002. Students at public colleges brace for large tuition increases. *Chronicle of Higher Education* 48 (25): A26. Available online at *chronicle.com.*

Newman, Frank, and Lara K. Couturier. 2001. The new competitive arena: Market forces invade the academy. *Change Magazine* (September/October).

National Association of Student Financial Aid Administrators and The College Board. 2001. *2001 Survey of Undergraduate Financial Aid Policies, Practices, and Procedures.* Washington, DC: Authors.

National Center for Public Policy and Higher Education. 2002. *Losing ground: A national status report on the affordability of American higher education.* San Jose, California.

Priest, D. M., W. E. Becker, D. Hossler, and E. P. St. John, eds. 2002. *Incentive-based budgeting systems in public universities.* Northampton, MA: Edward Elgar.

Pusser, Brian. 2002. Higher education, the emerging market, and the public good. In *The knowledge economy and postsecondary education,* ed. P. Graham and Nevzer Stacey. Washington, DC: National Academy Press.

Reich, Robert, B. 2000. How selective colleges heighten inequality. *Chronicle of Higher Education* 47 (3): B7.

Roherty, Brian, M. 1997. The price of passive resistance in financing higher education. In *Public and private financing of higher education: Shaping public policy for the future,* ed. P. Callahan, J. Finney, K. Bracco, and W. Doyle. Phoenix, AZ: American Council on Education and Oryx Press.

Rudolph, Frederick. 1962. *The American college and university: A history.* New York: Vintage Books.

St. John, Edward P. 2003. *Refinancing the college dream: Access, equal opportunity, and justice for taxpayers.* Baltimore: Johns Hopkins University Press.

St. John, Edward, and Ada Simmons. 2001. *Financial indicators for institutions of higher education: Indiana, peer states and the nation.* Bloomington: Indiana Education Policy Center.

Simon, Herbert A. 1997. *Administrative behavior: A study of decision-making processes in administrative organizations.* 4th edition. New York: Free Press.

Slaughter, Sheila, and Larry L. Leslie. 1997. *Academic capitalism: Politics, policies, and the entrepreneurial university.* Baltimore: Johns Hopkins University Press.

Snyder, Thomas, and Charlene M. Hoffman. 2002. *Digest of education statistics, 2001,* NCES-2002-130. Washington, DC: National Center for Educational Statistics.

Thelin, John. 1982. *Higher education and its useful past: Applied history in research and planning.* Cambridge, MA: Schenkman Publishing Co.

U.S. Department of Education. 2002. *IPEDS Peer Analysis System, 2002.* Available online at nces.ed.gov/ipedspas.

Whelan, David. 2002. U.S. colleges raised $24 billion in 2000–01. *Chronicle of Philanthropy,* 14 (12): 12–13. Available online at philanthropy.com/premium/articles/v14/i12/12003601.htm.

# CHAPTER NINE

# Reconstructing Rationales for Public Funding

## A Case Study

## Mary Louise Trammell

State support for public higher education has eroded substantially, especially in terms of direct subsidies to institutions. During the last two decades the taxpayer portion of higher education costs declined from more than 80 percent of educational costs in 1980 to less than 70 percent in 2000 (St. John 1994, 2003). Advocates of public funding have argued that the economic returns to education provide a sufficient rationale for public investment (e.g., Honeyman and Bruhn 1996), but higher education continues to have difficulty making a case for public funding. However, in spite of the decline in state support for public colleges (i.e., subsidies to institutions), science and technology have been targeted for investment by some states.

In this context, it is important to examine successful efforts to argue for public financing of public-private partnerships and scientific research based on rationales for economic development. This chapter presents a case study of the rationale that advocates of higher education developed in their effort in the early 1980s to lobby for the Louisiana Education Quality Support Fund (LEQSF), a state program that used revenues from oil and gas production for scientific research aimed at promoting economic development. After presenting background to situate the case and describing the methods used, the case analysis examines the ways that the human capital rationale was recontextualized in the lobbying process in Louisiana. The implications are also considered.

## Background

This case study examines the initial formulation to the adoption phases of Senate Bill 105 (SB 105) of the 1985 Regular Session of the Louisiana legislature, which created the Louisiana Education Quality Trust Fund (Permanent Trust Fund) and the Louisiana Education Quality Support Fund (LEQSF) programs. The LEQSF legislation provided for the protection of $700 million in escrowed petroleum tax revenues, the largest tax windfall in the state's history, for educational purposes. The debate embodied historical tensions between the dominant populist group that represented labor, agricultural, and other rural interests in the legislature and the subdominant reformist faction that represented the interests of higher education, business, and corporate leaders on issues of state financial management and educational policy.

For higher education institutions, the LEQSF program instituted a de facto state science policy modeled on the National Science Foundation's (NSF) agenda for science and engineering research and education enhancement. It also established a second source of state funding for higher education, especially for the state's more competitive research institutions. Thus, the creation of the program represented a departure in the course of educational finance policy in a state with a long, well-established history of underfunding higher education. To situate this case, we examine the national and state policy context for higher education finance in the early 1980s when the new bill was introduced as well as the changed policy context in which new coalition building seemed possible.

## The National Context

With the infusion of federal funding into universities during the post–World War II Cold War era, the influence of private industry was supplanted by interests of the federal government, especially for national defense (Noble 1991). Policies of the NSF, founded in 1950, and of other federal research agencies subsequently established, set an agenda for universities to emphasize basic research, largely leaving the applied research and development to the proprietary interests of industry (Kleinman 1995).

The decline of U.S. economic competitiveness in the global market precipitated a shift in crisis management reaction in federal and state policy practices. In an attempt to stimulate collaborative university investigation in technologies for economic development, federal agencies have, over the past twenty years, funded basic and applied research programs that promote cooperative support from industry and state agencies. The federal system has also provided special interest ("ear-marked") awards to universities, which increased yearly until 1993 ($763 million), and then began an incremental decline until 1997 (Brainard and Southwick 2001).

The passage of the Bayh-Dole Act (PL965-17) in 1980, allowing universities to retain title to technologies developed with federal funds, enabled the development of university-based technology transfer activities. Loosening of licensing restrictions also stimulated business sponsorships. Other federal incentives, such as the funding of cooperative research centers by the NSF, relaxing anti-trust laws to allow competing firms to collaborate on basic research, and changes in the U.S. Patent and Trademark Office, have stimulated university-industry partnerships.

Eric Bloch, former director of the NSF, framed the nation's economic crisis specifically in terms of human capital theory. Bloch maintained that a deficit in skilled scientists and engineers was at the core of the economic problem (Bloch 1990). However, after Bloch's retirement from the NSF, a federal report revealed that Bloch, also a former director of research for International Business Machines Corporation, manufactured reports of critical shortages of scientists and engineers to gain additional funding for the NSF (Rensberger 1992).

Conservative voices have blamed the economic crisis on the failure of the educational system to produce a skilled labor force and the failure of industry to bring new competitive technology quickly to the global market. Industrial management practices and the educational system, at all levels, have been seriously attacked as inferior to those found in Japan and Europe.

## The State Context

In 1982–83, Louisiana faced its worst fiscal crisis in fifty years, a $600 million state budget deficit due to shrinking revenues from oil and gas severance taxes. In 1981–82 oil and gas severance tax revenues constituted 31.5 percent of total state tax and permit revenues. By 1986–87, the year the LEQSF legislation was adopted as a constitutional amendment, severance tax revenues had fallen to 13.3 percent of total state tax revenues (*Louisiana Almanacs, 1986–87*). This was a devastating time for the state and for Louisiana's public higher education institutions, which suffered eight major cuts in state appropriations between 1982 and 1986, with a net budget loss of $80 million and the loss of 500 positions (Board of Regents 1986a). When the LEQSF program was proposed, Louisiana's funding on a per student basis ranked last in the southeastern region (Board of Regents 1986a). In 1981, the state's colleges and universities were funded at 97.7 percent of formula (based on student credit hours); by 1985–86, funding declined to 68.6 percent of formula (Board of Regents 1996), approximately where it remained in 1995.[1]

Louisiana higher education institution public funding suffered not only from the oil and gas fiscal crisis but also from effects of the 1982 national recession, which affected most colleges and universities in the United States. During the early 1980s, Louisiana institutions participated in a movement across the country in which administrators of elite research universities employed the ideology of human capital theory, restated as economic theory, in their arguments for public funding. They pointed to the link between higher education investment, economic productivity, and global competitiveness to legitimize their pleas for federal and state research support.

As Slaughter (1991) points out, the adoption of the reconstructed human capital theory by university administrators is rich with ironies and inconsistencies. With arguments for funding on the basis of ability, merit, and talent, the university presidents sought support for higher education institutions from the national research system. But the research system supported primarily graduate research education, and thus the requested funding would likely benefit mostly graduate students in the heavily funded science and engineering disciplines closely aligned with the national research agenda. These graduate students constituted only a fraction—albeit the most expensive fraction—of student enrollment. Some of the university presidents who also argued for equity and choice in higher education were apparently unaware of the ironic juxtaposition of a rationale based in research excellence.

The Louisiana legislature, in the early 1980s, followed national trends in education by enacting statutes to establish programs for targeted basic research[2] and endowed chairs. However, authorization was only symbolic, since the legislature did not appropriate funding for the programs. Funding these programs would have required the state to reduce support for health services—the only unprotected budget line other than higher education—or raise new taxes. In the early 1980s Louisiana's largest research institutions were receiving less than the national average in federal research funding, and private and corporate donations were diminishing with the decline of the state's monolithic oil and gas economy. Administrators of those universities were eager to have the tax windfall to enhance their institutions.

With multiple governing and management boards for public institutions, including one historically black three-campus system, reporting to the Board of Regents, the public higher education infrastructure was complex. Additionally, several private institutions, including minority universities, were under partial jurisdiction of the Board of Regents on issues related to public funding. Seventeen public and private universities offered graduate degrees in science and engineering; seven additional campuses had science and engineering undergraduate departments or programs. Interests of the diverse systems and campuses, especially those in rural areas, were topics of debate during the Educational Committee hearings on the LEQSF program. Their interests would profoundly shape subsequent implementation planning.

## Crafting a New Rationale

According to a 1986 Board of Regents report, 1985 federal data indicated that while the average U.S. higher education institution garnered 64 percent of their research funding from federal agencies, Louisiana's institutions received 35 percent. Remaining funding came from state and local agencies and institutional sources (Board of Regents 1986, app. 2, 7). According to the report, among the state's institutions, the Louisiana State University System, with its two medical campuses, an agricultural college, and a large private institution with a medical campus, attained dominant shares of research funding in the early 1980s. In fiscal year 1983, the Louisiana State University System campuses received 64 percent of the state's total research and development funding; the largest private university received 23 percent of total research funds. Of 1983 federal funding, the LSU System campuses received approximately 49 percent of the total, and the private campus received approximately 32 percent (Board of Regents 1986b). Senior administrators from the LSU System worked publicly for the enactment of the LEQSF. Senior administrators from both public and private universities worked on implementation planning under the direction of the state's Board of Regents.

The LESQF higher education implementation plan provided funding for: (1) endowed chairs; (2) basic and applied research, especially in discipline areas of economic importance to the state; (3) department and unit enhancement; and (4) recruitment of superior graduate fellows. An initial twelve-year funding schedule provided that after the first two years, most basic research disciplines (as defined by the NSF) would be eligible for funding on a staggered basis, with the exception of biological and earth/environmental sciences, which were eligible annually. The applied research program provided funding on a staggered basis for eleven topics related to the state's industrial interests, but annual funding only for oil and gas production, chemistry, materials science, and biotechnology. The enhancement program rotated all eligible disciplines on a three-year schedule. The superior graduate fellows program provided annual funding for five of the fourteen discipline areas: chemistry, physics and astronomy, earth/environmental sciences/ biological sciences, and engineering (Board of Regents 1987).

## Methods

The methodology for this study was threefold. To construct a set of issues for discourse analysis, the researcher compared the five versions of SB 105, which established the basis of the Louisiana Education Quality Trust Fund or Permanent Trust Fund, and the LEQSF. The bill was redrafted four times between April and July 1985 as amendments were brought to the Senate by the Senate Education Committee, the House Appropriations Committee and senators from the floor of the Senate. According to the official texts and the narratives, the primary issues of the debate were: (1) whether to protect the entire 8(g) windfall in trust for education; and (2) how to divide the portion protected for education.

In addition to the analyses of the dominant issues, the study also explored certain underlying problematics that emerged from the literature and from Board of Regents reports. These ideas became the basis for theoretical claims that framed the data analysis of the two primary issues noted above. This chapter focuses on one of those claims: *human capital theory was reconstructed for purposes of garnering state support for higher education based on a rationale of economic benefits to the institution and the state. Private or nonmonetary benefits to the individual were thus moved to the periphery of the discussion, consistent with lobbying for federal legislation* (Slaughter 1991).

### Official Legislative Record

At the first level, the researchers examined the official legislative record of SB 105 and compared five interim drafts and the final version of the bill to contemporary education and economic development policy texts. The interim drafts appeared related because they shared the same author and had common supporters, or because of similarities in stated purpose or language. Also, the researchers compared the LEQSF policy to a set of existing statutes that authorized higher education enhancement but remained unfounded. A third textual comparison was made with the Louisiana Science and Technology Foundation (LSTF) legislation (SB 947, 1984) that shared Senate sponsorship with the LEQSF program. The LSTF was one of twenty-four pieces of education/economic development legislation endorsed by the governor in his inaugural address and later enacted in 1984. The LEQSF program was also placed within the context of the Governor's Economic Development Commission report released in November 1985.

Proceedings of a portion of the Senate Education Committee hearing of May 30, 1985, were also examined from an audiotape recorded by the committee clerk. Present were the seven members of the Senate Education Committee; the senate sponsor of the LEQSF bill; and guests from higher education, secondary and elementary education, business, and other public domains, who participated in the debate. The event was interpreted as a ritual encounter bounded by the social rules and resources of the legislative culture (Giddens 1984).

## *Policymakers' Narratives*

At the second level of analysis, this study examined the narratives of policymakers, which enabled a greater understanding of policy construction than was possible only from official textual discourse. Therefore, the second level of analysis connected the official texts to policy actors' narratives to demonstrate their interests and motivations. Narrative analysis was employed on two levels: (1) for internal analysis of the interview content and setting (Riessman 1993); and (2) as a tool to analyze competing and contradictory claims between and among narratives (Roe 1994).

Policymakers' comments on the official texts were sometimes conflicting or contradictory, but the statements themselves appeared valid within the context and social structures of their respective policy domains. An explanation for the differences was found in Habermas's theories of "cognitive strategies," which allows individuals to organize and function within social systems based on three types of knowledge: that of work, of social interaction, and of power (Fischer 1985). Following Giddens' (1984) claim of structuration theory, state political practice was interpreted from the perspective of the social resources— meanings, morals, and power—that shaped it. And the emergent higher education policy was set within the historical context of higher education planning and budgeting practices.

As the author had managed the LEQSF research program at two universities, she had been curious about the influence the policy makers and the construction process may have had on subsequent program outcomes. The succinct language of the official policy texts, however, offered only limited clues. Because policy agents responsible for the LEQSF policy operated from positions of power within the higher education and legislative systems, their identities and interests were sought for insight into policy terms.

## Interview Process

Third, interviews were conducted with twenty-one officials who had been actively involved in the legislative process. They included university administrators and lobbyists, legislators, and other lobbyists and public officials. Early interview questions were instrumental in character and were designed to elicit information not found in the official texts. Questions were constructed to detect information about networks of policy actors and their values and interests and about the power struggle between the populist and reformist groups. Initial interview questions included:

1. Who originally formulated the goals of the LEQSF program?
2. Was there a relationship between the LEQSF (1985) legislation and the Louisiana Science and Technology Foundation legislation (1984)?
3. Was there a connection between the LEQSF initiative and the Governor's Economic Development Commission (1984–85)?
4. What do you know about the changes in the bill that occurred through the legislative process?
5. How did the division of the funds between higher education and elementary/secondary education occur?

Early in the series of interviews it became evident that the structured questions were interrupting the narrative process, for in the elite interviews, the respondents dominated the experience and constructed narratives according to their particular internal strategies (Marshall and Rossman 1989). Narratives were also expressions of how the narrator wanted to be known by the researcher. The face-to-face interactions of interview settings allowed the researcher to obtain data from conventions of gesture as well as talk. Two of the respondents occupied offices overlooking the capitol building, the site of their former professional activities, as they retold their LEQSF stories.

Interviewee remarks were constrained by the presence of the tape-recorder. Five respondents implied that their comments were limited by the recording. For instance, one interrupted himself, "So it was amazing that it did pass, given the climate." "Was [ . . . ] involved?" "I don't recall. Let me say this . . . could you turn off the recorder?" (Interview Q, 20, 6–10).

The interviews yielded contrasting and conflicting narratives, yet each story seemed grounded within the practices of the respondent's respective professional domain: higher education, government, business, or others. Policy actors' stories revealed the complexity, uncertainty, and polarity attendant to the policy construction process. An interpretive approach was adopted to give prominence to the agency of each respondent (Riessman 1993), and the questions were reduced to two "grand tour" questions (Spradley 1979) that elicited stories from the elite respondents:

1. What were the principle issues influencing the construction of the LEQSF program?
2. How were the compromises managed between the political factions? (If the respondent had not volunteered the information in the narrative.)

## Recontextualized Human Capital Theory

Perhaps the most compelling aspect of lobbying for the LEQSF related to coalition building. Louisiana had a strong populist tradition that valued spreading funding to reach the large segments of the population without a strong economic rationale (Miron 1992; Trammell 1996), a value base that would have support using the new fund for general support of schools. At the same time, there was an expanding group of new conservatives that believed in the new science arguments that were being used by NSF to argue for a reinvestment in scientific research. The recontextualization of human capital rationale played a crucial role in holding together these two interests in support of the legislation. The evolution of the new human capital rationale is examined below, followed by interviews that illuminated further how this new rationale evolved.

### Official Legislative Records

In the May 25, 1985, Senate Education Committee hearing testimony, a government elite used a reconstructed version of human capital theory to urge support for SB 105. He began his testimony with the rationale for funding higher education from a perspective of financing for higher education, explaining that Louisiana was $122 million below the regional average in expenditures for higher education (Sen, 3, 19–20). His statement repeated the adaptive strategy offered by an administrator at the flagship public institution, as Chaffee (1983) would have considered it, to use the LEQSF Trust Fund as an endowment for higher education (Interview Q). When his arguments met strong opposition from the committee, he invoked an ideology that had been used at the national level by those advocating the higher education–economic development linkage. Pressing his case, the government elite insisted:

> Louisiana can begin producing the brain power and the technology. Right now our economy is falling backwards, and the only way modern societies and states are now fueling an economy is through higher education . . . you've got a quick return in your investment in higher education. (Sen 6, 16–20)

After recurring challenges from the populist committee members, the government elite continued: "But higher education can absorb it [the tax windfall] almost instantly and can create the technology that's necessary" (Sen, 7, 19–21). He continued the economic development rhetoric with a description of how other states, such as Texas, were funding higher education to attract star professors into universities—stars who were luring industry:

> . . . and immediately [transferring] technologies that provide jobs. . . . I think that besides just education, the emphasis on higher education has to do with economic development. And this is what all of the other states, all of the consultants [LSTF economic consultants] say. This is where they are going. And we are frankly not competing. (Sen, 9, 35–10, 9)

From a perspective of linguistic analysis, the exchange was significant because although the bill's author repeated the higher education–economic development argument three times in response to committee members' challenges, the committee members never commented on his argument directly. The only reference to a theoretical human capital link between education and economic development was made by a committee member from the northwest region. He returned to the original (Becker 1964) interpretation of human capital theory, with a focus on education's benefit to the individual as well as to society:

> I have heard Mr. . . . [the state's leading business lobbyist] say ten million times, the main reason people want to come to a state is because they have a quality education system. . . . I am going to preach back what he's preaching to me (Sen, 10, 13–15) . . . . I'm going to be for putting some of this $700 million immediately in the blood of children in the first through the sixth grades, where that's the most

important place you can spend it. . . . I want some of it to go to the kids, and that's basically what we are going to do. (Sen, 11, 11–14)

The senior senator's last statement, "and that's basically what we are going to do," was the final statement of the formal exchange between the bill's author and the committee. It was a confidently delivered statement that carried all the weight of the populist power base of the Senate Education Committee.

From a theoretical perspective, the ideology used by the government elite reflected a reconstructed human capital theory as described by Slaughter (1991). Human capital theory (Leslie and Brinkman 1988) focused on the rewards of education as benefits to the individual as well as to society. The reconstructed version reflected classic structuralism in which the individual is decentered and the emphasis is placed on the institution and the state.

Bloland (1995) argued that the purposes and practices of higher education were being refocused on the performativity of the university in relation to the economic system. He characterized the link between higher education and economic development as "postmodern," based in part on the observation that the mission of universities in the latter half of the twentieth century was to create skills rather than "ideals." However, the top American graduate programs have sought industrial support for research since the late nineteenth century (Popkewitz 1991; Tyack 1974).

With the growth of federal research support after World War II, research universities were less dependent on private support. But as federal funding for higher education declined in the late 1970s and early 1980s along with the position of the United States in the global market, reliance on corporate sources again became important to higher education. Through policy statements of the National Academy of Sciences and federal funding agencies, universities were pressured to pursue financial partnerships with industry.

What may be "postmodern" or "postindustrial" in Bloland's (1995) analysis is that universities have, since the national recession of the late 1970s and early 1980s, found themselves to be less successful in garnering research support from industries that are shrinking their own research budgets. Consequently, these universities are going to the public trough for funds to enhance their research infrastructure and faculties with the professed goal of increasing competitiveness of private industry (Slaughter 1993).

In the LEQSF case, the higher education lobby adopted science and economic development rhetoric from the federal agencies to request state monies to enhance public and private higher education and graduate research, ostensibly for the benefit of the state economy. Adoption of federal policy and policy language to state educational initiatives has been a practice of long standing, and one that produces significant shifts in the original policy intent (Wirt and Kirst 1972).

The economy of Louisiana, based largely on agriculture and resource extraction, has few large industries headquartered in the state. The state's industrial plants, based on chemical research and chemical engineering (oil and gas or petrochemical companies), are headquartered outside the state. The state has three medical schools, but technologies developed at these sites have frequently been licensed to out-of-state or foreign companies. Thus, there are few opportunities for research faculty to partner with private corporate or industrial research laboratories in the state.

The professed mission of the LEQSF program was economic development, but the program lacked elements, such as venture capital pools or technology development programs, which were essential to the success of model state programs cited in Board of Regents planning documents. The California program cited was focused on microelectronics and was jointly funded by the state and industry. New Jersey had an established State Science and Technology Foundation that managed seven Centers of Advanced Technology, and a venture capital fund. Michigan also had created a number of technical centers with seed money from the state and partial industry sponsorship.[3] Ohio had a multifaceted Thomas Alva Edison Program that operated out of the State Department of Development, with seed capital for matching private sector support. Pennsylvania created the collaborative Ben Franklin Partnership that had functions similar to the Edison Program. Texas designed a highly targeted research program that involved mandatory industry support.

Ironically, the Louisiana Science and Technology Foundation (LSTF), which was authorized but not funded in 1984, did provide elements found in the model states but missing from the LEQSF program. The LSTF was not a program predominantly for basic research funding, but it covered the whole gamut of technology inducement, from idea generation through commercialization. The emphasis was on provision of seed and venture capital funding through public bonding authority. The program was private sector–oriented, with provisions for leveraging public funds with private investments (Gulf South Research Institute 1984).

The LSTF policy (SB 947, 1984) was an attempt to ameliorate the state's economic crisis precipitated by the rapid decline in the oil and gas industry in 1981–82. With the loss of revenues from oil and gas taxes and related revenues, the state's finances began a downward spiral not experienced since the Great Depression. As stated above, by 1982–83, the budget deficit had reached $600 million. (Louisiana is still servicing that debt.) Higher education appropriations were being trimmed annually.[4] The economic crisis triggered the Joint Committee on Economic Development and the Senate Commerce Committee to hire economic consultants from the northeast. The consultants had begun working in the late 1970s and early 1980s with legislatures in Massachusetts, Ohio, and Pennsylvania, states that had experienced rapid erosion in their major manufacturing sectors. The Louisiana study was done at about the same time as the studies for Arkansas, Kansas, Oklahoma, and Kentucky.

The central idea of the planning model was the remapping of traditional manufacturing economies into diversified, more versatile economies that emphasized small and medium-sized high technology business and industry. The primary outcome of the study was the Louisiana Science and Technology Foundation legislation, which was enacted in 1984 but not funded. The LSTF called for the encouragement of scientific and technological research (using an NSF model) that could be nurtured into commercial enterprises. It focused on:

- Creation of technology transfer mechanisms to move technology ideas into Louisiana businesses
- Fostering of entrepreneurial activity, including venture capital
- Creation of a science and technology policy board for the state. (Senate Bill 947, 1984)

According to one of the consultants interviewed, "Louisiana was one of our more depressing experiences. . . . The fatal flaw was that there were four key constitutional amendments, which were set to go before the voters regarding the funding mechanisms for the LSTF. But [the governor] was at that time faced with his indictment. He was not focused on legislation."

The LSTF policy language related to higher education was similar to that used by many higher education administrators at the time. Institutions in the early 1980s were experiencing the effects of the national recession, with declining enrollments and shrinking private support. In the process of retrenchment, administrators used adaptive fiscal strategies in seeking federal support for maintenance of laboratories, libraries, and research facilities. University presidents, in testimony before congressional committees from 1980 to 1985, used a reconstructed human capital ideology that linked higher education to economic development in order to seek funding from the national research system for their institutions, thus emphasizing benefits to the institutions and the state (Slaughter 1991). Ironies were embedded in the arguments, however, because higher education investments of interest to industry were (1) primarily for graduate education, and (2) usually restricted to science and engineering disciplines. Graduate education has been but a fraction, albeit a comparatively expensive fraction, of the total higher education need. The belief systems legitimated power structures while masking inequities. Policies allowed the power structure to help the institutions at the expense of the individual. By rebudgeting, institutional administrators were able to support new programs without requiring new money.

From a perspective of practice, the government elite's claim that higher education (graduate education and scientific research) could "almost instantly" (Sen 7, 19) produce technology was counter to what was known by the Board of Regents at that time (GSRI 1984). Gulf South Research Institute (GSRI), a quasi-public agency, prepared position papers that warned of the dangers in trying to link university research to economic development. For example, a GSRI report noted:

> Universities are generally represented in popular literature as important factors in industrial attraction. The empirical literature indicates that these relations are real but that they are far more modest than . . . suggested. . . . The major function of the university in economic development lies in the production of educated graduates. A special type of education is needed for technological development that should not be confused with issues of academic preeminence, even of preeminence in the sciences. (GSRI 1984, p. 12)

Thus, in a report prepared for the Board of Regents, the GSRI articulated the differences between the process of university education and the process of technology development. The GSRI author explained that many scholars were making the distinction between science and technology, but "they just weren't being heard" (GSRI 1984). In a report for the Board of Regents, GSRI (1985) offered a compromise position: "Nevertheless if technological activity is science-driven, then investments in science should then be the foundation of technological policy."

## *Policymakers' Narratives*

Statements by policy-actors revealed the ways in which specialized knowledge of higher education–economic development rhetoric, initially used by federal agencies, was used at the state level to influence public opinion. One higher education elite recalled:

> And Eric Bloch [director of the NSF] was around then, and doing a lot of stuff with NSF and how they could promote economic development . . . university-industry ties. And basically. . . . that was saying . . . if you . . . invest in these very specific areas in higher education, and you bring industry into this, you will get technology transfer and training in the right areas and economic development . . . we used the argument. I mean it wasn't only Erich Bloch that was doing it. . . . Bloch was making it visible . . . higher education is economic development in the nation, and productivity in the nation is dependent upon science. . . . Science is dependent upon higher education and so here's how you prime the pump to get economic development. (Interview A, 9, 9–35)

This long-term perspective, however, contradicts the public testimony of the bill's author in the Senate Education Committee hearing (May 30, 1985): "Higher education can almost *instantly* attract professors . . . get them into a nucleus at [a campus] and immediately transfer technology that provides jobs, a large number of jobs" (Sen, 9, 27–10, 1).

Another higher education elite explained why the federal rhetoric was adopted for the LEQSF program: "We added economic development to the LEQSF plan because of where the state was at the time—just at the precipice of the economic downturn. We knew Louisiana had to diversify to grow the economy. There was pressure from the Regents to add economic development to the plan" (Interview U, 4, 6–11).

A government elite said, "Those people who recognized that the revenues from oil and gas were starting to decline realized that something needed to be done and [the LEQSF program] kind of fit into a mind set that we already had and that was that education was important and that our natural resources should not just be exploited, but they should be used for spin-off industry that were more people-oriented" (Interview H, 3, 7–9).

"I don't think all of the nuances of what was taking place were generally understood," a government elite said. "But I think that . . . you can label something with education or economic development, and you . . . kind of mold it in such a way to make it palatable. And that's what we tried to do with the carrot of new jobs and a better economy. We were able to pull some people along that ordinarily wouldn't have voted for some . . . more esoteric sort of legislation (Interview H, 4, 12–18).

A higher education elite summarized the situation thus:

> As I recall, [economic development] was something they needed to make it pass. . . . around the time there were a lot of arguments about . . . trying to convince Louisianans they had to put more money into education because their economic problems were a result of bad education. And I know that was the first time I had seen it in the state where that issue had really been visible and kinda' crystallized, and really gotten across to the legislature. Previous to that, my impression from talking to people was, "Oh, yea, ho-hum, yea, sure, education and economic development." But this was a time when it really did seem to hit. Remember it was a time when oil had just gone down.

Success in the LEQSF case was attributable to skillful policy agents and timing. In the reformists' favor, the state's first major economic crisis since the Great Depression was looming on the horizon, and ideology used in the LEQSF campaign proposed to fix it. The program also fit within the general context of 1980s neoconservatism, because no new taxes were necessary. It was as if ideologies employed by the higher education and business elite had effectively assumed the status of hegemonic "common sense" ideology, as Miron (1992) would have described it. Other factors contributing to reformist success were that the tax windfall funds were anticipated but not in hand and that, because of his pending indictment, the populist governor did not interfere with the good government initiative. Finally, major media and grassroots campaigns were launched to make the project visible and to garner public support. The constitutional amendment to establish the LEQSF programs was approved by the legislature in July 1986 and established by public referendum in November 1986.

The reformist alliance borrowed the rhetoric of reconstructed human capital theory from federal agencies to justify the funding of higher education for purposes of state economic enhancement. Rather than focusing on education's rewards to the individual, the altered theory focused on rewards to society. Arguments used by proponents of SB 105 (1985) linked scientific research in the university, to be supported with tax windfall funds, to immediate technological rewards for the revitalization the state's crippled economy. Although some

higher education elites were aware of the illogical link between scientific research and immediate technological rewards, and although LEQSF policy
lacked provisions for venture capital funding or technology development and
commercialization, they used the economic rhetoric to persuade the legislature
and the voting public of the policy's virtues.

## Implications for Reconstructing Rationales

This case has implications for scholars who study lobbying in higher education and by lobbyists who construct new rationales for public funding. Three
aspects of the case are examined below.

First, the construction of new rationales seems necessary because of the decline of traditional patterns of public support for colleges and their students.
The decline was more extreme in Louisiana than in most other states, but most
states were confronted by some version of the decline in public support during the last two decades of the twentieth century. Moreover, with the new war
on terrorism and the desire to give taxpayers more money back, it is unlikely
that the old rationales for public funding will reinvigorate the public will to
fund higher education.

The Louisiana case mirrored the reconstruction of new scientific and economic rationales at the federal level. It also illustrates that appeals to economic
development and human capital were central to the construction of the new
political coalition. In addition, in Louisiana it was necessary to contend with
a populist version of human capital, an argument for putting money "immediately in the blood of children in the first through the sixth grades . . . the
most important place you can spend it." Many conservatives now argue that
funding schools should take priority over funding higher education. For example, Chester Finn (2001) recently argued against increasing support for federal student aid programs because K–12 reform was a higher priority if the goal
was to educate for the labor force. Ironically, Finn's reasoning for not refund-
ing federal need-based grants reads very much like the quote noted above. In
this context, the appeals for funding higher education, which has long-term
and indirect economic returns, is a difficult sell for lobbyists, especially if their
proposals are treated as alternatives to K–12 funding and programs.

In Louisiana, the new rationale that evolved had direct links to the interests
of business leaders and created a hope for new economy in the state. This rationale proved to play a role in fostering a new coalition of support for redi-

recting funds to higher education. The rationale of supporting technology transfer and applied research that can fuel economic development, in this instance, secured support for higher education. However, these arguments are persuasive not to general support, but for investment in crucial areas, such as information technology, science, and engineering. Therefore, advocates of funding colleges and studies must seek other rationales.

Second, the process of crafting new appeals for public funding is essentially political, requiring careful thought by lobbyists as well as by political and corporate representatives. However, different coalitions may be needed for different types of public funding. The coalition for funding scientific research might be different than the coalition that supports need-based grants in states. However, it is apparent that the nature of the appeals for and against funding will probably carry forward claims that appeal to constituents with different points of view. In Louisiana, it was necessary to hold the support of both populists and new conservatives.

The interviews with political elites in Louisiana revealed that they were aware that they were reconstructing the human capital rationale, a step that they viewed as necessary to extend their appeal to legislators with divergent points of view. Through the successive redrafts, legislation took shape that could hold together a coalition of conservatives and populists. The official texts—the bills and the testimony for the bills—made increasingly refined arguments that could hold together votes and public support for those votes. In Louisiana, it was crucial to bring some of the older populist rhetoric into alignment with the new conservative economic rationale. The interviews revealed that the lobbying community was aware of this process of incrementally reconstructing a rationale that held a new coalition together.

The implication of this finding is that to be successful, lobbyists should pay more attention to the types of rationales that different interest groups espouse as they reconstruct their proposals to build new coalitions for the support higher education. However, this process of crafting and recrafting arguments can be a slippery slope for higher education. For decades higher education sold itself based on its contributions to the economy and to human development. As new appeals are crafted to make appeals for funding, it is important to consider whether the arguments have merit and whether they represent the values of the academic community. Virtue should not be completely forsaken for funding. LEQSF had many virtues. However, human capital theory does not provide a sufficient rationale for creating an endowment of this type, especially

Table 9.1    State of Louisiana Economic Indicators

|  | 1980* | 1985 | 1990 | 1996 |
|---|---|---|---|---|
| *Per capita income*** |  |  |  |  |
| Louisiana | $8,672 | $11,634 | $14,279 | $19,824 |
| United States | $9,940 | $14,155 | $18,667 | $24,231 |
| Percent of average | 87 | 82 | 76 | 82 |
| *Gross state product, private industry sector**** |  |  |  |  |
| Louisiana | $58,364 | $76,581 | $84,341 | $102,980 |
| United States | $2,376,865 | $3,616,174 | $4,966,009 | $6,759,949 |
| Percent of total | 2.5 | 2.1 | 1.7 | 1.5 |

*Calendar years.
**U.S. Department of Commerce, Bureau of Economic Analysis, Regional Economic Measurement Division, Regional Economic Information System, CD-ROM. In DBER 1997.
***U.S. Department of Commerce, Bureau of Economic Analysis www.bea.gov/bea/regional/data.htm.

given that the funding could have long-term effects on technology but only modest effect on the labor force. But in the typical process of lobbying for higher education, the appeals were reconstructed to compete better with a wide range of political interests for constrained tax dollars. In the LEQSF case, a compromise was enacted that dedicated half of the funds to schools' improvement (Trammell 1996).

Third, it is crucial that advocates consider whether their claims will be borne out by empirical evidence if they are seeking ongoing funding. The interview results in this case indicate that the lobbyists and legislators were aware that they were making claims that might be difficult to prove. Funding research that focuses on local economic issues does not, in fact, have immediate economic returns (Table 9.1), as discussed above, but such claims were made as part of the rationale for LEQSF nevertheless.

According to a Board of Regents report (1996), since 1987 for every LEQSF dollar invested, $1.70 has been returned to the State of Louisiana. However, these dollars have not been adjusted for inflation. Furthermore, Bureau of Economic Analysis data indicate that between 1980 and 1990, average personal income in Louisiana declined slightly from 0.87 of the national average to 0.82 of the national average. Private Industry Sector productivity, as an indicator of state's economic health, actually declined from 2.5 percent of total National Gross National Product to 1.5 percent of GNP.

Since the fund was essentially an endowment based on a settlement with the oil industry, there was no reason to worry about the political fallout from this untested economic rationale. However, if new coalitions are trying to create rationales for funding colleges and college students from tax dollars, much more care should be taken to make arguments that have a chance for verification. Indeed, it is possible that higher education fell out of public favor because the public returns were not visible to the typical citizen or the majority of legislators. Therefore, while the rhetoric of the new science may provide a basis for arguing for funding of research and technology, it does not solve the problem of funding colleges and their students.

There is a clear need to think through the rationales used to argue for public funding for higher education. In most instances the new rationales for funding colleges and students will need to be made in ways that can be confirmed by empirical evidence. In these cases it is important that subsequent developments be related to the claims made when crafting new state finance policies, because legislators will remember the claims when voting on subsequent budgets. To lobby for funding year after year, colleges and their students need to point to the effects of public funding strategies.

The Louisiana case can help inform this process to the extent that lobbyists recognize the need to reconstruct their rationales and build new political coalitions. This will probably evolve through a reiterative process, much as the advocates of LEQSF collaborated on successive versions of the bill. However, unlike the Louisiana case, it will probably be necessary to think more critically and openly about the forms of evidence that will help the new political coalitions hold together year after year as they foster a new period of sustained investment in higher education.

NOTES

1. Formula funding for higher education fell rapidly in the first half of the 1980s. In 1981–82, formula funding was at 97.7 percent; in 1982–83, at 95.1 percent; in 1983–84, at 81.7 percent; in 1984–85, at 83.8 percent; and in 1985–86, at 68.6 percent (Board of Regents 1996).

2. House Bill 692 (1979) authorized the establishment of a research and development program to encourage basic research to promote the advancement of the state. The statute directed the Board of Regents to "promote strong links between industry and the public and independent colleges and universities in the state in conducting research." According to Sec. 3129.1(b) an advisory panel of representatives of industrial, scientific, and economic interests in the state were to make recommendations on research areas to be funded.

3. A note on the Michigan program indicated that there was a conscious effort to keep universities out of the economic development business since there was a tendency of universities and their boards to "bias decisions towards their own educational missions" (Board of Regents 1987, "Prosperity Through Academic Excellence," App. B, p. 2).

4. Board of Regents (1986), "Addressing the Budgetary Crisis in Higher Education: A Statewide Perspective," reported that public higher education institutions were facing a 5 percent cut, the eighth major cut in five years. The appropriation reduction for 1985–86 totaled $27,085,184; 60 percent of the cut would impact the LSU system (Attachment I).

REFERENCES

Becker, G. S. 1964. *Human capital: A theoretical and empirical analysis, with special reference to education.* New York: National Bureau of Economic Research and Columbia University Press.

Bloch, E. 1990. A Research and education base for the twenty-first century. In A. W. Betts and E. L. Gavlick, eds., *Proceedings of the forty-third annual conference on the advancement of research,* 77–88.

Bloland, H. G. 1995. Postmodernism and higher education. *Journal of Higher Education* 66 (5): 521–59.

Board of Regents. 1986a. *Addressing the budgetary crisis in higher education: A statewide perspective.* Baton Rouge, LA: Author.

Board of Regents. 1986b. LaSER (Louisiana Stimulus for Excellence in Research) implementation proposal for EPSCoR (Experimental Program to Stimulate Competitive Research) to NSF, March. Baton Rouge, LA.

Board of Regents. 1987. Louisiana higher education and economic development, prosperity through academic excellence, a white paper prepared by the LaSER Committee, June 1. Baton Rouge, LA.

Board of Regents. 1996. Information from Office of Fiscal Affairs, August 29. Baton Rouge, LA.

Brainard, J., and R. Southwick. 2001. A record year at the federal trough: Colleges feast on $1.67–billion in earmarks. *Chronicle of Higher Education* 47 (48) (August 10): A20–A38.

Chaffee, Ellen E. 1983. Role of rationality in university budgeting. *Research in Higher Education* 19 (4): 387–406.

Finn, C. E., Jr. 2001. College isn't for everyone. *USA Today,* 21 February, 14A.

Fischer, F. 1985. Critical evaluation of public policy: A methodological case study. In *Critical theory and public life,* ed. J. Forester, 231–57. Cambridge: MIT Press.

Giddens, A. 1984. *The constitution of society.* Berkeley: University of California Press.

Governor's Economic Development Commission. November 13, 1985. Report to Governor Edwin W. Edwards: Tax policy for economic development: Louisiana's expenditure policy; Future policy directions. Baton Rouge, LA: Author.

Gulf South Research Institute (GSRI). 1984. *A technology program for Louisiana.* Prepared for the Board of Regents, Office of the Governor, and the Department of Natural Resources. December. Baton Rouge, LA: Author

Gulf South Research Institute (GSRI). 1985. *A technology program for Louisiana: Background papers.* Prepared for the Board of Regents, Office of the Governor, and the Department of Natural Resources, April. Baton Rouge, LA: Author.

Honeyman, D. S., and M. Bruhn. 1996. The financing of higher education. In *A struggle to survive: Funding higher education in the next century,* ed. D. S. Honeyman, J. L. Wattenbarger, and K. C. Westbrook, 1–28. Thousand Oaks, CA: Corwin.

Kleinman, D. L. 1995. *Politics on the endless frontier: Postwar research policy in the United States.* Durham, NC: Duke University Press.

Leslie, L. L., and P. T. Brinkman. 1988. *The economic value of higher education.* New York: American Council on Education and Macmillan.

*Louisiana Almanacs, 1986–87.* Gretna, LA: Pelican.

Louisiana, House Committee on Appropriations, Minutes of Meeting, 1985 Regular Session, June 24, 1985.

Louisiana, Senate Archives, Legislative History of SB 105 (1985) and SB 522(1985).

Louisiana, Senate Education Committee Hearing, May 25, May 30, 1985. Cassette tape.

Marshall, C., and G. B. Rossman. 1989. *Designing qualitative research.* Newbury Park, CA: Sage.

Matkins, G. W. 1990. *Technology transfer and the University* American Council on Education/Oryx Press.

Miron, L. F. 1992. Corporate ideology and the politics of entrepreneurism in New Orleans. *Antipodes* 24 (4): 263–88.

Noble, D. D. 1991. *The classroom arsenal.* London: Falmer Press.

Popkewitz, T. S. 1991. *A political sociology of educational reform.* New York: Teachers College Press.

Rensberger, B. 1992. Scientist shortfall a myth—NSF study seriously flawed, panel is told. *Washington Post,* 9 April.

Riessman, C. K. 1993. *Narrative analysis.* Newbury Park, CA: Sage.

Roe, E. 1994. *Narrative policy analysis, theory and practice.* Durham, NC: Duke University Press.

St. John, E. P. 1994. *Prices, productivity and investment, assessing financial strategies in higher education.* ASHE-ERIC Report No. 3. Washington, DC: George Washington University Press.

St. John, E. P. 2003. *Refinancing the college dream: Access, equal opportunity, and justice for taxpayers.* Baltimore: Johns Hopkins University Press.

Slaughter, S. E. 1991. The "official" ideology of higher education: Ironies and inconsistencies. In *Culture and ideology in higher education: Advancing a critical agenda,* ed. W. G. Tierney, 59–86. New York: Praeger.

Slaughter, S. 1993. Retrenchment in the 1980s: The politics of prestige and gender. *Journal of Higher Education* 64 (3): 250–82.

Spradley, J. P. 1979. *The ethnographic interview.* New York: Harcourt Brace, Jovanovich College Publisher.

Trammell, M. L. 1996. An interpretive and critical analysis of the Louisiana education quality support fund policy construction. Unpublished manuscript. University of New Orleans.

Tyack, D. B. 1974. *The one best system.* Cambridge: Harvard University Press.

Wirt, F. M., and M. W. Kirst. 1972. *Political and social foundations of education.* Berkeley, CA: McCutchan.

# CHAPTER TEN

# Financing Instructional Technology and Distance Education

## Reviewing Costs and Outcomes

## James Farmer

In the late 1960s and 1970s computer-based training (CBT) appeared to provide new alternatives for meeting public policy goals of universal access to higher education, equal opportunity for success, and sharply lower unit costs of instruction. Research has confirmed that instructional and learning technologies, offered as distance learning or complementing classroom instruction, are as effective as traditional classroom instruction, especially for marginally prepared students, and that it increases access, retention, and completion.

But these benefits have been elusive because the cost of instruction using these technologies at most colleges and universities exceeds available funding. The history of technology funding in colleges and universities suggests students do not receive these benefits. In the traditional college delivery system, students incur the cost of traveling to class and the inconvenience or barrier of class schedules, and they benefit from more effective methods of learning. Students will evaluate the costs of instruction relative to the costs and convenience of alternatives. This suggests that in some cases students might be seeking lower costs, but in other cases students or employers might care more about convenience.

In public colleges and universities, states subsidize a share of the costs of higher education as well, which is why the costs of technology are of concern to states. If technology is to be treated as a lower-cost option than traditional delivery systems, then it is essential that the costs be comparable to the alternative. In particular, some state officials might be concerned about the economies achieved by distance education.

For distance education to become economically viable, it will take changes in colleges and universities that transcend the boundaries of finance and instruction. Some faculty must become more specialized in authoring learning materials. Academic planners will have to segment the market based on student characteristics and then make the most appropriate methods of teaching and learning available to each segment. Business officers will have to explore market segment pricing. Federal, state, and local governments will need to recognize the benefits of improved learning technology and increase their contribution to higher education for these benefits—a sharp departure from the trends of the past decade. If all of these can be accomplished, new models of course delivery will become viable, and students and society will benefit from this cooperative effort.

This chapter examines the rationales for public funding of distance education in colleges and universities, using costs and outcomes as considerations. It then presents a case study examining the instructional cost of interactive instructional television (IITV) in Arizona to illustrate the financial challenge facing efforts to reduce cost through distance education. Recommendations for improved use of the technology and funding follow.

## Rationales and Realities

The investment in course materials can become a barrier to widespread use of instruction and learning technology. As computer-savvy, Internet-using, computer-game-playing youth become the new students, their expectations for the quality of instructional materials may increase the cost the way the cost of motion pictures increased—about 10 percent per year—to meet the expectations of the young audience. As more students work while attending college, the methods of instruction will have to accommodate these limitations the way Executive MBA programs have accommodated harried executives, and community colleges have turned to new forms of instruction that exploit the flexibility and effectiveness of learning technology. To have a long, useful life, learning materials will have to be designed for the student of 2005 or 2010, not for the student today. Knowing the trend in the quality of learning materials, projections can be made about the level of investment that must be made.

There are price constraints, however. The cost of learning materials and the associated networking infrastructure must have sufficient utilization—class size—to amortize the investment over a large number of users. The key to amortizing the high cost of multimedia learning materials for a large number of students is to standardize learning content and ensure that it is interoperable with almost all learning management systems and virtual learning environments. If this were done, then the publishing industry or collaborations could play a major role in supplying learning content to colleges and universities at prices that yield costs of instruction comparable to those of the traditional classroom.

Some college presidents, especially in rural community colleges, are making the decision to employ instruction and learning technologies to provide access even though this requires internal subsidization from other programs. Some college presidents are also making the decision to employ these technologies solely to benefit students who otherwise could not attend the scheduled classes, again accepting higher costs in order to better serve the community.

To better understand the actions that need to be taken to achieve sustainable costs of instruction and the trade-off decisions that must be made both at the local level and at the state and federal level, it is useful to analyze what is known about these students and the experience in offering broadcast television, interactive instructional television, and Internet delivery. Some limited experience demonstrates the benefits of using multimedia learning materials in the traditional classroom.

The new students will come to college when use of the Internet is as ubiquitous as television and they use new media every day. A recent study shows that current eighth graders already play computer games more than they read for enjoyment. This still remains less than the time spent watching television.

With the support of the U.S. Department of Commerce, colleges began installing microwave links providing two-way video and audio links between the source of the class and students at remote locations in the 1980s. Called Interactive Instructional Television (IITV), this approach was successfully used by Arizona community colleges to bring instruction into remote small towns throughout the state. Broadcast television was successfully used by Coast (California) Community College District and the Dallas County Community College district to make courses available throughout a large urban area, and they became major suppliers of broadcast video courses. The University of Nebraska used broadcast television to bring classes to rural areas. Policymakers funded such projects to make rich and varied academic programs available in areas where low population density could not support a college or university.

The availability of the Internet has moved learning from the computer laboratory to learning at work and home. It has moved the source of learning from the nearby college or university to anywhere in the world. And it has sharply reduced the cost of networking.

With these successes, what are the barriers to widespread use of instructional technology? These barriers are investment in learning materials, a major capital expense; computing infrastructure, now almost complete; and quality control. And who will pay? Students, as they do with books or special computing fees? Faculty who have contributed to both textbooks and early eLearning materials? Or the colleges and universities as part of the education expenditures such as the library?

The key to low unit costs will be the number of students who use the same learning material, not the cost of development. Funding for this effective method will be a combination of lowering unit costs—to make it economically viable—and some additional revenue reflecting the improved productivity. This will require several steps on the part of the colleges and universities collectively; or ultimately, the free-market, morphing from the training perspective, will extend the corporate training model into postsecondary education.

There are several models of success in distance learning. One is the use of networked audio and video, which has effectively increased class size and lowered unit costs. Several of the colleges became sources of video material that was licensed to other colleges, sharing the investment for their development. Typical license costs were $600 to $1,500 per semester course, independent of the number of students. The costs of the broadcasts were generally contributed or subsidized as a "public service" required as a condition of having a television broadcast license. This model was especially effective in urban areas that would have larger student enrollments within the area of broadcast reception. Another use of networked audio and video was the remote classroom, which increased the class size. Often the additional networking cost would still reduce unit costs as class size increased. This was particularly effective in community college districts that had several remote campuses in small cities or towns. Another, more contemporary model is Internet delivery, a return to the computer-based training (CBT) model using current technology.

Perhaps the most successful example is the British Open University that began using the broadcast technology model in 1975 and is continuing its transition to the Internet delivery model. Open University has demonstrated how a large investment in learning materials can be amortized over a large student enrollment to achieve low unit costs. The British Open University has succeeded when the publishing industry in the United States failed because of one factor—the ability to attract large enrollments. Open University's US$1 billion investment in its undergraduate curriculum is being amortized over an average class size of 11,000, with the lowest class size of 800.[1]

Rio Salado College, a Maricopa County (Phoenix) community college specializing in nontraditional instruction, provides a large number of Internet courses. Their courses are typically developed by their faculty. The college has created a teaching model that is effective and a business model that is viable, with course delivery costs comparable to, or lower than, the other Maricopa community colleges.[2]

Most distance learning now combines the features of all of the early models. In addition, distance learning techniques have been added to many "traditional" courses to improve learning. In general, distance learning instruction has been found to be as effective as, but perhaps no more effective than, classroom instruction. Crump (1928) found no difference in test scores of college classroom students and correspondence students enrolled in the same subjects. Hanna (1940) even found correspondence study students performed as well as or better than their classroom counterparts. Similar results were recently reported for interactive instructional television. Recent results showed no significant difference between the remote and non-remote groups (McGreal 1994b). Recently Schlosser and Anderson (1994) reported that students learn equally well from lessons delivered with any medium. Face-to-face or at a distance, there is no inherent significant difference in the educational effectiveness of media. Sorensen (1995) reported no differences in achievement between students in traditional classes and those in distance-delivered classes, or between distance students at remote sites and those at origination sites where a teacher is present. If this is true, then the focus can be on the costs rather than differences of effectiveness.

Two observations suggest that there are differences that effect enrollment. First, focus groups continue to report that students prefer classroom instruction. An unpublished study shows that students will commute further to a traditional classroom that they will to an IITV classroom offering the same course.[3] This suggests that traditional student enrollments may be minimally affected by the type of media used in a course. However, this observation may not be relevant since distance learning is primarily used where students cannot conveniently be in a classroom because of either distance or schedule. And second, Rio Salado College has observed that text-based Internet courses are enrolling a larger proportion of older students than other courses with multimedia. This suggests the use of instructional media may affect enrollment of younger more than older students (Farmer 1996).[4]

Yavapai College introduced multimedia in the classroom for Biology 101—a key course for allied health and pre-medicine professionals (Farmer 1996; Gaff, Ratcliff, and Associates 1996). When it was introduced, course completion rates increased from 60 to over 80 percent. Increases were greatest for a section that taught using graphic media, in a linear format. Subsequent developments included a hypermedia format to permit immediate changes in response to student needs and interests (Gaff, Ratcliff, and Associates 1996).

Over the past decade, computer-based instruction (CBI) or computer-based learning (CBL) and computer-based training (CBT), both based on the same educational technologies, have taken on different meaning and different economics. The term *training* is typically used for corporate programs; the terms *instruction* or *learning* for colleges and universities. As used here, training and instruction have sharply different economics. Employees are students of corporate training; their wages and travel expenses are part of the corporate "cost of instruction." For professionals such as airline pilots, these costs can be as high as $500 per hour of instruction.[5] The number of students taking the same training tends to be much higher than the average course size in higher education. For this reason, the unit cost of instruction for corporate training tends to be insensitive to the investment cost of course materials.

Because the course content for training can be similar for a number of companies or agencies, commercial training materials are frequently used. Because of the quantity and low price sensitivity, an active market for corporate training materials exists for common subjects. Sophisticated learning materials that reduce student time are cost-effective for business. These economics are not available in higher education, where students bear the cost of their time and travel and these costs are not included in the cost of instruction borne by the college or university. The students, their employers, and society, rather than the college or university, benefit from increased productivity.

The economic models of instructional technology and distance learning in this chapter use the cost of instruction as defined for colleges and universities. As the knowledge economy grows and the scope of corporate training expands, "publishers" of these courses are beginning to market them to traditional colleges and universities. The University of Phoenix has adopted some of the corporate training practices. Course content is determined and course materials developed centrally; course and instructor evaluations are used to continuously revise both the course materials and teaching methods and to insure the quality of course delivery at any location.[6]

There are two important differences in the cost of distance learning as compared to the traditional classroom. Except for interactive instructional television, which uses an instructor teaching in a classroom, there are significant costs for the development of instructional media. In the past, the instructor had the responsibility for writing textbooks. These textbooks were in turn printed and sold to students. The cost of the textbook principally was the cost of printing, binding, and distribution. The professor wrote the text at no cost to the institution and for a small royalty from students who purchased the text. The professor "subsidized" the preparation of the instructional materials, and the cost of the professor's royalty, if any, was borne by the student, not the college.

The textbook business has changed. Textbooks are "published" where the publisher has responsibilities for contributing to the development of the content, for choosing images such as charts and graphs that are included in the textbook, for developing workbooks and other student materials, and for producing multimedia instructional materials and instructor's guides that accompany the text. These costs are borne by the student in terms of higher costs for textbooks.[7]

With new forms of instruction such as Internet courses, television courses (telecourses), and computer-based instruction courses, the costs for the development of the media is being borne by the college producing the materials or by the author—which may be someone other than the professor. When these costs are borne by the college, then they should be included in the cost of the course in computing course costs and unit costs.

Some colleges have attempted to license course materials to others. This has been successful for telecourses used for broadcast television. Users pay a fixed fee plus an increment for each enrollment. Some Internet courses are being licensed for similar amounts, but it appears there is insufficient enrollment at this time to make this economically viable.[8] When media are licensed, then the cost of the license rather than the cost of media development is included in the course costs and unit costs.

Typical costs of instruction range from several hundred dollars per course

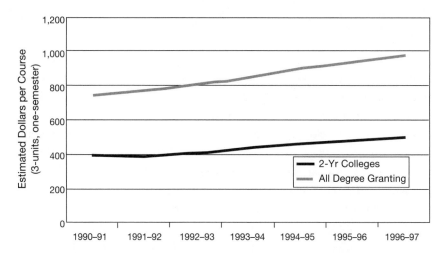

*Figure 10.1.* Average National Cost of Course Delivery. (Based on *Digest of education statistics 2001,* National Center for Education Statistics, Tables 349 and 351.)

for low-tuition public colleges to several thousand dollars per course for private colleges and universities. National averages for two-year and for all colleges is shown in Figure 10.1. As seen in Figure 10.1, it is difficult for any college to absorb the cost of development of television courses or even computer-based instruction courses. Internet courses take several hundred enrollments over the life of the course to achieve costs per enrollment that are comparable to current costs of instruction or textbook costs.

Although it is possible to achieve break-even enrollments for the most popular courses—much as telecourses do—significant issues will arise in developing multimedia materials for specialized courses.

In summary, although there are indications that multimedia course materials associated with instructional technology will increase enrollments and completions, these benefits are not sufficiently acknowledged to include in the analysis (Farmer 1996).[9] There are also indications that "screenager" students will prefer multimedia with their higher and increasing development costs. This will affect enrollments; however, this effect will not be included in the analysis until it has been quantified.

## Case Study

In the 1990s, I consulted with the community college system in Arizona on the evaluation of IITV courses. Interactive Instructional Television (IITV) refers to teaching using two-way video and audio between a classroom with an instructor and a remote classroom. The instructor can see students in the remote classroom on a television monitor. If there is more than one remote classroom, then multiple classrooms can be shown on the instructor's monitor or monitors, or the monitor can show remote classrooms in sequence, or show only the classroom from which a student may be speaking. The students will always see the instructor or the classroom from which a student is speaking on the monitor in the student's classroom. In some installations the student's voice is always heard—the sounds of a typical classroom—and in others the student speaks using a "press to talk" microphone or an automatic sound control that transmits sound only from the location with the highest volume.[10]

To analyze the costs for interactive instructional television, it is useful to begin with a typical configuration (Figure 10.2). Four levels are shown: Classrooms that originate or receive the instruction and the control center are typically found at colleges and community college district. When colleges are linked together, an additional layer—the "distributor" is added. As national networks expand, the typical IITV network will also be connected to extranet course suppliers. The case study below summarizes results of the evaluation using this framework.

In this typical IITV network, Site 1 is a college or community college district that has communications with one or more campuses or sites. As shown, Sites (campuses) 2, 3, and 4 have electronic classrooms. They are connected through a "control center" that, as shown, is located at Site 1. The control center typically has a nearby electronic classroom. The control center has electronic equipment for switching video and audio, and equipment for video and audio conferencing.[11] It may have full-time staff—the typical implementation—or it may have part-time staff with automatic switching that has been set up previously.[12] Most electronic classrooms may be used to both originate and receive IITV instruction.

The network diagram in Figure 10.2 shows a "distributor." Colleges and universities are now planning to connect to other networks that are originating instructional television. For example, Western Governors' University has considered originating IITV instruction and has identified institutions that may

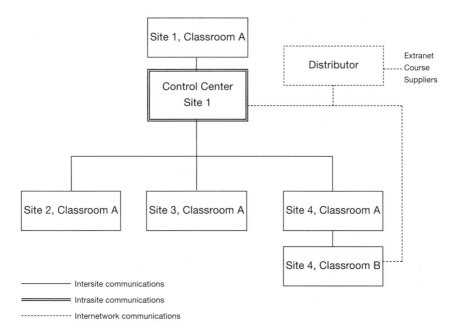

*Figure 10.2.* Typical IITV Network

serve as sources of IITV. Broadcast television, usually obtained by satellite transmission, could be a source of instruction on the IITV network as well.[13] In Virginia, the Northern Virginia Community College plays this role by scheduling instruction originating at one community college to be received by one or more other community colleges. Arizona Learning Systems is planning a similar role for the Arizona community colleges. Both rely on ATM communications networks.[14] In this diagram both could be considered "distributors" of IITV, whether the courses originated from one of their "customer" colleges or from an external source such as the Western Governors' University or the Dallas County Community Colleges.

Distributors may have equipment used for switching and have multipoint control units for conferencing classrooms. In general, the distributor may have the same functions, equipment, and staff as a control center, but the distributor operates at a different organizational level.

The distributor could be connected to external providers of broadcast television, audio programming, and video conferencing as well as interactive instructional television.[15] Depending on the communications technology, the

*Table 10.1    Costs of a Typical College IITV Control Center*

| Description | Typical | Estimated |
|---|---|---|
| ATM communications switch | $10,000–25,000 | $20,000 |
| Multipoint control unit | 100,000–150,000 | 125,000 |
| Audio mixing and control | 10,000–25,000 | 25,000 |
| Video conferencing station | 4,500 each | 9,000 |
| Video monitors | 1,000–2,000 each | 6,000 |
| Speakers and headsets | | 1,400 |
| Racks and furniture | | 4,000 |
| Total, manual operation | | $190,400 |
| Computer for automated operation | | 5,000 |
| Software for scheduling communications circuits | | 15,000 |
| Software for scheduling classrooms | | 12,000 |
| Total, automated operation | | $222,400 |

"distributor" could connect to a classroom through the control center or could connect directly to an electronic classroom.[16]

Costs for IITV are developed at three levels. There are costs associated with the control center, which should be allocated to all of the classrooms. Generally this allocation is made on the basis of the number of hours the classroom is used per week.[17] For term-based colleges and universities, the number of course hours in all of the classrooms that are used for IITV under that control center is used for this allocation.[18] If the control center is used for courses from a distributor or extranet course supplier, then that use would be included as well.

Each classroom has costs associated with it as well. These costs can be allocated to courses on the basis of the course hours. Thus, a course has two allocated costs—the cost of the control facility that are allocated across all classrooms in accordance with their utilization, and the cost of the classroom based on the course hours for a particular course.

For consistency, the examples in this chapter will use cost per course to mean the cost of education or cost of instruction for a three-credit-hour lower-division course. Other units may be more appropriate in a different context. The configuration of equipment, typical costs, and an estimated cost is given in Table 10.1 for control centers that are being installed now.[19] The cost for manual operation assumes that an operator is available at all times that a classroom is being used.

By adding computer hardware and specialized software, it is possible to auto-

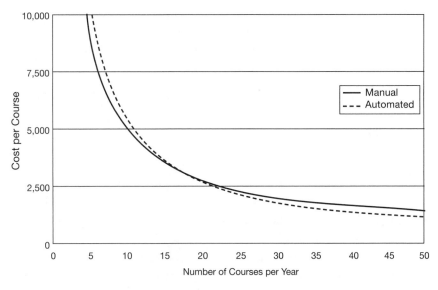

*Figure 10.3.* Average Cost per Course for Control Center Operations

mate the operation of the Control Center.[20] In this example, it is less expensive to automate the control center if more than 17 IITV courses are offered per year. The real value of automation comes when the number of courses per year is more than 25, as shown in Figure 10.3. A typical college with a two-channel system will use the IITV system more than 50 hours per week, which would be more than 60 courses per year.[21] However, even with this level of utilization the course costs will be significant as compared to other costs (Table 10.2).

Table 10.3 gives the detailed costs per course for 50 courses per year. Equipment amortization is the most significant cost for either manual or automated

*Table 10.2  Average Course Costs for Control Center Operation*

| Number of Courses per Year | Manual | Automated |
| --- | --- | --- |
| 25 | 2,323 | 2,163 |
| 50 | 1,401 | 1,081 |
| 75 | 1,094 | 721 |
| 100 | 941 | 541 |
| 125 | 849 | 433 |
| 150 | 787 | 360 |
| 175 | 743 | 309 |
| 200 | 710 | 270 |

*Table 10.3    Distribution of Course Costs for Control Center Operations*
(50 courses per year)

|  | Manual | Automated |
|---|---|---|
| Amortization of equipment | $685 | $801 |
| Equipment maintenance | 190 | 222 |
| Maintenance and operation of plant | 46 | 46 |
| Personnel costs | 480 | 160 |
| Total | $1,401 | $1,229 |

operation. The costs for control center operation do not include the costs for a director or manager. The decisions on which courses to offer and when to offer these courses should be included as academic support and are not included in these direct costs.

Each electronic classroom has provisions for displaying a received video channel at sufficient size and resolution to be seen by all in the room and accompanying audio with high-fidelity speakers that can be heard throughout room. The display should have sufficient microphones that all students can be heard. There should be sufficient video cameras to cover the entire classroom. These cameras may be locally or remotely controlled—the typical configuration when staff are used to control videography—or they can be automated to focus on the speaker (regardless of site) or on the person who has pressed a microphone "push to talk" switch.

Electronic classrooms used for the origination of instruction have cameras to show the instructor and any blackboard (whiteboard) or easel pad used by the instructor; a camera to show documents or displays such as experiments—called a "pad" camera; and connections to show videos, computer displays, or other sources of video, images, or audio the instructor has selected.

Following the television paradigm, early installations of IITV used an engineer to operate the cameras, usually remotely, and to select the source of the video and audio.[22] This choice was necessary because of the complex wiring and switches and because of the knowledge and effort that were required to produce a video stream that followed the instructor's needs and to focus on students in either the local or remote classroom who had comments or questions.

Digital technology has permitted some of these tasks to be automated. Wireless transmitters are now followed by a camera; the instructor wears a micro-transmitter. Computer programs can now analyze the video stream and focus

Table 10.4  Typical IITV Electronic Classrooms

|  | Type S | Type C | Type T |
|---|---|---|---|
| Number of students | 4–12 | 1–3 | 8–24 |
| Location | Conference room | Cubicle | Classroom |
| Technology | Videoconferencing | Desktop videoconferencing | High-resolution video |
| Classroom and equipment costs | $35,000 | $9,000 | $100,000 |
| Utilization for coursework (typical hours per week) | 39 | 36 | 57 |
| Site personnel | None | None | 1 |
| Space, site (in square feet) | 200 | 70 | 1200 |
| Communications | 0.5 T1 | 0.25 T1 | T3 |

the camera on motion—typically the instructor moving or talking.[23] Similarly, cameras can be preset and focus on students who "press to talk."

Characteristics of three typical classrooms are given in Table 10.4. The most frequent in Arizona community colleges is Type S. Each classroom is equipped with television monitors for faculty and students. One or more cameras are used in the originating and each remote classroom, and microphones and sound system are installed in all classrooms. This could be analog broadcast television operated over microwave (Arizona Western, Mohave, and Yavapai Colleges, for example) or could be operated over digital circuits (Central Arizona College and Northland Pioneer College). Type C is a proposed method of extending participation to very small groups—one or two students at a cubical. This arrangement would use the current ISO-standard desktop videoconferencing equipment and protocols.[24] The Type T electronic classroom includes large screen projection displays or several extra large monitors with sufficient luminance to permit students to read and take notes, automated "follow me" cameras, and direct connections to such sources as computers, Internet, VCR decks, and live television under control of the instructor.[25]

Although most Type S classrooms currently require an operator, Central Arizona College has demonstrated that camera automation and instructor control can replace the operators at each site. Operators may be required for the electronic classroom, though forthcoming implementations suggest an operator at

*Table 10.5   Fixed Costs for Receiving Sites*

|  | Type S: Conference Room | Type C: Cubicle | Type T: Classroom |
|---|---|---|---|
| Equipment amortization | $6,300 | $1,620 | $18,000 |
| Equipment maintenance | 1,750 | 450 | 5,000 |
| Operation of physical plant | 2,280 | 2,280 | 7,980 |
| Communications | 7,800 | 3,900 | 54,000 |
| Total fixed costs | $18,130 | $8,250 | $84,980 |

the remote site is not necessary and may even impede an instructor's responding to classroom activity. To meet broadcast television standards, a high bandwidth (T3) communications channel or analog television channels would be required. Currently, Central Arizona College is transmitting and receiving two channels on a standard T1 telephone line. Northland Pioneer is using similar bandwidth.[26]

The configurations will continue to evolve as commodity-priced electronics replace classical analog television equipment and as automation becomes more widely available.[27] The fixed costs for the remote receiving site for the three typical implementations of IITV distance learning are given in Table 10.5.[28]

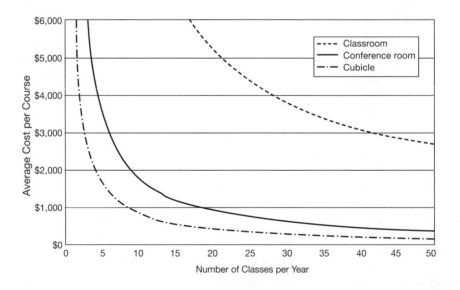

*Figure 10.4.* Average Allocation of Fixed Costs per Course for an Electronic Classroom

Table 10.6 *Incremental Cost per Course for Typical Number of Courses at a Single Site*

| | Case S | Case C | Case T |
|---|---|---|---|
| Location | Conference room | Cubicle | Classroom |
| Technology | Videoconferencing | Desktop videoconferencing | Electronic classroom |
| Courses per term | 13 | 12 | 19 |
| Incremental cost per course | | | |
| Equipment amortization | $194 | $54 | $379 |
| Equipment maintenance | 54 | 15 | 105 |
| Communications | 240 | 130 | 1,137 |
| Site personnel | 0 | 0 | 720 |
| Space, lease and maintenance | 70 | 76 | 168 |
| Total direct costs per course | $558 | $275 | $2,509 |
| Allocation of control center costs (single site) | 1,690 | 1,802 | 1,150 |
| Total costs per course | $2,248 | $2,077 | $3,660 |

These fixed costs are then distributed over all courses that use the classroom. The average allocation is dependent on the number of courses that are taught per week.[29] The average allocation of those fixed costs per course associated with the classroom is shown in Figure 10.4.

Using costs for the configurations of electronic classrooms described above (Table 10.5), allocating the fixed costs in Table 10.6 over the number of courses offered per year (approximately 2.5 times the number offered per term), the course costs are given in Table 10.6 for a single three-credit course. These costs include costs of the Control Center allocated to a single site. It is important to note that it requires 12 to 19 courses being offered at the same time to achieve the average course costs in Table 10.6.

Table 10.6 provided the per-course costs of instruction. This is a single site example; all of the costs of the Control Center as well as the classroom costs were allocated to these courses. In Figure 10.5 the cost per student enrollment is shown for average class sizes. This assumes that class size applies to all of the courses that are offered at that site. The same data are shown in Figure 10.6.

The average class size for rural community colleges in Arizona is reported to be 16 to 20 students. The average class size for distance learning is 24 to 32 students at one to two remote sites.[30] These data can be used to develop an example.

Those community colleges with established IITV programs typically use

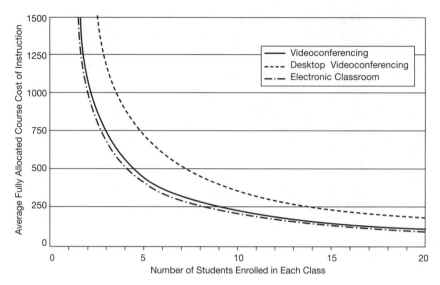

*Figure 10.5.* Average Fully Allocated Cost of Instruction per Student Enrollment for a Single Site

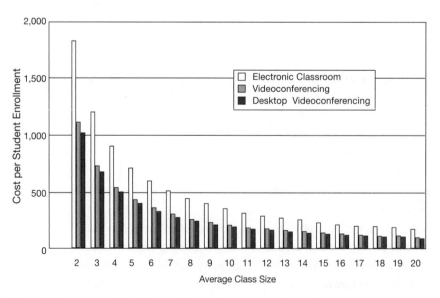

*Figure 10.6.* Average Fully Allocated Cost of Instruction, Single Site

Table 10.7   Computation of a Typical Number of Student Enrollments in a Course

| Factor | Number |
|---|---|
| Courses per term | 10 |
| Terms | 2.5 |
| Students per remote site | 10 |
| Remote sites | 2 |
| Student originating site | 12 |
| Number of units at remote sites | 500 |

their systems from 40 to 56 hours per week; an average of 15 courses is reasonable. Using recent data, there would be 10 students at a remote site with 12 at the originating or "local" site for a total of 32 students per course. Although most Arizona community colleges have one remote site, recent enhancements have increased the number of remote sites from one to two. These values are listed in Table 10.7, and the resulting number of student enrollments in distance learning courses provides the basis for developing unit costs—that is, cost per course enrollment. The cost of instruction at the originating site is adjusted from 16 to 12 students, increasing this cost from $230 to $307 per student. The costs at the remote site are based on the 500 units from Table 10.7.

The cost of the control center is allocated to the courses and then to the student enrollments. This remains the most significant of the distance learning costs.

In Arizona community colleges, distance learning is typically used to increase access rather than to increase class size. That is, additional instructors or teaching assistants are not required to accommodate additional students since the combined class size is not greater that the maximum class size.[31] For this reason, the cost of the instructor is not included in these distance learning costs, assuming that the increased enrollment can be accommodated by the classroom instructor. In this example the instructor had 12 students in the classroom at the originating site and 20 students at remote sites. This is a total of 32 students, still less than the maximum class size of 35 for teaching this subject.

The costs in Table 10.8 are incremental unit costs for distance learning and do not include the costs of academic support, student services, institutional support,[32] and maintenance and operation of physical plant. The costs in Table 10.9 include these costs, using the adjustments to student services for the reduced use of these services and to physical plant operations for facilities that

Table 10.8    *Cost of Instruction per Student Enrollment in a Course*

|  | Originating Site | Remote Site |
|---|---|---|
| Cost of instruction | $307 |  |
| Amortization of equipment |  | $25 |
| Equipment maintenance |  | 7 |
| Maintenance and operation of plant |  | 5 |
| Personnel costs |  | 16 |
| Communication costs |  | 16 |
| Total direct classroom costs | $307 | $68 |
| Control center |  | 180 |
| Total | $307 | $249 |

are not used and therefore do not require maintenance. These costs are also shown in Figure 10.7.

The costs of IITV instruction is compared with those with those of traditional classroom instruction in Table 10.10 and Figure 10.8. These costs include the cost of maintaining facilities, but not the cost of building the facilities.

Although one of the interests in instructional technology has been to avoid the cost of buildings, this analysis does not include those costs. Brief computations show that these costs may not be significant compared to other costs associated with IITV. For example, a 70-square-foot student workstation can support 20 student course enrollments per term, or 50 per year at full utilization. The cost of building the physical facilities would be about $10,000 to $20,000. With a 20-year life, this would add about $10 to $20 per course enrollment to the cost of education. Better estimates of this cost would depend upon additional data on the cost of construction and the cost of plant maintenance—which were included in this analysis—and utilization rates of these facilities.

The average costs developed in the examples use data from the Arizona

Table 10.9    *Fully Allocated Cost of Education per Student Enrollment in a Single Course*

|  | Originating Site | Remote Site |
|---|---|---|
| Cost of instruction | $307 | $249 |
| Academic support | 50 | 50 |
| Student services | 44 | 22 |
| Institutional support | 83 | 83 |
| Physical plant operations | 46 | 23 |
| Total cost of education | $530 | $427 |

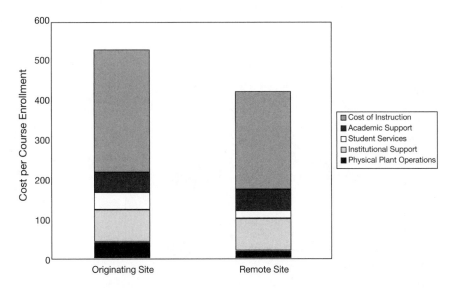

*Figure 10.7.* Costs per Course Enrollment, Recent IITV in Arizona Community Colleges

community colleges—a group of colleges that rank high nationally in efficient instruction. The examples are those where a college has, over a period of time, developed an effective IITV programs and where there is still unmet need in remote locations.

Unit costs increase sharply when utilization rates are not high. A college must offer from 10 to 20 courses per term in order for the costs to be reasonably comparable to those of the traditional classroom. This implies a major investment in facilities and, by the faculty, in course development.

The model developed here was based on traditional costing methodologies developed for colleges and universities. This makes some assumptions about instruction and about the student's need and use of academic support, student

*Table 10.10   Comparative Cost per Course Enrollment*

|  | Traditional Classroom | IITV |
|---|---|---|
| Cost of instruction | $230 | $280 |
| Academic support | 50 | 50 |
| Student services | 44 | 34 |
| Institutional support | 83 | 83 |
| Physical plant operations | 46 | 35 |
| Total | $453 | $483 |

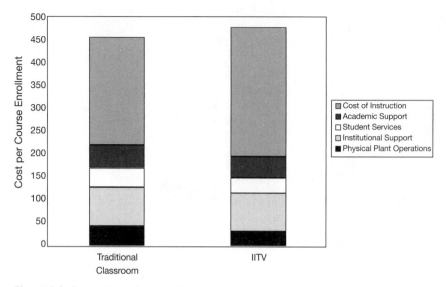

*Figure 10.8.* Comparative Course Enrollment Cost of Education, Typical Community College Implementation

services, and the administration of the institution. These assumptions may not be valid as the type of student in higher education continues to change.

The investment cost in multimedia on-line course materials is not likely to decrease. The current generation of college students grew up with the Internet. They are accustomed to motion pictures and television with extensive visual effects as well as lavishly illustrated textbooks and magazines. Students will not be satisfied with course materials that are not designed for the ways they learn and that are not visually rich and convenient. These preferences imply high-cost multimedia learning materials delivered over the Internet at the same time that the cost analysis shows how little cost recovery can be borne by traditional college and university funding.

In Arizona, policy decisions about the level of costs of IITV and other distance education were made incrementally as part of a political decision-making process. Having higher per student costs in distance education than in traditional classrooms was acceptable for political reasons. In reality it was cheaper to provide distance education to rural locales than to provide new traditional classrooms in low-demand locales. Thus, politics may have resulted in rational choice that could be illustrated by comparing average classroom costs for traditional courses and IITV courses.

## Conclusion

There are two separate actions that colleges and universities can take to achieve economic viability. One is to sharply increase the number of students who use the course materials—that is, to increase the divisor of unit costs. This suggests a publishing model, but for the publishing model colleges and universities must have learning management systems (virtual learning environments) that use "standard" learning materials. At the present time there are a number of proprietary systems that cannot use open standards-based "learning objects." Interoperability tests conducted in late 2002 by the United Kingdom's Joint Information Systems Committee (JISC) Centre for Educational Technology Interoperability Standards (CETIS) commented that "90% of the interoperability problems are trivial and will be corrected soon. The others can be resolved later." If this is true, and if this work continues, and if the learning management systems software suppliers continue to participate in interoperability testing, then "publishing" learning materials will become economically viable. So far the chief business officers of colleges and universities have not mandated software procurement and funded course development that comply with these standards. This is imperative for the publishing industry to be able to serve higher education.

It may also be necessary to increase unit revenue for multimedia courses. The benefits that accrue to students—convenient times and locations, improved retention and success rates—and those that accrue to society may suggest a long-term benefit to increased tuition or fees over traditional courses or increased funding by federal, state, and local government much as special education in K–12 is funded.

Alternatively, education can evolve toward the corporate model. When the new patterns of education and employment are considered, some students will be willing to pay a higher cost for convenience and different ways of learning. The University of Phoenix is an example where students make this trade-off of cost for benefits. This model begins to divide the development of course materials from the faculty to central teams of experts and to standardize "course delivery." It begins to segment method of instruction—classroom, on-line, or a mix (often called "blended learning")—that matches market segments.

The U.S. community colleges and the regional universities offer a combination of facilities and environment that many students find desirable. The focus becomes a network-equipped library, the "learning center" with counselors; or a "computer laboratory"; or even a student union that combines informality, food and beverages, and "hot spots"—wireless support of student laptops. The availability of library, computing resources, teaching faculty, and counselors and tutors make learning much easier. Perhaps the bookstores have shown that coffee and books, and the coffee shops have shown that coffee and laptops, attract knowledge workers—or was it that bookstores and coffee shops watched that evolution at college campuses?

The executive MBA programs have shown that some students will pay significantly more for a different learning environment, convenient times and places, and students who share similar interests and responsibilities—and that some of the costs can be shifted to employers. Similarly, contract education has demonstrated that specialized content and delivery and "branding" are attractive to businesses and their employees. The priorities include:

- Sharable learning content to encourage publishing
- Convenient and effective methods of instruction for each learning market segment
- Change at colleges and universities to accommodate this new diversity
- Market segment pricing

If these strategies were implemented broadly, then the dream of lowering cost through technology might be realized. Yet this dream may continue to be difficult to realize in the United States, which has a highly decentralized, market-oriented system of higher education. The comparison between the United Kingdom and the United States illustrates the perplexing nature of the challenge facing policymakers. In the United Kingdom, college access was constrained through the 1960s. The British Open University was designed to provide mass higher education at a low cost (Ferguson 1975; Perry 1977), so it was relatively easy to integrate technology as part of the development process over three decades. In contrast, the United States had mass access to higher education in the 1960s. Technology integration has added to the costs of higher education (Davis 1997), making the dream of lower costs difficult to realize.

It is crucial that policymakers in states and in public colleges and universities begin to realize the complexity of technology integration in the United States. New students often have a choice to attend traditional colleges or to take courses online. The decentralization of the system makes it more difficult to achieve efficiency gains when implementing new technologies. The rationales used to argue for public funding should be adapted to recognize these complexities.

NOTES

1. Based on an analysis of Open University's financial statements, Justin E. Tilton and the author estimated this investment to be US$500 million. Subsequent discussions with Open University at the NASSGAP/NCHELP Conference corrected the investment to US$1 billion. The class sizes were estimated from enrollment data for the 1999–2000 academic year.

2. In a sense, the faculty are "subsidizing" course development since they were selected for their special interest in distance education and they work intensely on their course materials. Like Open University, the faculty are continuously monitoring student performance and are adjusting their instruction to improve student retention and performance.

3. From an unpublished study by the author (Farmer 1996) of the affect of distance on student enrollments of Pima Community College District.

4. This observation was made by Rio Salado College's Carol Wilson. Karen Mills developed statistics that confirmed the observation. The needs and preference of "screenagers" was documented in an unpublished paper by John C. Kennel of instructional media + magic, inc.

5. A planning value given by Lufthansa Airlines at an Aviation Industry CBT Committee Meeting.

6. Personal conversations with Apollo Group, Inc. chairman, Dr. John G. Sperling, in 1997 through 1998 while working with Rio Salado College and subsequent meetings with CEO Todd Nelson while working with the Arizona Board of Regents. According to the 2002 Annual Report of the Apollo Group, the University of Phoenix has 176 campuses in 37 states and the province of British Columbia serving 157,800 students.

7. This explains why today's high-quality color textbook is more expensive than those only with text.

8. Rio Salado College may be an exception because of its low cost of course development and the large number of enrollments.

9. One example is Yavapai College's experience. Professor Jon Freriks increased completion rates in his Biology 180 course and subsequent enrollments using a multimedia instructional presentation developed from his notes and images by Justin E. Tilton of instructional media + magic, inc., as documented by Jim Farmer (1996).

10. Equipment has been developed for distance learning that both "turns on" the microphone and directs the camera to focus on the speaker. As distance learning becomes more pervasive, such advances are being developed and priced at commodity prices. This suggests continued decline in costs and increases in performance.

11. IITV systems that use digital video require the use of multipoint control units (MCU) to both switch the video and conference the audio. These are located at the control center.

12. Northern Virginia Community College operates the control center for the Virginia community colleges. All switching and communications circuit and facilities (classroom) assignments are done automatically from a schedule database.

13. The line between IITV and broadcast television begins to blur as networks are connected together. For example, Northern Arizona University has IITV classes that are also carried on cable television. Students who receive instruction via cable television may call into the originating classroom or may send e-mail to the classroom as the instruction is presented. In this case the broadcast television is more like radio's "talk show" format.

14. Asynchronous transfer mode digital communications networks are usually high bandwidth networks. These networks communicate two-way video consistently within the acceptable delay for two-way conversation and observation. Virginia has a statewide ATM network that is used by colleges and universities and can also be used by school and state agencies. Arizona's Project Eagle expects to implement a similar network. The network and technology also support packet switching used for the Internet, and voice and data circuits as well. Arizona Learning Systems will be one statewide customer of the network.

15. In the past there was a difference in the analog television technology used for IITV and the digital technology used for video conferencing. Newer IITV implementations used digital video and audio following the H.3xx standards of the International Standards Organization. These standards support the different rates and resolutions that are used for IITV and both low- and high-quality video conferences.

16. Northland Pioneer College in Holbrook, Arizona will be one of the first colleges to implement this technology when their electronic classrooms and the supporting ATM communications network are connected to Arizona Learning Systems. This is expected early in 1998. North Virginia Community Colleges ATM network supports this type of distribution but current practices require control at the local campus.

17. "Course hours" is a vague term that can be viewed as the number of hours a classroom is used per week for a course or, in a different context, for all courses. This is acceptable for term-based instruction that anticipates the same, or nearly the same, number of hours per week throughout a 15 to 18 week term that the classroom is used by a course. More precise analysis is required for instruction formats that vary significantly or for colleges or universities that do not follow terms.

18. Allocation of costs when courses are received from extranet course suppliers would be made only if the use of the control center was required.

19. Cost data for manual operation was based on board reports at Northland Pioneer College. Costs of automation were based on costs by Northern Virginia Community College District. Northland Pioneer College converted to automated operation in Fall 1998.

20. Although it is possible to automate the operation of a Control Center for analog video, the costs are significantly above those listed in Table 3.

21. This is based on utilization rates of Mohave and Yavapai Colleges in Arizona. These colleges have used IITV for almost a decade to cover the rural areas in their service area.

22. The "video engineer's" task is similar to the producer or director's role in a live television broadcast. Because of the several possible sources of video and the several sites, producing an instructional session "live" is similar to producing a sports event.

23. This technology has been mass-marketed for security cameras, first displaying and then focusing on moving objects.

24. Central Arizona College is using this technology to connect the Learning Resources Centers at three sites. The system was used for classes beginning in Spring 1998.

25. This type of classroom was used by Northland Pioneer College in Spring 1998. However, for the first semester "operators" were available to assist instructors using the equipment.

26. The two colleges are using different codecs that convert analog to digital. Although the decompression algorithms are standard, the compression algorithms are proprietary with performance in terms of resolution, color accuracy, and motion differing

roughly according to price. Because each codec and compression equipment must provide a signal that can be decoded by standard receiving equipment, signals from both can be received with all ISO-standard equipment configurations. The difference in quality of the compression algorithms explains much of the difference in cost between Central Arizona's and Northland Pioneer's implementations.

27. For example, analog switcher equipment that cost $100,000 in 1996 can be replaced with high-definition digital switching at $4,995—a 95 percent reduction in price. Similar equipment price reductions can be expected as digital equipment becomes available and companies are willing to sharply lower the prices to achieve volume sales and production—that is, use "learning curve" pricing.

28. The cost of space per square foot is estimated to be $6.50 per square foot per year, representing typical lease rates for rural community colleges. The cost of maintenance is estimated to be $5.70—more than is being paid by Arizona community colleges, but about $1.00 less than costs for colleges and universities in the West. Equipment is depreciated to 10 percent residual value over five years. This is reasonable for digital equipment that may be used elsewhere as equipment is upgraded. Otherwise, a three-year life is more appropriate.

29. The number of courses for the electronic classroom is the number of courses that Yavapai College transmits to its Verde Valley campus from Prescott. The other two cases are based on a reasonable number of courses to be offered during typically available student schedules. This requires scheduling courses at the transmitting site in accordance with the needs of both local and remote students and the availability of communications channels and remote-site classroom and cubicles.

30. President John Klein reported the average class size for IITV courses at Central Arizona College was 31 for Fall 1997.

31. Northern Arizona University has class sizes that exceed the maximum class size for an instructor. The university provides the instructor with teaching assistants to support the larger combined class. One NAU administrator said that 100 students per class would be an ideal number.

32. Often called administration, though this classification is somewhat broader. Student records costs are included in student services.

REFERENCES

Crump, R. E. 1928. Correspondence and class extension work in Oklahoma. Ph.D. dissertation, Teachers College, Columbia University.
Davis, J. S. 1997. *College affordability: A closer look at the crisis.* Washington, DC: Sallie Mae Education Institute.
Farmer, J. 1996. Using technology. In *Handbook of the undergraduate curriculum: A comprehensive guide to purposes, structures, practices, and change,* ed. Jerry G. Gaff, James L. Ratcliff, and Associates. San Francisco: Jossey-Bass.
Ferguson, J. 1975. *The Open University from within.* London: University of London Press.
Gaff, Jerry G., James L. Ratcliff, and Associates. 1996. *Handbook of the undergraduate cur-*

*riculum: A comprehensive guide to purposes, structures, practices, and change.* San Francisco: Jossey-Bass.

Hanna, L. N. 1940. Achievement of high school students in supervised correspondence study. Master's thesis, University of Nebraska.

McGreal, R. 1994a. Canadian province utilizes distance learning in new "Knowledge economy." *ED, Education at a Distance* 9 (1): 6–9.

McGreal, R. 1994b. Comparison of the attitudes of learners taking audiographic teleconferencing courses in secondary schools in Northern Ontario. *Interpersonal Computing and Technology: An Electronic Journal for the 21st Century* 2 (4): 11–23.

National Center for Education Statistics. 2001. *Digest of Education Statistics 2001.*

Perry, W. 1977. *The Open University.* San Francisco: Jossey-Bass.

Schlosser, C. A., and Anderson, M. L. 1994. *Distance education: Review of the literature.* Ames, Iowa: Research Institute for Studies in Education, Iowa State University.

Sorensen, C. K. 1995. Evaluation of two-way interactive television for community college instruction. ACEC Conference, Ames, Iowa.

# Part IV / New Understandings

In the preceding sections, the collaborating authors explored how the contexts for public policy have been transformed in recent decades, along with some of the ways the rationales for public funding have also changed. Lobbying for higher education has become more fragmented but is not less pervasive. While claims are often made about research-based reform, research results are more often used to support ideological arguments than to evaluate the course of public policy. This final section turns to problems of theory and practice facing lobbyists and policy researchers.

Michael D. Parsons (chapter 11) examines the new understanding of lobbying that is emerging. While the notion of community once prevailed in the literature on higher education, this ideal now seems elusive. Yet there continues to be a need for a common understanding of the practice of lobbying. Parsons concludes that while the practice of power provides one of the few common threads in the policy literature, there is no common ground or shared sense of purpose for higher education lobbyists in the period ahead. He warns that the public sector as we have known it remains threatened by new policy rationales, but lobbyists for public colleges have little choice but to seek a new consensus of support for public institutions.

While researchers must also contend with this fragmentation, St. John (chapter 12) concludes that the research community can work with policymakers to create a new common ground. He examines the role of evidence in building new rationales, focusing on the importance of policy studies that seek to fill the void in information about the influence of policy decisions on movement toward common goals. He suggests that Rawls's theory of justice provides a starting point for a new framework for policy analysis in higher education but recognizes the political nature of policy. After all, researchers, like policymakers, must contend with the roles of power and ideology that shape many public decisions affecting higher education.

# CHAPTER ELEVEN

# Lobbying in Higher Education

Theory and Practice

## Michael D. Parsons

In the 1990s, I argued that the federal higher education policy arena could be defined as a communication community in which power rested on the ability of actors to define and solve problems (Parsons 1997, 1999a, 1999b, 2000). Policy actors could use this theoretical and conceptual construct of a policy community as they sought to understand and influence policymaking. This framework for explanation and understanding also provided a foundation for examining the development of rationales used to advocate for public support of higher education. In addition, the definition of a communication community of policy actors bonded by emotional, historical, intellectual, and social bonds could be used to inform policy development.

By the late 1990s, the community that had developed slowly over some thirty years came to a swift end (Parsons 2000). The federal higher education policy arena was hit by highly partisan politics, ideological divides, retirements by major policy actors, shifting public opinion, demands for accountability, a declining trust in government, and a movement in emphasis away from equity in favor of privatization. The problem solving and seeking of common ground that had defined the arena was replaced by a more primitive form of power as neoconservatives and neoliberals sought to enforce power over the policy-making process (Cook 1998; Gray 1995; Parsons 2000; Waldman 1995b).

In the Introduction to this text we lamented the decline of consensus that had guided policy researchers and actors and suggested that it might be possible to identify the basis for a new common ground. In addition, we hoped that the beginning of a new theoretical framework might be established that could be used to advocate for better-informed policy choices. These are rather lofty goals for a single edited volume, but policy scholars have an obligation to critique, to identify problems and solutions, and to dream.

The paragraphs above represent a summary of my position before reading the contributions of the invited scholars. After reading their chapters, I have reinterpreted past events and reconsidered how higher education advocates might best position themselves as they seek to influence public policy. The first section of this chapter briefly reexamines the old common ground and suggests that it was an illusion based on a small area of consensus and a large supply of federal funds. The next section questions the ability to find a new common ground. The policy arena of the last century has fragmented into multiple arenas that make a new common ground difficult, if not impossible, to achieve. The last section considers the use of postmodernism as a heuristic device for understanding and influencing public policy. Policy researchers and policy actors need not consider themselves postmodernists, but they will need to approach the policy arena with a strong sense of "irony and contingency" (Rorty 1989).

## The Old Common Ground

The formation a common ground for the higher education policy started in the spring of 1964 when President Lyndon Johnson began planning for his next term of office. Sensing what would soon become reality, Johnson anticipated an overwhelming victory over Republican candidate Barry Goldwater and large Democratic majorities in the 89th Congress. Not wanting to miss a historic opportunity, Johnson instructed his staff to organize a number of task forces to work on legislative proposals for immediate presentation to the new Congress. The president wanted to present Congress with a massive social reform program and enabling legislation when it met in January 1965 (Graham 1984).

With the Higher Education Act of 1965, Johnson not only created a legislative program but laid the foundation for the development of a higher education policy arena. Over the next twenty-seven years, HEA would be reauthorized six times. From these common experiences, a communication community developed. One of the prerequisites of such a community is a common language that can be used and understood by all of the members. In the beginning, it did not have a common language; but today terms such as equity and access, Congressional methodology, direct lending, GSL, loan-grant imbalance, needs analysis, Pell Grant, Sallie Mae, TRIO, and dozens of others need no explanation or definition for community members.

Language by itself is not enough to foster fully understood communications. The community also needed widely understood signs and symbols to convey shared meanings. The hearings associated with each reauthorization were an opportunity to display these signs and symbols of the community. In addition, community members need to interact in cooperative activities because "the pulls and responses of different groups reinforce one another and their values accord" (Dewey [1927] 1988, p. 148). The various reauthorizations and associated activities provided scores of opportunities for cooperative activities between 1965 and 1992. The shared activities also produced emotional, intellectual, and moral bonds that helped bind the community. These prerequisites for a communication community produced a community that transformed the power of domination into the power of problem solving.

In addition to its focus on problem solving, the policy arena was characterized by low internal complexity, high functional autonomy, strong unity within types of participants, and cooperation among different participants. A small group of policy actors worked together on virtually every reauthorization. The White House was primarily a non-actor after 1965, leaving the field to the congressional committees and the higher education associations. In the House, Representative Gerald Ford had been an active participant starting with the Great Society programs. He was joined by long-term Republican members such as Representatives E. Thomas Coleman and William F. Goodling, who valued educational opportunity for students above party politics.

In the Senate, Edward Kennedy and Claiborne Pell had been there from the first days of HEA. Pell guided the 1972 reauthorization that created the framework for the major student aid programs. He was so highly regarded by his colleagues that they gave his name to the largest student grant program—the Pell Grant. As in the House, Republican senators such as Nancy Kassebaum and James Jeffords worked more closely with committee members than with their own party to fashion higher education legislation. Vermont Republican Senator Robert Theodore Stafford was so respected by his fellow senators that they gave his name to a student loan program.

Congressional staff members also played an important role in the community. Thomas R. Wolanin, who worked for Ford, was known in Congress for his detailed knowledge of HEA and in academe for his writing on higher education policy issues. David V. Evans started working for Pell in 1978. Given the broad jurisdiction of Senate committees, Evans shared the higher education workload with Sarah A. Flanagan, who joined the subcommittee in 1987. Terry

W. Hartle was a key aide to Senator Kennedy on higher education issues. Hartle, a former policy analyst with the American Enterprise Institute, had also written on federal student aid programs.

While there are a large number of higher education associations, only a few were recognized as active policy actors. The major higher education associations are housed in the National Center for Higher Education at One Dupont Circle in Washington, D.C., and the address became a shorthand way to refer to higher education associations. Of the twenty plus associations that reside at One Dupont, only the American Association of Community and Junior Colleges (AACJC), the American Association of State Colleges and Universities (AASCU), the American Council on Education (ACE), the Association of American Universities (AAU), and the National Association of State Universities and Land-Grant Colleges (NASULGC) have been consistently active policy actors in the higher education policy arena. ACE, an umbrella organization, has often attempted to forge consensus positions on policy issues, getting as many associations as possible to speak with one voice on the issue before attempting to influence Congress or the Executive. The other five associations, all of which are institutional associations, provide the expertise on the issues that most affect their member institutions.

The higher education associations that work with the committees to shape higher education legislation benefit from an extensive circulation and flow of personnel within the policy arena. For example, Beth B. Buehlmann, William A. Blakey, John Dean, Rose DiNapoli, Jean S. Frohlicker, Richard T. Jerue, Patty Sullivan, Lawrence S. Zaglaniczny, and other professional staff have remained in the community for many years but have moved between positions within the community. While the leaders of the associations and congressional committees changed, the staff remained, providing an institutional memory. This movement contributed to the maturation of the communication community as policy actors gained shared experiences and multiple perspectives.

Over a nearly thirty-year period, the higher education policy arena evolved into a communication community devoted to problem solving. Higher education associations were powerful policy actors because of their ability to work with other policy actors to solve student aid and other higher education policy problems. Problem solving rested on an axiomatic system of beliefs, institutional relationships, and personal relationships that guided the higher education policy arena in the construction and design of student aid programs. Problems were frequently addressed on the basis of a recommendation from a policy actor with whom other policy actors shared personal relationships. The reason for following the recommendation was explained by policy actors in terms of knowledge, longevity, respect, trust, and other characteristics that define personal relationships. Institutions were defended because they were the institutions that policy actors knew. Programs were created and defended on the basis of what a member believed to be right.

## Foundations of Power

The foundations of power concept calls on earlier concepts of power developed in communicative action theories. It goes beyond the work of Arendt (1968, 1969, 1986), Dewey ([1927] 1988), Habermas (1979, 1984, 1986, 1987), and others to search for the foundations of power. Power rests on three broad foundations. These foundations, suggested by the historical and social context of the higher education policy arena, interact to give form, shape, and meaning to power. One foundation of power is formed by *society's defining institutions and structures*. Visible structures of power are the products of decisions made in earlier policy arenas. Institutions are the "structures [that] define interactions among individuals and groups" (Rorty 1987, p. 10). They also house the persons and social relationships of the community. The institutional foundation answers the "where" of addressing problems, while persons and social relationships represent the "who," and beliefs and values the "why" of policymaking. As such, these structures represent the exercise of power in the past but are not generative sources of power in the present. Instead, these structures represent "the greatest achievement of power . . . its reification" (Clegg 1989, p. 207). These monuments to past power form the relatively fixed, obligatory passage points of power in the present. While they do not generate power in the present, problems must be addressed within these structures. Institutions become important when occupied and manipulated by humans who are addressing problems.

While institutional structures form the channels and boundaries within which the higher education communication community functions, alone, they are not generative of power. Without human occupants, the institutional structures are mere monuments to the past. Power in a communication community is generated through interactions between the foundations of power. The social foundation of power consists of the *rules governing the relationships between policy actors and programs* in a policy arena and includes, in addition, the personal relationships that develop between policy actors apart from any formal relationships created by the rules of the game. Over time, these relationships, formal and informal, become relatively fixed, but this stability should not be interpreted as permanence. Instead, what is being observed is adherence to customs, loyalties, and norms that have developed over the years and that guide the policy arena in the conduct of its affairs.

The third foundation of power is formed by *the beliefs, principles, and values of the community.* Many of these are well-defined, but the community often works with a tacit understanding of its beliefs and values. At times the values and beliefs that underlie student aid policies are unconnected, compartmentalized, and even conflictual. The policy arena does not seek philosophical coherence, nor does it have a mechanism for value clarification. Over the years, new programs and policies have been created to match policy actors' assumptions about problems without any concern over whether or not the guiding assumptions and beliefs mesh to form a coherent philosophy. This explains why supporters of seemingly contradictory policy proposals can each claim that his/her problem solution is grounded in the values of the arena and vital to its future. While the values and beliefs that guide policy are not always well defined and articulated and are at times conflictual and contradictory, successful problem solving is dependent on solutions that are grounded in the beliefs and values of the higher education policy community.

In addition to beliefs, principles, and values, traditions and emotional experiences serve as a basis for problem solving without first being developed into abstract principles or clearly articulated beliefs. These emotional reactions and responses to events are proto-beliefs that sometimes evolve into fully articulated beliefs, principles, or values. In considering the beliefs' foundation, it is important to recognize that beliefs may follow from the actions of policy actors as much as their actions follow from beliefs. Interaction between the three foundations generates power, regulates power, and provides the channels and boundaries of power in the higher education policy arena.

Communication communities, as defined by Arendt, Dewey, and Habermas, exist to solve problems. Problem solving in the higher education policy arena did not match the Habermasian ideal of communicative competence, nor is it an irrational activity that produces problem solutions through some random or accidental confluence of events that results in a policy decision. Instead, problem solving depended on, and was framed by, an axiomatic system of beliefs, institutional relationships, personal relationships, and values that guide the community in the construction and design of student aid programs. Successful problem solvers were those who built their solutions on these foundations and showed how the community's past and future were linked to acceptance of those solutions.

## Collapse of the Community

The most remarkable thing about the communication community and the old consensus is that it was built on such a narrow base and that it lasted for so long. When President Johnson's task force fashioned what would become HEA, they put together a diverse group of interests. The intent of the legislation and the composition of its constituency are reflected in HEA's eight titles. Title I attempted to expand the land-grant extension concept to urban universities. This was included as a concession to ACE and to the U.S. Office of Education (USOE). Title II provided money to expand college and university libraries and to train librarians. This was supported by the USOE, the American Library Association, and the Association of Research Libraries as a necessary program to meet the demands of a rapidly expanding college population. Title III was designed to aid historically black colleges and universities but was drafted in terms that veiled the basic intent. Title IV, with its four-part package of financial aid, is the heart of HEA. The Democrats were finally able to gain student scholarships in the form of Educational Opportunity Grants to institutions. To forestall support for tuition tax credits and to undermine Republican opposition, a guaranteed student loan program for the middle class was included. College work-study and an extension of the NDEA loan program completed the aid programs. Title V established the National Teachers Corps. The Corps was to provide teachers to poverty-stricken areas of the United States. Title VI created a program of financial assistance for improving undergraduate instruction. Finally, Title VII amended the Higher Education Facilities Act, while Title VIII contained the law's general provisions.

Over the years each title has developed its own constituency, advocacy groups, and budgets. Still, the focus of most policy analysts and researchers has been Title IV. The narrow focus on Title IV caused most researchers to miss the fact that Title IV and other programs rested on a common ground no larger than a metaphorical dime. The narrow overlap of social and economic rationales shared by liberals and conservatives was enough to nurture, develop, and support a massive higher education policy arena. Obscured by the focus on student aid was the development of multiple interests within the policy arena, multiple centers of power, and multiple levels of decision making. It is not surprising that once the common ground vanished, there were no metanarratives to support new rationales for public funding of higher education. The possibility of creating a new common ground from which to lobby for higher education is addressed in the next section.

## Seeking a New Consensus

In the Introduction we suggested that it might be possible to develop a new common ground by focusing on the public interest and considering how lobbyists might develop rationales to help us reach the common goals represented by the public interest. Reading the chapters submitted by the contributors makes the possibility of finding a new common ground seem remote. This is not pessimism. It is simply recognition of the new context of policymaking. What once was is gone and may never be again.

The generation of policymakers and education leaders that crafted federal policy between 1965 and the mid-1990s has now left the arena. A new generation will make higher education policy in the 2000s. Unlike the earlier period, higher education is today seen as a private consumer good rather than a social good whose benefits are publicly shared. Without higher education's status as a social good, universities and colleges become just one more special interest group seeking a public handout for its own private benefit. As such, they find themselves in competition with other interest groups seeking a portion of the federal budget. The federal higher education policy arena of the early 2000s is characterized by fragmented, specialized associations, with each one seeking to protect and expand its share of the budget.

Historically, the fault lines of the community can be seen even before it started to form into what we call the higher education policy arena in the mid-1960s. Thelin notes that the federal government has long supported the divergent goals of research and undergraduate student assistance. This helped produce different power centers with divergent beliefs, values, goals, social relationships, and institutional structures. The contemporary practice of earmarking further divided postsecondary institutions. On one level, those with the research infrastructure to receive earmarks were separated from those who did not. Within this group, those with powerful congressional sponsors were separated from those without powerful sponsors. Another level of institutions with no known ability or merit emerged simply because they enjoyed the support of congressional leaders who wanted funds to flow to their home states. With the expansion of earmarks, a new language emerged to justify earmarks and to distinguish the privileged from the disadvantaged. Merit, peer review, research performance, and similar long-used academic terms were replaced by fair share, equal distribution, need to develop research ability, and other terms more closely associated with entitlement politics.

Federal support of undergraduate student assistance highlights the development of different types of postsecondary institutions. Land-grant colleges and universities, historically black colleges and universities, research universities, and community colleges can trace their development to federal funding and/or federal policy decisions and recommendations. The growth of this array of institutional types was followed by the development of a full range of student aid programs. Today any student, from the truly needy to the truly comfortable, qualifies for some form of federal student aid. Given the diversity of goals and missions, it is not surprising that institutions, the various aid programs, and representative organizations developed different constituents, interests, and needs. What is surprising is that the flow of federal student aid funds was so successful in papering over these differences for so long.

Hearn and Holdsworth (chapter 3 in this volume) may be correct when they suggest that what we see today is "a *return* to dissensus." The brief period of consensus that we saw in the 1970s was an aberration from the norm that existed before the passage of HEA. Even during this period of relative consensus, policy actors could not agree on program "goals, participants, and delivery systems." As programs multiplied, constituent groups grew around each program, offering different rationales for the support of their program at the expense of other programs.

While much of the focus of policy analysts has been on federal policy, actions at the state level and in the courts have also contributed to the fragmentation of the policy arena. One can read Zumeta, Hossler, and Trammel (chapters 5, 8, and 9) together to get a good sense of what is happening in the states and how it changes the way postsecondary institutions position themselves. As state support declines, public institutions increasingly position themselves as private institutions. Trammel notes that an even more dangerous turn could occur as institutions are tempted to craft appeals for state support that lack merit and do not "represent the values of the academic community."

Judicial policymaking is a political process that represents the intersection of federal, state, institutional, and individual interests. It is reviewed here to re-inforce the claim that higher education policymaking has fragmented into multiple arenas and occurs on multiple levels. The shifting of issues such as af-firmative action to the states clearly illustrates and supports this claim. As Brown, Butler, and Donahoo (chapter 6), as well as Conrad and Weerts (chap-ter 4) note, higher education affirmative action cases are still decided in the federal courts, but the states are now the focus of power. States and institutions are the originators of policies and practices that produce decisions such as *Adams, Fordice,* and *Hopwood.* In addition, some states have moved to opt out of affirmative action, leaving unresolved the national commitment to higher education desegregation. Those states that have abandoned affirmative action justify their retreat by declaring that it is no longer needed to insure access and equity. States are also using the current budget crisis as an excuse to reduce their commitment to access and equity.

It is not necessary to review each of the contributions to this text to demon-strate the fragmentation of the higher education communication community. The fragmentation has made it impossible to find a new common ground from which to lobby for public support of higher education. One need not accept Thelin's metaphor of the public trough (chapter 1) to accept that institutions are seeking the largest possible share of the $18 billion in federal grants and contracts and are not seeking to define an overarching rationale of the public interest. Hearn and Holdsworth have established that institutions use multiple rationales to lobby for federal student aid. The chapters that address affirma-tive action establish that any consensus that might have existed around access and equity has long since exploded. Each of the growing number of fragments that once were part of the old common ground now has formed, or seeks to form, its own set of rationales, arenas of action, centers of power, and institu-tions of control. It is within this context that advocates of public support of higher education must navigate in the early 2000s.

## Conclusion: Theory and Practice

Understanding the fragmented, decentralized higher education policy arena of the early 2000s calls for a postmodernist perspective. The use of the term *postmodern* will immediately produce as many definitions as there are readers of this text. The purpose here is not to define postmodernism. Instead, I want to use a postmodern perspective as a heuristic device for understanding and influencing public policy. What that means in this setting is defined below. In addition, I will combine a postmodern perspective with the foundations of power concept to show how it can be used to organize and use insights gained from use of the perspective.

## *Taking a Postmodern Perspective*

Postmodernism has so often been used to undermine what are viewed as modernist perspectives that we forget that it also can be used to gain insight into possible solutions to modernist problems (Cahoone 1996). The intent here is not to attack but to discover. The use of a postmodern perspective as a heuristic device requires that the user accept certain positions. One is that there are no metanarratives that provide a single foundation for a uniform higher education policy arena. A second is that discourses over public funding of higher education are struggles over the production of meaning. A third is that rationales, or language used to define and support policy, do not carry meaning outside the context in which they are developed and used. Fourth is that rationales exist primarily within the social network in which they are created, thus the power of rationales can be expanded by increasing the scope of the social network. Finally, to borrow from the very modernist historian Richard Hofstadter (1970), one must be both "playful and pious" in using these positions. Playful in the sense of being open to new ideas and insights that might result from their application, and pious in the sense of treating seriously the obligation of scholars to act as social critics and social constructors.

A good beginning point in the application of a postmodern perspective is to accept that the metanarrative of access and equity that drove public support for higher education in the last half of the twentieth century is gone. Accepting this, advocates can then begin to explore and "play" with the narratives that explain student aid, state higher education financing, desegregation, institutional positioning, technology, and the many other higher education policy arenas. Each arena will have its own set of rationales, meanings, and social networks that characterize successful advocacy. Policy advocates must learn and apply the rules of success for each arena in order to effectively lobby for public support of higher education.

Advocates must also be "pious" and understand that postmodernism tends to be anti-communitarian, whereas higher education is dependent on communities. In seeking to understand the various narratives that define the multiple higher education policy arenas of the 2000s, advocates must apply postmodernism loosely. A strict application would focus on the differences that differentiate and divide the fragments of the old common ground. A loose application provides a way to understand the fragments while listening for elements that might be woven into a larger narrative capable of uniting some of the diverse fragments.

In the 1990s, advocates lost control of the evolving language of public support for higher education and remained mired in the old language of the policy arena even as the arena itself fractured. Liberals and neoliberals lost ground as neoconservatives and the right appropriated what had been the language of liberalism. In an effort to be more inclusive, liberals and neoliberals celebrated difference and rejected any discussion of commonality as essentialism (Martin 2000). Neoconservatives and the right were able to capture rationales for equal opportunity, equal educational opportunity, merit, and other arguments that had once belonged to liberals, and to use those arguments in ways that damaged affirmative action, equity and access, and public funding of higher education.

A strict application of a postmodern perspective is also dangerous in that it removes the foundational basis for rationales. If rationales have no ethical or moral foundation, then there is no claim of privilege for access, equity, desegregation, public funding, or other rationales designed to make higher education fair, open, and available. Without the ability to claim a special role or privileged position in society, higher education is nothing more than another special interest group feeding at the public trough.

Advocates need to be "playful" with rationales—listening to what is said in different arenas and then playing with those rationales outside the context in which they were first used. This may seem like a violation of the positions listed as a condition for taking a postmodern perspective, but it is not. The purpose of taking a postmodern perspective is to gain insight and understanding of policy advocacy. Recognizing that different fragments of the old common ground now speak in different tongues is one way to gain insight into those fragments. Carrying rationales from one fragment to another may be a way to increase lobbying effectiveness as different rationales are tested and used. Developing rationales that work across multiple arenas might build small islands of common ground from which to advocate for broader support of higher education.

Higher education advocates might also use this playfulness to sharpen their understanding of arenas of discourse as struggles for power. Discourse is not about conversation, debate, messages, or knowledge. Discourse is about the relationship between power and knowledge and should be seen as a contest to impose hegemony (Clegg 1989). The winner gains the right to impose meaning on the discourse. Lobbyists for higher education seem to have forgotten this in the 1990s. As a result, they often fell into the trap of using their critics' language in an effort to defend themselves and to develop rationales of support for higher education (Cook 1998; Parsons 1997; Slaughter and Leslie 1997). When one side controls meaning in the discourse, then it also controls the range of possible outcomes (Schattschneider 1970). If advocates are unable or unwilling to be "pious" about discourse arenas as arenas of contest, then they will continue to have the higher education policy agenda defined in ways that are not supportive of public funding for higher education.

The last position required for a postmodern perspective is that rationales exist primarily within the social network within which they are created and used. If lobbyists want to increase the power of their arguments for public support of higher education, then they need to increase the scope of their social networks. Advocates would seem to have ample opportunity to expand the scope of their networks, given that higher education has moved from access for the elite to access to the masses in a relatively short time. As we have seen in this text, higher education is now more important to more individuals, groups, and organizations than it ever has been. The multiple higher education policy arenas are teeming with potential friends and allies who could join the traditional advocates of higher education to form a powerful lobby.

Ironically, the traditional Washington, D.C.–based advocates of higher education seem to have moved in the opposite direction, becoming more exclusionary and aligning themselves with a corporate vision of education (e.g., Slaughter and Leslie 1997). This behavior might be attributable to several factors: the original HEA was created in secrecy; the Washington, D.C.–based associations have long worked inside the policy process; and the associations and other higher education advocates have seen themselves as being cleaner and more pure than common lobbyists (Cook 1998; Gladieux and Wolanin 1976; Parsons 1997). If advocates for higher education are going to be effective in the 2000s, they will have to become more like common lobbyists looking to form coalitions that will expand their social networks as well as expand the reach and power of their rationales.

## *Foundations of Power: Revisited*

A postmodern perspective helps provide insight and understanding for policy actors who are willing to play with the positions. It helps us see that any "truth" about public support for higher education is not "the product of free spirits" but "is produced by virtue of multiple forms of constraints" (Foucault 1980, p. 131). Foucault and other postmodernists contribute to our understanding of constraints but not to our understanding of power. Nancy Fraser (1989) summarizes the problem of using Foucault and other similar postmodernists to understand power by noting that "the problem is that Foucault calls too many sorts of things power and simply leaves it at that. . . . Phenomena which are capable of being distinguished . . . are simply lumped together . . . a broad range of normative nuances is surrendered, and the result is a certain normative one-dimensionality" (p. 32).

How then can higher education policy actors and advocates play with a postmodern perspective and use the results to influence public policy? The foundations of power concept can be used as an approach to organizing knowledge about the multiple higher education policy arenas gained from the application of a postmodern perspective. In some ways this approach is similar to Foucault's effort to apply an archaeological approach to discourse. Here our concern is not with the rules of discourse but with the meaning of power in each of the policy arenas. More specifically, it is about using power, however it might be defined in an arena, to successfully lobby for higher education in each of the arenas that affect public policymaking.

Each arena, regardless of its nature, will have an institutional foundation, a social foundation, and a beliefs/values foundation. Understanding this, policy actors and advocates can use the foundations of power concept to organize knowledge gained from the application of a postmodern perspective. Each arena can be mapped, models of operation can be developed, and a classification system of power can be established. None of these can bring back the old common ground or create a new consensus for public support of higher education. At the very least, the proposal to combine a postmodern perspective with the foundations of power concept will increase lobbyists' level of understanding and possibly their level of effectiveness as they advocate for public support of higher education. At the very best, this approach may create some small islands of consensus in a sea of dissensus.

Finally, while this approach promises an opportunity for success in the new context of higher education policymaking, the ability of higher education advocates to take advantage of the opportunity remains questionable. The post-1992 success of higher education advocates is attributable more to institutional conflict than to any actions taken by the higher education associations and advocates. Important policy issues such as national service and direct lending were neither developed nor embraced by the higher education associations. The defense and protection of student aid in the 1995–96 budget battle between the Clinton administration and the Republican Congress was not, as Cook (1998) claims, due to the power and influence of the associations, but it was due to Clinton's willingness to close the federal government rather than accept Republican cuts in AmeriCorps, direct lending, and other student aid programs. With a different president controlling that obligatory passage point in the institutional foundation, the results could have been very different.

Federal and state higher education policymaking in the 2000s will be marked by fragmentation, conflict, and coercion. The new context will not be friendly to an expansion of public support for higher education. Indeed, any change, including program elimination, will be difficult to achieve because there is no common ground that spans the entire policy arena and because groups are more willing to engage in conflict. It remains to be seen if the higher education advocates will be able to meet the challenges of the new millennium. To understand higher education policymaking, one must understand the meaning of power in the policy arena. To understand power, one must understand the institutional, social, and beliefs foundations on which it rests. If the past is a prelude to the future, then higher education advocates and associations have shown neither the ability to respond to the challenge nor an understanding of the changes in the new context of higher education policymaking.

REFERENCES

Arendt, H. 1968. *Between past and future: Eight exercises in political thought.* New York: Viking Press.
Arendt, H. 1969. *On violence.* New York: Harcourt, Brace, and World.
Arendt, H. 1986. Communicative power. In *Power,* ed. S. Lukes, 59–74. New York: New York University Press.
Cahoone, L. 1996. Introduction. In *From modernism to postmodernism: An anthology,* ed. L. Cahoone. Oxford, UK: Blackwell Publishers.

Clegg, S. R. 1989. *Frameworks of power.* London: Sage Publications.

Cook, C. E. 1998. *Lobbying for higher education: How colleges and universities influence federal policy.* Nashville, TN: Vanderbilt University Press.

Dewey, J. [1927] 1988. *The public and its problems.* Athens, OH: Swallow Press.

Foucault, M. 1980. *Power/knowledge.* Brighton, UK: Harvester Press.

Fraser, N. 1989. Foucault on modern power: Empirical insights and normative confusions. In *Unruly practices,* ed. N. Fraser, 17–32. Minneapolis: University of Minnesota Press.

Gladieux, L. E., and T. R. Wolanin. 1976. *Congress and the colleges: The national politics of higher education.* Lexington, MA: D. C. Heath.

Graham, H. D. 1984. *The uncertain triumph: Federal education policy in the Kennedy and Johnson years.* Chapel Hill: University of North Carolina Press.

Gray, J. 1995. Senators refuse to save national service program. *New York Times,* 27 September, D22.

Habermas, J. 1979. *Communication and the evolution of society.* Boston: Beacon Press.

Habermas, J. 1984. *Theory of communicative action,* vol. 1, *Reason and the rationalization of society.* Boston: Beacon Press.

Habermas, J. 1986. Hannah Arendt's communications concept of power. In *Power,* ed. S. Lukes, 75–93. New York: New York University Press.

Habermas, J. 1987. *The theory of communicative action,* vol. 2, *Lifeworld and system: A critique of functionalist reason.* Boston: Beacon Press.

Hofstadter, R. 1970. *Anti-intellectualism in American life.* New York: Knopf.

Martin, J. R. 2000. *Coming of age in academe.* New York: Routledge.

Parsons, M. D. 1997. *Power and politics: Federal higher education policymaking in the 1990s.* Albany: State University of New York Press.

Parsons, M. D. 1999a. The higher education policy arena. In *Foundations of American higher education,* ed. J. L. Bess and D. S. Webster, 615–33. Needham Heights, MA: Simon and Schuster Custom Publishing.

Parsons, M. D. 1999b. The problem of power: Seeking a methodological solution. *Policy Studies Review* 16 (3/4): 278–310.

Parsons, M. D. 2000. The higher education policy arena: The rise and fall of a community. In *Higher education in transition: The challenges of the new millennium,* ed. B. Fife and J. Losco, 83–107. Westport, CT: Greenwood Publications.

Rorty, R. 1987. Method, social science and social hope. In *Interpreting politics,* ed. M. T. Gibbons, 241–59. New York: New York University Press.

Rorty, R. 1989. *Contingency, irony and solidarity.* New York: Cambridge University Press.

Schattschneider, E. E. 1970. *The semisovereign people.* New York: Holt, Rinehart and Winston.

Slaughter, S. E., and L. L. Leslie. 1997. *Academic capitalism: Politics, policies, and the entrepreneurial university.* Baltimore: Johns Hopkins University Press.

Waldman, S. 1995a. *The bill: How the adventures of Clinton's National Service bill reveal what is corrupt, comic, cynical—and noble—about Washington.* New York: Viking.

Waldman, S. 1995b. Sallie Mae fights back: The brutal politics of student-loan reform. *Linguafranca: The review of academic life* (March/April): 34–42.

# CHAPTER TWELVE

# Policy Research and Political Decisions

## Edward P. St. John

The political landscape of higher education policy has changed substantially over the past two decades. University officials have long lobbied public officials for tax dollars, as Thelin (chapter 2) so eloquently documents. However, the older claims about economic productivity and public investment are no longer treated seriously by most state legislators. Instead, new arguments about privatization, reductions in tax support, merit aid, and accountability for public dollars influence state and federal policy (Parts I and II).

In this political context, university officials have made incremental adjustments in the rationales they use to argue for public funding (Trammell, chapter 9), while public research universities have begun to use private college pricing and student aid strategies (Hossler, chapter 8). After more than a decade of experimentation with distance education strategies, it is clear that distance education has not solved the college cost problem in the United States (Farmer, chapter 10). Economies of scale remain elusive, even when the new technologies are used. Thus, colleges and universities in both the public and private sectors of higher education are faced with the challenge of developing new rationales that captivate both the public and policymakers sufficiently to provoke thoughtful reinvestment in higher education.

These new policies—especially the privatization process—may have marginally increased the efficiency in the use of tax dollars (St. John 2003). Yet privatization has had another unintended consequence as well: an increased inequality in the college enrollment rates for Hispanic and black high school graduates as compared to whites (St. John 2002, 2003). Some policymakers and researchers have begun a process of rethinking the assumptions used in policy research (ACSFS 2002; Fogel 2000; St. John 2003), but this process is far from complete. There is no longer a consensus about the rationales that should be used as a basis for policy decisions about higher education finance (Parsons, chapter 11), but there is an opportunity to engage in both academic and policy discourse about possible foundations. While researchers might like to think they lead the discourse on public policy in higher education, it appears that much of policy research remains on the sidelines of policymaking.

As a conclusion to this volume, I suggest a new approach to policy research. First, as a way of further illuminating the problems facing policy researchers who work with policymakers, I consider how politics influences policy research on higher education. Then I revisit the theory problem, suggesting a way of using the theory of justice (Rawls 1971, 2001) as a basis for rethinking the rationales used for research on education reforms and higher education finance. I conclude by suggesting strategies for policy research that recognize the political nature of policy research.

## The Politics of Policy Research

It is clear from reviews of federal policy on student financial aid that mainstream research has not influenced policy, that policy decisions have remained essentially political in recent decades (Hearn 1993, 2001; Hearn and Holdsworth, chapter 3; Parsons, chapter 11). Instead, most of the highly visible research used to argue for public funding for higher education (e.g., Choy 2002; King 1999b; NCES 1997a) has been craftily constructed to support the rationales of the new conservatives and new liberals. In other words, policy research has been used to rationalize new policies rather than to inform the public and policy development. Therefore, it is important to consider how policy research has been used in new conservative and new liberal rationales. I review two recent examples below, then summarize a few new studies that have used a more balanced framework.

### Research Supporting New Conservative Rationales

Since the middle 1980s the new conservatives have sought explanations for inequalities across income groups in postsecondary opportunity. Initially, they argued that differences in high school math explained disparities that developed after 1978 (Pelavin and Kane 1990), a theme that has evolved over the past decade. An examination of two examples of this research trend can help clarify how policy research and advocacy have been intermingled. Federally funded analyses of the longitudinal databases (e.g., the National Education Longitudinal Study of 1988 and follow-ups, or NELS:88) provide one example. For decades the National Council for Education Statistics has produced reports that overlook the role of student financial aid in promoting access. The analyses using this model (NCES 1997a, 1997b, 2000) systematically overlook the idea that finances could influence enrollment behavior, even when they report statistics on financial aid. The following conclusion illustrates the interpretative position typically taken in these federal reports:

> Although there are differences by income and race-ethnicity in the four-year college enrollment rates of college-qualified high school graduates, the differences between college-qualified low-income and middle-income students, as well as differences among college-qualified black, Hispanic, Asian, and white students, are eliminated among those students who have taken the college entrance examinations and completed an application for admission, the two steps necessary to attend a four-year college. (NCES 1997a, p. iii)

This statement clearly argues that by taking college entrance tests and applying in advance to four-year colleges,[1] minority students could gain access to four-year colleges. Ironically, this report presented information related to the role of finances, controlling for academic preparation, but failed to even consider the possibility that financial aid influenced college enrollment by low-income students who took the steps to prepare for college.[2] Like most other studies by NCES that have analyzed NELS:88 (NCES 1996, 1997b), this report ignored the possibility that the decline in federal student aid after 1980 could have influenced the opportunity gap. Other studies using this logic have also been widely disseminated.

Recently the American Council on Education (ACE) published a summary essay on NCES research using NELS:88 to study access. The summary report concluded that parents' education was the most important predictor of college enrollment (Choy 2002), leaving the impression that two decades of decline in federal grants and growth in privatization had no influence on the growing inequality in postsecondary opportunity. The extreme nature of these claims about academic access necessitates a rethinking of the logical models used in federal studies of financial access.

## *Research Supporting New Liberal Rationales*

A recent book sponsored by the ACE provides an example of new liberal rationales[3] for public funding. *Financing a College Education: How It Works, How It's Changing* (King 1999b) examines changes in federal student financial aid policy during the 1990s but fails to consider the consequences of new federal policies. Part I focuses on how student financial aid works, at least in a technical sense, but fails to consider how well student aid works relative to the access goal underlying federal programs. Then the essays in Part II provide the reader with information on recent changes in federal student financial aid but fail to critically examine the consequence of these changes. For example, Gladieux and Swail (1999), in an essay titled "Financial Aid Is Not Enough," outline why postsecondary encouragement has become a central concern in the higher education policy community but fail to even consider whether there is enough need-based student grant aid to enable enrollment by college-prepared, low-income students. In the concluding essay, the editor reveals the position that led to these oversights: "Higher education generally, and student aid advocates in particular, must do as much as possible to bolster the college participation and success rate of low-income students. This is important both to create a record of what need-based aid can accomplish when paired with other efforts and to demonstrate higher education's commitment to equal educational opportunity" (King 1999a, p. 201).

This statement is clear. It argues that the rationale for funding encouragement and academic preparation should be dominant in policy analysis on student aid. It explicitly argues that "student aid advocates in particular" must focus their research on the outcomes that drive these arguments. Unfortunately, this advocacy position overlooks four decades of research in economics that focuses on the impact of finances on enrollment. There is overwhelming evidence from research in the economics of education that tuition charges have a substantial, direct, and negative effect on enrollment by low-income students (Heller 1997; Jackson and Weathersby 1975; Leslie and Brinkman 1988; McPherson 1978). Economic and higher education research document that low-income students respond to grant aid in enrollment decisions and persist as well as other students, controlling for background and achievement, if they receive adequate grant aid.

*Financing a College Education: How It Works, How It's Changing* largely ignores research on the impact of prices and student financial aid. The informed reader is left with no option but to conclude that the failure to recognize the implications of this large body of research on the economics of higher education and higher education finance represents a new liberal view, given that ACE essentially sponsored the project. Not only is the twenty years of neglect of need-based grants a problem, but it is frightening to think about the consequences of this new liberal position, given the new inequalities in access (ACSFA 2002). There are few advocates for equity left in the policy research community.

## Finding a New Balance

While many higher education researchers have followed the new conservative rationale by ignoring the consequences of the decline in need-based grants when arguing that new programs merit aid and early interventions should be funded (e.g., King 1999a; Gladieux and Swail 1999), there have been a few recent attempts to reframe the debate. The examples below illustrate how some researchers have attempted to fill the policy void created by the new conservative policy dominance and the new liberal response by the lobbying community in Washington.

Recent efforts to reexamine NCES reports reveal that there is a link between reductions in federal need-based grants and the growing inequality in educational opportunity. The Advisory Committee on Student Financial Assistance documented that the rise in net prices for low-income students after 1980 created an access problem: large numbers of college-prepared low-income students lack the opportunity to attend college. In 2001 the ACSFA published *Access Denied,* a report that compiled statistics from NCES publications to document how the decline in need-based financial aid paralleled the growing disparity in opportunity. The report argued: "The opportunity gap for low-income students that exists today stands in stark contrast to the unparalleled prosperity of many American families and the large budget surpluses of the nation. In order to address the current opportunity gap and avoid a potential access crisis in the future, the federal government must renew the nation's commitment to a broad access strategy" (ACSFA 2001, p. vi).

Critics of this report argued that improvements in K–12 education were a priority over investing in need-based grants and that if sufficient improvement were made in schools, reinvestment in grants would not be needed (Finn 2001). This type of criticism illuminated the need to deal more directly with the claims about academic preparation that had been made by the new conservatives and the ways the modest federal investment in "postsecondary encouragement" had captured the liberal establishment. Subsequent studies by the ACFSA and their allies focused on the question: Were some low-income students who prepared for college left behind as a consequence of the decline in need-based grants?

The ACSFA and their consultants reexamined the statistics on NELS:88 reported by NCES when they argued that the income differences in college enrollment were explained by academic preparation (NCES 1997a). These reexaminations of NCES reports used the same definitions of—and statistics on—college qualification as the earlier report. The reexamination revealed:

> NCES argued for encouraging more low-income students to take (and pay for) college entrance exams. Many low- and lower-middle-income students attend less expensive colleges that do not fit the analytic model NCES used in its studies of college access using NELS:88. Fully 81% of the college-qualified, low-income group took the exam, but this analysis reveals that 22% of this group did not attend. Further, many low-income students met the qualifications and took the entrance examination, but decided they could not afford to attend any college. The pipeline analysis led to fundamentally misleading conclusions about access, conclusions that totally overlooked the role of finances. (St. John 2002, p. 22)

Based on this type of reexamination, the ACSFA released *Empty Promises,* documenting that large numbers of college students were left behind for financial reasons (2002). They estimated that four million college-qualified students from low-income and lower-middle-income families would be left behind in the first decade of the twenty-first century if there were no improvements in federal need-based student financial aid. These studies started to build a new rationale: even after academic preparation was taken into consideration, inequities in opportunity were still evident. The decline in need-based student aid after 1980 increased inequalities between low-income and high-income students who had prepared for college.

## Political Rationales and Policy Research

These recent examples illustrate that political ideologies must be contended with by policy researchers if they are to generate studies that can inform policy development. However, they also reveal a fundamental problem. The research that is typically disseminated to policymakers by NCES, ACE, and the ACSFA is different than the research on policy issues published in academic journals. While academic research may be summarized in policy reports, these reports are often politically constructed to support positions of powerful constituents, a pattern that helps explain why there is a disconnect between research and policy (Hearn 1993).

However, it would be a mistake to merely sanction the misuse of research without thinking critically about the implications. The review above illustrates a different usage of theory in policy research. In prior generations, policymakers often used commonly accepted economic rationales like human capital theory to rationalize new federal programs (Slaughter 1991). As these older programs and funding policies are dismantled, it is important to develop ways to test the assumptions made in the newer rationalizations used to argue for dismantling aid programs and for decreasing support for public colleges. Somehow, as part of the political process, we need to evolve a new common ground that can be used to reconstruct the financial strategies in ways that overcome the misuse of research.

My argument is based on the hope that it is possible to build a new consensus, an issue discussed in the introduction (St. John and Parsons, chapter 1). However, as the review above illustrates, some distance must still be traveled before this new progressive dream can be realized. To create a new common ground, it is necessary to dig deeper into the rationales used in political arguments about funding in higher education.

## Rethinking the Role of Theory in Education Policy Research

If one accepts the argument that policy development is a political process, then it is easier in some sense to explain the tendency of many policy researchers to reinterpret academic research to support political rationales. However, it still is not easy to accept this practice. The notion that there is a public interest of which both politicians and researchers should be cognizant remains compelling, even if this goal seems elusive. The chapters in this volume offer a vantage point on the need for a new rationale but do not solve the problem.

Clearly, an incremental reframing process is now underway in higher education finance (St. John and Paulsen 2001). The chapters in this volume have added substantially to critical thought on policy rationales, but the task of creating a new common ground is far from complete. Public institutions are building new arguments for funding that appeal to specific interests. Hossler described the process of leveraging student aid in public universities as a response to the new priorities (chapter 8). Trammell described the new economic development rationale that was used to argue for research funding in one state (chapter 9). Farmer described how the logic used to argue for distance education is being reconstructed to deal with the economic realities of higher education finance (chapter 10). A close reading of these chapters, however, reveals that these are marginal adaptations to longstanding policy arguments, but they stop short of presenting a new rationale for public finance policy. A theory problem underlies the policy debates on finance. If economic theory is no longer an adequate basis for public finance policy, given the efforts to dismantle programs and funding formulae constructed based on the old progressive assumptions, what theories *should* inform a rethinking of policy rationales?

Given the political nature of public policy, it is crucial to use political theory in the reformulation of financial strategies, especially theory that deals with justice principles that underlie Western democracies. While economics often appear to be neutral politically, the rationales developed by economists are often as political as the arguments developed by most other groups. Below, after reexamining the theory of justice, I revisit political, economic, and education theories with a view toward suggesting a new basis for thinking about finance policy.

## *Theory of Justice*

John Rawls's theory of justice (1971, 2001) provides a starting point for suggesting a new framework for higher education policy research. While this theory has been criticized because it does not fully consider basic rights in ways that are compatible with justice and economic issues in developing countries (Nussbaum 1999; Sen 1999), it holds up as a basis for thinking critically about policy in Western democracies, including the United States. Rawls distinguished two principles:

a. Each person has the same indefeasible claim to a fully adequate scheme of equal basic liberties, which scheme is compatible with the same scheme of liberties for all; and

b. Social and economic inequalities are to satisfy two conditions: first they are to be attached to offices and positions open to all under conditions of fair equality of opportunity; and second, they are to be the

greatest benefit of the least-advantaged members of society (the difference principle). (2001, p. 42)

These principles relate directly to the current debates about higher education finance (St. John 2003). The arguments about academic preparation relate
to schemes related to basic rights, with a focus on the nature of requirements
for a high school education. In contrast, the debate about whether students
who are prepared for college had equal opportunity relates to the difference
principle. New conservative arguments about academic preparation have
shifted attention away from equity, which had been the original basis for creating federal need-based student aid programs. By focusing on measures related
to the two principles, it is possible to identify related issues.

However, if we are to view an adequate, quality education as a basic right,
and equal opportunity to attend college as an equity right related to the distribution principle, then we also need to think about the role of taxation.
Rawls's "just savings principle" provides a basis for rethinking the role of taxpayer support. He argues that cross-generation tax support provides a means
of promoting across generations. However, equity remains a priority: "The
principle of just savings holds between generations, while the difference principle holds within generations. Real saving is required only for the reasons of
justice: that is, to make possible the conditions needed to establish and to preserve a just basic structure over time" (2001, p. 159).

Taxation, according to Rawls, represents the primary method democracies
use for just savings and cross-generation support. According to this widely accepted moral philosophy, equal opportunity (i.e., the distribution principle)
should hold priority in the use of tax dollars, even when efficiency (or reduced
costs of taxes) is a public priority. During the last two decades of the twentieth century, the federal government promoted savings and tax credit programs
over need-based student aid as priorities in public funding (King 1999b; St.
John 2003), a pattern that directly contradicts the just savings and distribution
principles outlined above. Achieving lower taxpayer costs may be a priority for
some experts in higher education finance, but students from low-income families should not be excessively disadvantaged by policies implemented to reduce
taxpayer costs (St. John 2003).

Thus, Rawls's theory provides the moral and philosophical basis for rethinking policy on higher education, a basis that overcomes the limitations

of economic theory and the new conservative rationales now used in higher education finance. While it may be important to consider efficiency concerns, given the conservative priorities of the majority of voters in this generation, overlooking equity can not be excused in the name of efficiency.

## Economic Theory and Research

Economic rationales are appropriately examined within a political theory that is justice-based, rather than treated as rationales that support various political arguments. The reconstructed theory of justice provides a way of thinking about research and theory in the economics of education:

- The nature of basic education rights (i.e., Rawls's principle a), including the content and quality of K–12 education, is an issue in education reform that has implications for research in education and economics. However, basic rights should not be treated as a priority over equal opportunity (i.e., the distribution principle).
- The equitable distribution of resources in support of equal educational opportunity, especially equal opportunity for college enrollment for students who are academically qualified, should be central to policy research, including research in the economics of education and student demand.
- Efficiency in the use of resources necessary to provide K–12 and higher education in ways that are consonant with the difference principle (i.e., equal opportunity) and the just savings principle (i.e., this generation's concerns about tax costs) remains a concern. By focusing on efficiency in the use of tax dollars, it may be possible to separate the discussion of privatization from claims of low-cost options.
- The willingness of taxpayers to support higher education influences the prices of attending as well as the nature of the basic educational rights, including the quality of preparation in K–12 schools and access to college. Both academic preparation and the ability to pay influence access.

Economic theory and research consistently support the claim that attainment of higher education improves individual earnings (Paulsen 2001a, 2001b; St. John and Paulsen 2001), a conclusion that supports both individual and public investment in higher education. However, while some economists claim K–12 preparation should be a priority (e.g., Bishop 1992, 2002), such speculation generally fails to consider social theory related to equity, and education theory related to preparation. Therefore, access to higher education is a basic right that relates to investment decisions both within and across generations.

Historically, economists were concerned about equity in higher education finance. There is a sound research base for the claim that low-income students are more price-sensitive than the majority of students (Heller 1997; St. John 2003). However, the net price rationale does not hold up well in policy (Hansen 1983; Kane 1995), especially when it is applied only to need-based student aid. Analysis of the impact of changes in public funding for all types of student aid—need-based and specially directed (e.g., veterans benefits)—shows that change in enrollment does correspond with changes in public funding (St. John 1994, 2003). Therefore, there is a sound basis for using economic theory and research to assess the impact of reductions in student aid and increases in prices. However, net price theory has proven tautological: it is true that students respond to net prices. Yet changes in one aspect of net price (e.g., federal grants) can be shown to have no effect on enrollment (Hansen 1983; Kane 1995) unless the effects of different types of costs and subsidies are considered (St. John 2003).

Tax dollars are used to support public institutions, colleges, students, and research that supports economic and social development. Earlier chapters illustrated that the rationales for all three forms of public investment are changing, becoming more specific and targeted. After 1980 the taxpayer costs of higher education (the sum of subsidies to students and institutions), as measured by spending per student enrolled in the national system of higher education, actually declined (St. John 2003). And while taxpayers' costs rose again in 1990, tax dollars spent per FTE were still lower in 2000 than in 1980 (St. John 2003). These trends illustrate that taxpayer costs must become an integral part of the policy discourse on higher education finance, especially since conservative arguments about the costs of higher education and reductions in tax rates merely disguise a deeper concern about tax rates.

The cost of attending college, an issue that is of concern to most families with students of college age, is complicated by the politics of privatization. Not only was there a shift between 1980 and 2000 in who pays for college, from taxpayers to students and their families, but a new inequality emerged as a result of the way privatization was implemented. Unfortunately, we lack a common basis for discussing college costs in spite of decades of economic research on the issue. More specific consideration of college costs in relation to the justice issues outlined above might help clarify this policy debate. There is clearly a need for further analyses of the public and private returns to the public investment in higher education.

## Social Theory

Social theory and research are also crucial to building a new understanding of the public role in higher education finance, especially given official publications that focus on the role of parents' education (Choy 2002). A correlation between parents' education and college enrollment does not mean that public policy cannot influence college enrollment. Untangling how policy changes influence enrollment patterns requires a better understanding of social theory than has been exhibited in these recent applied policy studies (e.g., Choy 2002; NCES 1997a).

Social theory has long focused on cross-generation uplift, a concept integral to the theory of justice. Mainstream theories focus on the influence of family income and parents' education as indicators of social class but also recognize that education achievement and other forces influence attainment across generations (Alexander and Eckland 1974, 1977, 1978; Blau and Duncan 1967). Social reproduction theory illuminates some of the ways in which social class is reproduced by educational and social institutions (Berger 2000; McDonnough 1997), but this theory also illuminates the potential for cross-generation uplift. Indeed, both theories suggest that finances can play a facilitating role in cross-generation uplift if resources are adequate, or an inhibiting role if financial support is inadequate (St. John and Musoba 2002).

Recent analyses of Indiana's Twenty-first Century Scholars Program revealed that a comprehensive approach to early intervention that combines encouragement and adequate aid can overcome some of the social barriers to access. An analysis of a cohort of students, following middle school students through the first year of college, revealed that encouragement increased the chances that students would prepare for college and that grant aid had a substantial direct influence on enrollment (St. John, Musoba et al. 2002). A follow-up analysis of the white and black students indicated that (1) parents' education was associated with enrollment by whites in Indiana but not for African Americans; and (2) that student grant aid had a more substantial influence on enrollment by African Americans than by whites (St. John and Musoba 2002).

Second, a recent study of postsecondary aspirations in the state of Washington provides further insight into the influence of parents' education in states with adequate grant aid. In a study of high school students in Tacoma, Washington, Hirschman and Lee (2002) found that for white high school students, parents' education had a substantial and direct influence on aspirations to attend a four-year college, but this variable was not significant for African American high school students. Washington is a state that has managed to provide adequate state grants (St. John 1999), so it appears that the financial environment enabled more minority students to aspire to attend four-year colleges.

In combination, these analyses illustrate that adequate grant aid can overcome social barriers to access. In the Indiana case, there is also a substantial state investment in postsecondary encouragement through the Twenty-first Century Scholars Program. Without adequate aid, it is doubtful that encouragement would make much difference in promoting college preparation and access, given that many college-qualified, low-income students currently lack financial access (St. John 2003).

## Education Policy Research

Education research has also emphasized correlation statistics over theoretically sound reasoning about the influence of policy decisions on colleges and college students. There has been a tendency to abstract policy remedies from correlation statistics, a logical fallacy embedded in many policy reports focusing on academic preparation (NCES 1997a, 1997b; Pelavin and Kane 1990).

There should be little reason for surprise that students who take more advanced math courses are more likely to enroll in college (e.g., NCES 1997a; Pelavin and Kane 1990), but this correlation may not be causal. In fact, students who aspire to go to college are more likely to take advanced courses, a fact that disputes the causal logic of these official reports. Furthermore, such a correlation does not mean that a policy that requires more advanced math courses for high school graduation will influence more students to prepare for college or will induce more high school graduates to enroll in college. After all, it is just as likely that stiffer requirements—be they high-stakes graduation tests or mandates for more advanced math courses for high school graduation—can induce more school dropout and have little or no influence on preparation and enrollment (Jacob 2001; Manset and Washburn 2000).

Researchers need to consider the consequences of implementing stiffer requirements. There have been two decades of the new excellence reforms. It is time to consider how well these reforms have served urban schools (Miron and

St. John 2003), as well as whether the standards-driven reforms have improved rates of high school graduation and college enrollment. Research that tests whether the reform policies have had their intended consequences is crucial. Unfortunately, not only have correlation statistics been used to make false claims about academic preparation, but they also have also been used to obfuscate the role of finances in college access (ACSFA 2002; St. John 2002).

By evaluating the effects of education reforms, it is possible to raise the level of debate about college access and public finance. It is important for policymakers to have information on the effects of education reforms, just as it is important for them to have information on the effects of college prices and student aid. Such information can inform policy development.

## A New Challenge for Researchers and Policymakers

Thus, the theory of justice—informed by economic, social, and education policy theory and research—can frame the development of a new generation of policies in higher education finance and education reform. It is crucial, however, that policy researchers and policymakers transition from making broad claims based on the study of one aspect of the problem, to evaluating the consequences of the policies that have actually been implemented. It is crucial to assess the consequences—intended and unintended—of policies that are now in place, if we are to identify new, more workable approaches to public finance and education reform in the future. Specifically, it is important to balance three issues in the evaluation and refinement of education and finance policies:

- *The nature of the basic right for education:* Do education reforms improve the chances students will graduate from high school and be prepared to enroll in college?
- *The equity aspects of college finance:* Does the combination of prices and aid provide ample opportunity for low-income students who are prepared to enroll in college?
- *The efficiency aspect of finance and education reform:* Are tax dollars invested in ways that optimize education attainment and economic returns from the taxpayer investment?

Privatization, standardization, and accountability are strategies used to improve education and to refocus public policy on the efficient use of tax dollars (Finn 1990; Paige 2003), but these rationales ignore equity altogether. By balancing the three aspects of education policy—the basic right, equity, and efficiency—and evaluating how new policies influence the balance among these concerns, it may be possible to make better policy decisions. There is no higher aim in policy research on education and public finance than to frame analyses in order to inform the public interest in ways that are fair and just.

## Contending with the Political Aspect of Policy Research

Three steps are necessary to generate policy research that can inform policymakers about a more balanced approach to education and public finance policies: (1) recognize that there are divergent claims about policies and outcomes; (2) design studies that test divergent claims, with an emphasis on building a balanced understanding of the role of public policy; and (3) provide information that facilitates debates about basic rights, equity, and efficiency, rather than constraining interpretations to a single priority.

### Recognize Divergent Claims

Educational research has been captured by new conservative and new liberal political ideologies over the past few decades. The new conservative contingent argues for reducing public support for higher education, increasing the emphasis on academic preparation in high school and distance education higher education, and using standards and accountability to ensure the public interest is realized. The new liberal argument works around the edges of the dominant conservative position, building funding rationales for new programs that hold up to new conservative critiques.

The old liberal opposition argued that public investment is needed for quality schools, that investment in higher education promotes economic development, and that academic freedom is essential to a quality education. This universal rationale gave way to a series of new arguments for funding over the past few decades. However, the new arguments are based largely on correlation statistics and fail to consider the influence of policy decisions. Taking more demanding courses is correlated with high graduation and college enrollment. Net prices are related to the probability of enrollment, especially for low-income students. But such correlation statistics are meaningless for policy unless there are sound theoretically and empirically based reasons behind the correlations.

It is crucial to evaluate whether public policies influence education achievement (the basic right), equity in the opportunity to attain an education, and efficiency in the use of tax dollars. Therefore, policymakers and researchers need to ask evaluative questions such as:

- Has the implementation of education reforms (e.g., education standards, high-stakes graduation tests, and/or increased graduation requirements) improved the quality of education outcomes as measured by standardized scores (achievement) and attainment by diverse groups (equity)?
- Given the decline in federal grants, does the adequacy of state grants improve college-going rates? Is high tuition–high aid more efficient than low tuition?
- Has the decline in need-based grants adversely affected equal opportunity? Specifically, do the new privatization strategies—lower public subsidies for colleges and low-income college students—foster a system of access that discriminates unfairly against college-prepared students from low-income families?

Evaluative questions like these must be addressed by policy researchers if we have any hope of finding a new common ground. After more than twenty years of new policies aimed at improving educational outcomes and reducing the taxpayer costs of higher education, it is time to evaluate the consequences of these policies. Both the new claims about policy and the old claims must be evaluated in ways that can inform a new generation of education and public finance policies. Resting policy on correlation statistics generated with sophisticated modeling does not answer basic questions about the consequences of the new policies that dismantle longstanding public programs. Policymakers and policy researchers should move beyond correlation into the domain of policy evaluation, which starts in critical thinking about the ideological claims that have influenced current and past polices.

## Use a Balanced Framework

There was a sustained period of public investment in the development of a system of K–12 and higher education across the states between 1880 and 1980. There was also a generally accepted common ground in education and public finance. However, the progressive assumptions that guided the century of growing public investment—from 1880 to 1980—have fallen apart. In this new period, sophisticated analytic methods have been used to overlook the obvious and to make untested claims about new policy directions. However, it is possible to evaluate the effects of these new policies on their own terms, considering the intent of the new conservatives while also considering the unintended consequences of their policies, the decline in equal opportunity that has been overlooked for more than two decades.

The new conservative policies have emphasized redefining the nature of the basic right to an education and the public interest in efficient use of tax dollars. Both are legitimate concerns that merit consideration in policy development. There have been modest gains in efficiency and gains in college rates since 1980 (St. John 2003). However, it is also abundantly apparent that twenty years of overlooking equity has had a high cost: a slight reduction in high school graduation rates and an increased disparity in college enrollment rates for low-income students compared to high-income students (St. John 2003).

These equity considerations merit attention, but this does not diminish the importance of even modest efficiency gains. If there is a shared goal of expanding access, we must find more efficient means for the public finance of higher education. Otherwise there would be a need for substantial tax increases. Privatization—having students pay a larger share of the cost of public colleges and encouraging more students to attend private colleges—improved taxpayer efficiency in the 1980s and 1990s, but equity declined because need-based grants were not adequate. Maintaining adequate need-based grants in states proved even more crucial during this period of privatization (St. John 1999; St. John, Hu, and Weber 2002; St. John, Musoba, et al. 2002). Gains in taxpayer efficiency, when coupled with reduced equity, illustrates false efficiencies rather than real improvements in cost-effectiveness (St. John 1994).

Gains in the quality of education are also important, but it is time to evaluate the efficacy of this new generation of education policies, using serious and thoughtful evaluation frameworks. It is apparent that urban schools have not benefited from most education reform policies since 1980 (Miron and St. John 2003). Clearly, there is a need for more evaluative research that focuses on the impact of standards, graduation requirements, high-stakes graduation tests, and so on.

The framework outlined above provides a starting point for a more balanced approach to the evaluation of public policies in education and higher education finance, but it does not answer the many questions that linger about effects of the policy paths consistently chosen over the past two decades. Policy researchers have an obligation to use a balanced approach to provide policymakers with balanced information, including research that considers equity along with efficiency and excellence. This obligation is moral and relates to the fundamental precepts of democratic society.

## *Provide Information to the Public and to Policymakers*

Education in the United States is in miserable condition, but not for the reasons that are widely espoused by the new conservatives. The fact that there have been modest gains in the quality of education in some locales as a consequence of education reform over the past two decades merits acknowledgement. The efficiency gains of the 1980s are also noteworthy (St. John 2003). However, education policy and higher finance reform are speeding down new pathways that have gone largely unexamined. They have resulted in new inequities. After twenty years, it is time to rethink the direction of education reform and public finance of higher education.

Not only are we in a period of rapid privatization, but further movement in this direction will probably be necessary if America is to expand access to higher education without substantially raising taxes. This means increased tuition. In the past decade, targeted tax credit programs were implemented to ease the burden for the middle class, but the increased inequality for low-income college-qualified students was ignored. Researchers and policymakers need to consider equity along with the efficiency effects of privatization.

The notion of public accountability has been used to wage war against the liberal education establishment over the past twenty years. It is important to evaluate how well twenty years of education reform policies have improved the quality of education students have received. It is also essential to evaluate the equity effects of these reforms. Such studies are important for higher education for two reasons: (1) studies that focus on the impact of recent school reforms are essential to efforts to inform the national conversation about academic preparation; and (2) higher education is facing a similar push for accountability systems. Therefore, research on the consequences of standards and accountability can inform lobbying efforts in higher education as well as the development of accountability systems in the states if they are mandated in the next reauthorization of the *Higher Education Act.*

Finally, equity and diversity merit attention because of the new conservative policies that attempt to dismantle affirmative action and shift the focus of desegregation to historically black colleges (Brown, Butler, and Donahoo, chapter 6; Conrad and Weerts, chapter 4). Certainly, the equity effects of reductions in student-need-based grants and of increased education requirements merit attention for the reasons outlined above. However, given the recent history of inequality, it is too soon to dismantle affirmative action policies. We still experience the residual effects of *de facto* and *de jure* segregation and racial isolation in higher education. Clearly, greater attention should be given to equity concerns as part of a more balanced approach to education policy in United States.

NOTES

1. The NELS:88 questions about college applications were asked during the senior year, which means that students answering affirmatively on these questions had applied to a college that required an advanced application. Many less selective institutions do not require students to make applications in advance.

2. A subsequent section of this chapter presents a reexamination of analyses reported by NCES (1997a) to illustrate that because of the interpretive assumptions, NCES has systematically overlooked the role of finances in promoting equal educational opportunity in the United States. This is both sad and ironic, given that the goal of promoting equal opportunity remains an intent of federal student financial aid, the primary form of federal investment in higher education.

3. Increasingly, it is possible to distinguish a new liberal position in the policy literature. When we look critically at the literature, a new liberal position is evident as policy analysts argue for funding of new programs while remaining silent about the inequalities created by cuts in federal need-based grants.

REFERENCES

Advisory Committee on Student Financial Assistance (ACSFA). 2001. *Access denied: Restoring the nation's commitment to equal educational opportunity.* Washington, DC: Author.

Advisory Committee on Student Financial Assistance (ACSFA). 2002. *Empty promises: The myth of college access in America.* Washington, DC: Author.

Alexander, K. L., and B. K. Eckland. 1974. Sex differences in the educational attainment process. *American Sociological Review* 39 (5): 668–82.

Alexander, K. L., and B. K. Eckland. 1977. High school context and college selectivity: Institutional constraints in educational stratification. *Social Forces* 56 (1): 166–88.

Alexander, K. L., and B. K. Eckland. 1978. Basic attainment processes: A replication and extension, 1999. *Sociology of Education* 48 (4): 457–95.

Berger, J. B. 2000. Optimizing capital, social reproduction, and undergraduate persistence: A sociological perspective. In *Reworking the student departure puzzle,* ed. J. M. Braxton. Nashville, TN: Vanderbilt University Press.

Bishop, J. H. 1992. Why U.S. students need incentives to learn. *Educational Leadership* 49 (6): 15–18.

Bishop, J. H. 2002. A prospective policy evaluation of the Michigan Merit Award Program. Presented at "Taking Account of Accountability: Assessing Politics and Policy," Kennedy School of Government, Harvard University, June 10 and 11, 2002.

Blau, P., and O. D. Duncan. 1967. *The American occupational structure.* New York: Wiley.

Choy, S. P. 2002. *Access and persistence: Findings from 10 years of longitudinal research on students.* Washington, DC: American Council on Education.

Finn, C. E., Jr. 1990. The biggest reform of all. *Phi Delta Kappan* 71 (8) (January): 584–92.

Finn, C. E., Jr. 2001. College isn't for everyone. *USA Today,* 21 February, 14A.

Fogel, R. W. 2000. *The fourth great awakening and the future of egalitarianism.* Chicago: Chicago University Press.

Gladieux, L. E., and W. S. Swail. 1999. Financial aid is not enough: Improving the odds for minority and low-income students. In *Financing a college education: How it works, how it's changing,* ed. J. E. King, 177–97. Westport, CT: Oryx Press.

Hansen, W. L. 1983. The impact of student financial aid on access. In *The crisis in higher education,* ed. J. Froomkin. New York: Academy of Political Science.

Hearn, J. C. 1993. The paradox of growth in federal aid for college students: 1965–1990. In *Higher education: Handbook of theory and research,* vol. 9, ed. J. C. Smart, 94–153. New York: Agathon Press.

Hearn, J. C. 2001. Epilogue to "The paradox of growth in federal aid for college students: 1965–1990." In *The finance of higher education: Theory, research, policy, and practice,* ed. M. B. Paulsen and J. C. Smart, 316–20. New York: Agathon Press.

Heller, D. E. 1997. Student price response in higher education: An update to Leslie and Brinkman. *Journal of Higher Education* 68 (6): 624–59.

Hirschman, C., and J. C. Lee. 2002. *Race and ethnic inequality in educational attainment in the United States.* Paper presented at the Jacobs Foundation Conference on "Ethnic Variations in Intergenerational Continuities and Discontinuities in Psychosocial Features and Disorders," October 24–26, 2002, Zurich, Switzerland.

Jackson, G. A., and G. B. Weathersby. 1975. Individual demand for higher education. *Journal of Higher Education* 46 (6): 623–52.

Jacob, B. A. 2001. Getting tough? The impact of mandatory high school graduation exams on student achievement and dropout rates. *Educational Evaluation and Policy Analysis* 23 (2): 99–122.

Kane, T. J. 1995. *Rising public college tuition and college entry: How well do public subsidies promote access to college?* Working paper series No. 5146. Cambridge, MA: National Bureau of Economic Research.

King, J. E. 1999a. Conclusion. In *Financing a college education: How it works, how it's changing,* ed. J. E. King, 177–197. Phoenix, AZ: Oryx Press.

King, J. E., ed. 1999b. *Financing a college education: How it works, how it's changing.* Phoenix, AZ: Oryx Press.

King, J. E. 2002. *Crucial choices: How students' financial decisions affect their academic success.* Washington, DC: American Council on Education.

Leslie, L. L., and P. T. Brinkman. 1988. *The economic value of higher education.* New York: American Council on Education and Macmillan.

Manset, G., and S. Washburn. 2002. Equity through accountability? Mandating minimum competency exit examinations for secondary students with learning disabilities. *Learning Disabilities Research and Practice* 15 (3): 160–67.

McDonnough, P. M. 1997. *Choosing colleges: How social class and schools structure opportunity.* Albany: State University of New York Press.

McPherson, M. S. 1978. The demand for higher education. In *Public policy and private higher education,* ed. D. W. Breneman and C. E. Finn Jr. Washington, DC: Brookings Institution.

Miron, L. F., and E. P. St. John, eds. 2003. *Reinterpreting urban school reform: Have urban schools failed, or has the reform movement failed urban schools?* Albany: State University of New York Press.

National Center for Education Statistics (NCES). 1996. *National Education Longitudinal Study: 1988–1994, Descriptive summary report with an essay on access and choice in postsecondary education.* NCES 96-175. Washington, DC: Author.

National Center for Education Statistics (NCES). 1997a. *Access to postsecondary education for the 1992 high school graduates,* NCES 98-105. By Lutz Berkner and Lisa Chavez. Project Officer: C. Dennis Carroll. Washington, DC: Author.

National Center for Education Statistics (NCES). 1997b. *Confronting the odds: Students at risk and the pipeline to higher education.* NCES 98-094. By Laura J. Horn. Project officer: C. Dennis Carroll. Washington, DC: Author.

National Center for Education Statistics. 2000. *Mapping the road to college: First-generation students' math track, planning strategies, and context of support,* NCES 2000-153. By Laura Horn and Anne-Marie Nunez. Project Officer: Larry Bobbitt. Washington, DC: Author.

Nussbaum, M. C. 1999. *Sex and social justice.* Oxford, UK: Oxford University Press.

Paige, R. M. 2003. More spending is not the answer. *USA Today,* 10 January.

Paulsen, M. B. 2001a . The economics of human capital and investment in higher education. In *The finance of higher education: Theory, research, policy and practice,* ed. M. B. Paulsen and J. C. Smart, 55–94. New York: Agathon Press.

Paulsen, M. B. 2001b. The economics of the public sector: The nature of public policy in higher education finance. In *The finance of higher education: Theory, research, policy and practice,* ed. M. B. Paulsen and J. C. Smart, 95–132. New York: Agathon Press.

Pelavin, S. H., and M. B. Kane. 1990. *Changing the odds: Factors increasing access to college.* New York: College Board.

Rawls, J. 1971. *A theory of justice.* Cambridge, MA: Belknap Press of Harvard University Press.

Rawls, J. 2001. *Justice as fairness: A restatement.* Edited by E. Kelly. Cambridge, MA: Belknap Press of Harvard University Press.

St. John, E. P. 1994. *Prices, productivity and investment: Assessing financial strategies in higher education.* ASHE-ERIC Higher Education Report No. 3. Washington, DC: George Washington University, School of Education and Human Development.

St. John, E. P. 1999. Evaluating state grant programs: A case study of Washington's grant program. *Research in Higher Education* 40 (2): 149–70.

St. John, E. P. 2002. *The access challenge: Rethinking the causes of the new inequality.* Policy Issue Report # 2002-01. Bloomington: Indiana Education Policy Center.

St. John, E. P. 2003. *Refinancing the college dream: Access, equal opportunity, and justice for taxpayers.* Baltimore: Johns Hopkins University Press.

St. John, E. P., S. Hu., and J. Weber. 2002. State policy and the affordability of public higher education: The influence of state grants on persistence in Indiana. *Research in Higher Education* 42 (4): 401–28.

St. John, E. P., and G. D. Musoba. 2002. Academic access and equal opportunity: Rethinking the foundations for policy on diversity. In *Equity and access in higher education: Changing the definition of educational opportunity,* vol. 18, *Readings on Equal Education,* ed. M. C. Brown, 171–92. New York: AMS Press.

St. John, E. P., G. D. Musoba, A. B. Simmons, C. G. Chung, J. Schmit, and C. Y. J. Peng. 2002. *Meeting the access challenge: An examination of Indiana's Twenty-first Century Scholars Program.* Presented at the Association for the Study of Higher Education Annual Meeting, November 2002, Sacramento, CA.

St. John, E. P., and M. B. Paulsen. 2001. The finance of higher education: Implications for theory, research, policy, and practice. In *The finance of higher education: Theory, research, policy and practice,* ed. M. B. Paulsen and J. C. Smart. New York: Agathon Press.

Sen, A. 1999. *Development as freedom.* New York: Anchor Press.

Slaughter, S. E. 1991. The official "ideology" of higher education: Ironies and inconsistencies. In *Culture and ideology in higher education: Advancing a critical agenda,* ed. W. G. Tierney. New York: Praeger.

# Contributors

*M. Christopher Brown II* is an associate professor of education and a senior research associate in the Center for the Study of Higher Education at the Pennsylvania State University. He earned a national reputation for his research and scholarly writing on higher education policy and administration, meriting him both the ASHE (2001) and AERA (2002) early career research awards. He is the author or editor of *The Quest to Define Collegiate Desegregation* (1999), *Organization and Governance in Higher Education* (2000), and *Black Sons to Mothers* (2000) with James Earl Davis.

*Jason L. Butler* recently received a B.S. in sociology from the University of Illinois. Recognized as a member of the Academic All–Big Ten Team and the Dean's List, Butler was also a participant in the Summer Research Opportunities Program and the McNair Summer Program, where he conducted research with M. Christopher Brown II. His research experiences include investigations of affirmative action programs, diversity in schools, and educational achievement.

*Choong-Geun Chung* is associate director of the Indiana Project on Academic Success, Indiana University, Bloomington. His major interest is in statistical models for school reform, the effect of state and federal finances on students' access and persistence in higher education, and issues in minority representation in special education and school discipline.

*Clifton F. Conrad* has been Professor of Higher Education at the University of Wisconsin-Madison since 1987. His books include *A Silent Success: Master's Education in the United States* and *Emblems of Quality: Developing and Sustaining High-Quality Academic Programs*. Since 1980 he has been an expert witness—notably on academic program quality and program duplication in higher education, desegregation in higher education, and higher education curriculum—for the U.S. Department of Justice in six civil rights cases involving race and gender in higher education.

*Saran Donahoo* is a doctoral candidate in higher education administration at the University of Illinois at Urbana-Champaign. She earned her B.A. in secondary education at the University of Arizona and her M.A. in history at the University of Illinois. Her research interests include higher education history, law and policy, women and minorities in higher education, and curriculum and assessment.

*James Farmer* is project administrator for the JA-SIG uPortal software development. Previously he taught the Information Systems and Strategy Planning modules at Harvard University's Graduate School of Education. He graduated from the University of Oklahoma with a B.S. in mathematics, from Harvard University with an S.M. in applied mathematics, and from UCLA with an MBA. He also did graduate work in economics at UCLA on the value of information.

*James C. Hearn* is Professor of Public Policy and Higher Education at Vanderbilt University. His research has appeared in education, sociology, and economics journals as well as in several edited books. Among his recent projects are studies of P-16 cooperation and planning at the state level, the influences of state policies on student learning in postsecondary education, and the effectiveness of policies oriented to improving postsecondary access in the United States and in several states.

*Janet M. Holdsworth* has a Ph.D. from the University of Minnesota and is a research analyst and research associate at the Midwestern Higher Education Consortium. Her research has focused on the influence of state policies on student learning in postsecondary education, public perceptions of access and equity in higher education, an environmental analysis of accountability in higher education institutions, and the impact of state policies on distance learning initiatives.

*Don Hossler* is Professor of Educational Leadership and Policy Studies, Professor of Philanthropic Studies, Vice Chancellor for Enrollment Services at Indiana University Bloomington, and Associate Vice President for Enrollment Services for Indiana University system wide. His areas of specialization include college choice, student financial aid policy, enrollment management, and higher education finance. His books include *Mapping the Higher Education Landscape* and *Going to College: How Social, Economic, and Educational Factors Influence the Decisions Students Make* (1997).

*Michael D. Parsons* is Professor and Chair of Educational Leadership and Policy Studies, College of Education, Florida International University. He has served as the chair of the Department Human Development, Leadership and Technology, Indiana University Purdue University Indianapolis. Parsons was a visiting faculty member at the College of William and Mary, 1994–1995, and a Fulbright Scholar at Karaganda State University in Karaganda, Kazakhstan, in 1999.

*Edward P. St. John* is Algo D. Henderson Collegiate Professor of Education at the University of Michigan's Center for the Study of Higher and Postsecondary Education. St. John has published numerous studies of the impact of student financial aid on college choice and persistence. He recently published *Refinancing the College Dream: Access, Equal Opportunity and Justice for Taxpayers* (2003) and co-edited *Incentive-Based Budgeting in Public Universities* (2002). He holds an Ed.D. from Harvard and an M.Ed. and B.S. from the University of California Davis.

*John R. Thelin* is University Research Professor at the University of Kentucky, where he is a faculty member in Educational Policy Studies. He received his M.A. in history and Ph.D. in history of education from the University of California, Berkeley. He is author of *Games Colleges Play*, a history of college sports scandals.

*Mary Louise ("Mike") Trammell* is currently Senior Licensing Associate for Life Sciences, Office of Technology Transfer, at the University of Arizona. She has an A.B. from Randolph-Macon Women's College, an M.A. from Tulane University, and a Ph.D. in higher education administration from the University of New Orleans.

*David J. Weerts* is a visiting scholar at the Wisconsin Center for the Advancement of Postsecondary Education (WISCAPE) and adjunct assistant professor in the Department of Educational Administration at the University of Wisconsin-Madison. David earned a Ph.D. and an M.S. in higher education from the University of Wisconsin–Madison, and a B.A. in communication and journalism from the University of Wisconsin–Eau Claire. His 2002 book, *State Governments and Research Universities: A Framework for a Renewed Partnership,* discusses political, structural and cultural issues that are central to the development of research institutions that are well-funded and poised to effectively partner with their states to serve societal needs.

*William Zumeta* is Professor of Public Affairs and Education Policy and associate dean of the Daniel J. Evans School of Public Affairs at the University of Washington. He has written in recent years about policies toward graduate education and science, state policy and private higher education, state finance of higher education, and budget-linked accountability policies in higher education. He has served on the editorial boards of *Review of Higher Education, Journal of Public Administration Research and Theory,* and *International Public Management Journal.*

# Index